Notes & Apologies:

★ After twenty-plus years, here we are, at issue 150 of *The Believer*. To celebrate, we decided to print a commemorative poster, by Kristian Hammerstad, featuring the many interview portraits he's done for us over the past few years. We've also included a special letters section and a comprehensive index of every issue we've ever published, as best as we can remember things—it's been a long time!

We remain ever grateful to you, dear *Believer* readers. Thank you for helping us to keep on keeping on. Here's to 150 issues more. Rejoice! Believe! Be strong and read hard!

★ Annual subscriptions to *The Believer* include four issues, one of which might be themed and may come with a special bonus item, such as a giant poster, free radio series, or annual calendar. View our subscription deals at *thebeliever.net/subscribe*.

★ We now have our very own Substack. Head to *believermagazine.substack.com* for themed archival posts, new articles liberated from our paywall, weekly picks from our interviews section, and much more.

THE BELIEVER

TWO DECADES OF THE BEST ESSAYS, INTERVIEWS, JOURNALISM, AND MORE, RIGHT AT YOUR FINGERTIPS

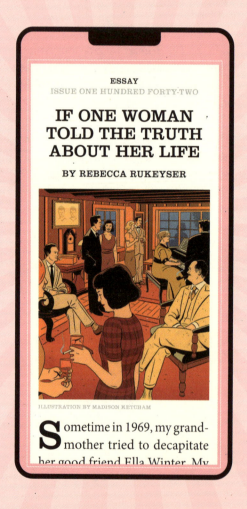

Subscribe now and get exclusive access to
The Believer's entire twenty-year archive.

SUBSCRIBE NOW AT
thebeliever.net/subscribe

DEAR THE BELIEVER

849 VALENCIA STREET, SAN FRANCISCO, CA 94110

letters@thebeliever.net

Dear Believer,

Happy 150th! I remember when you were just a glint in our eyes, in the fall of 2002. We were going to call you "The Balloonist," then thought better of it. It had to be *The Believer*! There was a movie called *The Believer*, I remember, and over the years some people thought we were a religious periodical—well, maybe we are, at that. The religion of writing! Of interesting articles! Of unorthodox trim size and Charles Burns's portraits!

I remember your debut, in March 2003. You looked like nothing else on the newsstand. I'm looking at the issue—your baby picture—now. A friend of mine, Michael Carter, did six of the interior illustrations. They're marvelous: e.g., for Heidi Julavits's "Rejoice! Believe! Be Strong and Read Hard!," he drew what appears to be a hot-air balloon—but it is actually a smaller version of that conveyance, hoisting a typewriter high above a gentle landscape. For my piece on Charles Portis, he conjured a few floating landmasses, no bigger than paint chips, busy with ladders, a Ford Torino, a house, some soft-looking trees, and, yes, a weather balloon. Michael drew a delightful card catalog to kick off Paul La Farge's piece on Nicholson Baker, and a stout gentleman with an indignant expression sitting in front of a fireplace. (The gentleman has the head of a bird.) Inexplicably, Michael's name was not listed anywhere in that first issue (this was redressed subsequently). I haven't looked at these drawings in a very long time, and I like them a lot.

Today's readers won't find these elusive drawings on the website, but they may want to search for them on the secondary market. (Ebay is selling issue one for $132—that's $22 for each illustration.) Dreams are everything that's not online.

Ed Park
New York, NY

Dear Believer,

I write to you in the midst of a crisis of faith. I don't know if the things I value—many of which overlap with *The Believer*'s—matter much to the world in the same way they used to. The political scene is full of liars and history-deniers who don't value human life, let alone the most tender, credulous, but also aptly skeptical expressions of what it means to live. Bad faith and tendentiousness rule the day. Tech companies encourage the exploitation of our attention spans, and, by and large, we acquiesce. The stakes for dissension seem to be climbing considerably higher. I feel like I've lost something, and I'm not sure if I'll ever get it back.

A little over five years ago, in February 2020, I was in Los Angeles, in a Lyft. The person driving said that she was also a screenwriter and network television administrator and then she asked me what I did. I told her I was a writer and an editor for this magazine. Before I could go into my usual spiel about *The Believer*'s history and the type of work published within it, she asked me if the magazine is about "African American spirituality." I remember being a little surprised by the ask. She may have flicked on her signal, and made a left, or a right; I know that she dropped me off eventually. But even after I'd arrived at my hotel, I was still back there—at the intersection of the conflation she'd made. I found it really funny and also *funny*. Because of the magazine's name, I'd heard variations on this question before, but I had never had anyone openly link the editorial content to *Black* spirituality based on its title and my association with it. Of course, this kind of thing happens all the time; I'm a book (or a magazine) and also a cover.

Shortly after that ride, the entire world shut down. In the middle of a chaotic summer that saw protests over the murders of George Floyd and Breonna Taylor, I found myself weirdly obsessing over the Clark Sisters, a revered gospel group. One of the first things I watched during lockdown was a Lifetime biopic about the Sisters, which sent me down a YouTube rabbit hole of all their live performances. I teared up while watching the women sing about how God has delivered them a life of grace, salvation, and unyielding awe. It was nice to see people hold space for conviction about mystery, cradling it in harmonious, unifying notes, able to wade into waters unknown at a time when everything felt precarious. I've been to church, and flirted with a few religions, but nothing has ever stuck. I'm not a joiner. The closest I've come to religious adherence is my belief that attention and care matter. Mostly, I've practiced this commitment in my criticism. To me, reading, watching, and thinking deeply are like a form of prayer.

I've attended to my affection for the Clark Sisters. I went to see them at the Brooklyn Academy of Music in 2023, and, along with other members of the audience, responded as they called, forming a rolling wave of praise up and down the aisles. I was happy to be in that number. As dismissive of religion as I've been in the past, I don't feel that way about gospel today. As a devotee of Black artistic traditions, I know that popular American music as we know it would not exist without them. As a searching person in the middle of a crisis, I find the mix of confidence and doubt in the best gospel music revealing of the tensions in my own soul.

"Is My Living in Vain" and "You Brought the Sunshine" are the most famous Clark Sisters compositions, and they were both written by Twinkie Clark. While "Sunshine" is undoubtedly sunnier, a hit beloved by both Studio 54 and gospel audiences, "Is My Living in Vain" is the more moving song. On YouTube, there's one video of the original lineup of all five Sisters singing the song back in the late '70s or early '80s. It's in this video that Twinkie Clark pauses to cry before asking, at the end of a list of actions, "Is my playing the organ in vain?" Her youngest sister, Karen, is caught onscreen crying, wiping tears away as she stares at her sister's lyrical and existential inquiry. (The movie reveals that Twinkie sold the rights to her songwriting catalog to buy a car.)

"Have I let my light shine?" is another question the Clark Sisters ask in the song. I wonder if that question had multiple connotations for them. According to lore, the Sisters' mother and teacher, Dr. Mattie Moss Clark, was reprimanded by the all-male leadership council of the Church of God in Christ, the family's denomination, for appearing on the Grammys with her daughters in 1988. She was shining too much. She was banned from performing with them, and apparently adhered to that order until 1994, when she died. By leaving, Dr. Clark moved out of the way to let her daughters receive praise and honor, and to carry out her vision. In doing so, her absence created a gulf that is only barely filled by her immense legacy.

In Garth Greenwell's interview with Nellie Hermann, which I edited, in *The Believer*'s June/July 2020 issue, Greenwell mentions the theological term *via negativa*, or "the way of negation," which is used to describe the experience of what God is not, and which is characterized by the idea that "one's awareness of divine transcendence, or of God's unfathomable love, reveals the inadequacy of all human images and vocabulary to talk about God meaningfully." Before editing that piece, I had never heard of the concept. But I realize I have observed it in practice, and can recognize it when I listen to music or sermons. There is via negativa in a singer's pause, in a scat riff, in Dorinda Clark's raspy vocal runs, in one of Karen Clark's drum fills, in the "ghost notes" created by the expectation of an intentionally muted note that still has a rhythmic value but no discernible pitch. There is via negativa in Twinkie's hesitation before tinkling the keys, and in the moment when she stopped singing to question the purpose of her labor. It's there in the spell of time after the Sisters sing "Is my living in vain?" and answer "No, of course not," the implication being that everything God creates is purposeful and part of a divine plan. Is the work of Twinkie, "the Queen of the Hammond B3 Organ," in vain? No, of course not. See the light coming through the stained-glass window in one video, as the crowd turns into an extension of the choir? See Karen's awestruck appreciation of her sister? Both are visions of ecstatic experience.

Recently, in a year of yet more political upheaval, when I've undergone lots of personal changes, including leaving my editing job to write full-time, I find myself feeling simultaneously bolder and more insecure than ever—about the future, and about my own abilities, about whether it matters. I've been returning to the Clark Sisters intermittently. My friend Daniel Gumbiner, this magazine's editor, asked me if I'd like to write a letter, which got me thinking about what *The Believer* means to me, which subsequently sent me back to the question my Lyft driver asked before the pandemic. Using the principle of via negativa, I can offer a different response to her question: *The Believer* is not a magazine about African American spirituality, but it's not *not* one either.

People often talk of solo singers' intonational "gymnastics" and "acrobatics," but the only vocal displays I've ever seen that are worthy of sports analogies involve people harmonizing together. Harmonizing well is like synchronized swimming. The Clark Sisters have demonstrated the beauty of blending; Dr. Clark, who is often credited with innovating a way of teaching three-part harmony to gospel choirs, taught them well. Making magazines is an intensely collaborative effort, and here, in these pages, I blend with other people, as a reader and as a writer and, in the past, as an editor, a kind of choir director. For most of my adult life, *The Believer* has been a sacred space, a place for me to have the kind of awakenings prompted by good writing, the mix of what my favorite critic, Ian Penman, favors in music: "an unconscionable swerve, heretical detail, some shiver of incomprehension." *The Believer*, being a profoundly secular project, uses human images and vocabulary to describe the mysterious presences and absences that life leaves in each of us. It values a different way of negation, or the idea of doing more with less, of showing rather than telling, whenever possible. It's only recently, in the age of AI and of Donald Trump's second term, that I have wavered, and questioned whether there's a future for any of this. All the time now I'm asking myself if my work is in vain, if the work of magazines like *The Believer* is in vain. I wake up from nights of short, fitful sleep and try to compose an email, or a sentence, and find myself flattened by some decree or intentionally shocking news item from the White House. I end up looking for distractions—at YouTube or Instagram, or for something to clean—when I should be dropping to my knees, finding a book or long-form piece to pore over. But faith is the evidence of things not seen. I know it might sound a little pat, but I swear it's true: every time I read this magazine, I find my faith restored a bit more, or rather, I see more reason to have faith in the idea of faith. The work in these pages doesn't come with answers, but instead with hundreds of inciting questions (in features and reviews, and not just in the interviews section). When I read *The Believer* I become more and more certain that even if I can't be sure whether other institutions will hold up, I know there are people who care about what life looks like and who want to document it, no matter how strange or niche its provenance. In their tiny corners of the world, the writers who pitch and write for *The Believer* are drafting missives from vanishing places, presenting them for the interest of its readers like Sunday-school children at a show-and-tell. Out of the voids this country's minders are trying to make—in federal employee logs, in logic, in history, in an already frayed social fabric—something else will emerge. And I hope we'll be here to push back against the administrative embrace of holes and to fill them with stories and reviews. In 150 issues, these pages have been a place to be an apostate and a believer. I pray we get 150 more.

Niela Orr
Brooklyn, NY

Dear Believer,
I often compare you to an ex-girlfriend. I dropped out of college to be with you—your second issue was my first, and I spent nearly all my waking hours with you. It never felt like work, even if there were extreme emotional highs and lows; I have vivid memories (primary smell: burritos) of crying on Dolores Avenue into a 2004-era Nokia with my mom on the line, telling her that I didn't think I could handle this, being the managing editor (and sole full-time employee) of a new national magazine as a college dropout. There was a similarly burrito-scented, weepy Nokia session with my best friend, when I told him I really thought I was going to bail this time; I couldn't hack it. I listened carefully as he told me he thought that would be a decision I'd regret for the rest of my life. He was right—I'm so glad I stuck it out.

Eventually, though, after eight or so years, it became clear that I had given all I could to the relationship, at least in that form, at that time. You were giving me carpal tunnel syndrome. I didn't think we were growing together. The truth is, I met someone else. She happened to be a person, and not a magazine. Instead of dropping out of college to be with her, I dropped back in: I followed her to Missouri, where she got her first assistant professor job, and I finished my BA as a thirty-two-year-old. I felt like Rodney Dangerfield in a more subdued and politically correct remake of *Back to School* (1986).

At first we stayed close—I took over for Ed Park for a while, assigning and editing features from Missouri. But that role faded, and as the years ticked by, whenever I heard about you, or got issues in the mail, I got increasingly extreme ex-girlfriend energy. Like, *Oh, she moved to Las Vegas? Huh. That's interesting. I wonder if she'll like it. Wait: No. I can't think about this right now.* I tried to stay out of it, didn't want to meddle; you were doing your own thing. But I couldn't help but feel invested in your journey, particularly when I heard about your near-death experience, and something about selling sex-toys and working in e-commerce.

As a kid, I read magazine mastheads. I remember being curious and confused about what a contributing editor was—one of those alluring but opaque job titles, like associate producer, that seemed important and probably fun as far as jobs went, but what did one actually do? Now that I've been a contributing editor for so many years, I feel like I've grown into the job, and I understand it intimately: Being a contributing editor is like being a magazine's ex-boyfriend, one with whom you're on good terms. He still sends you book recommendations, and puts you in touch with people he thinks you'll find interesting. There's no more of that jealous *ex* energy; you're just old friends, happy to be in touch when it makes sense, picking up the thread, without resentment, after long intervals. I'm so glad you're still in my life. Love,

Andrew Leland
Northampton, MA

Dear Believer,

Now that you are 150 and I've known you half my life, I may as well admit what you've long since sussed out about me: I was never really an intellectual.

Sure, I met you at the University Library Bookstore. Oh, I could drop a few obscure writers' names: Jimmy Kerouac, Jen Austen, Ernest Hemsworth. I knew that *lit* probably meant "literature." I had a rough idea of what it took to become a McSweeney.

But you and I both know what beguiled me about you. It was those Charles Burns cover portraits, that beautifully confounding comics page. I loved you for the reviews of power tools and of children. Hell, the first thing I did when picking up an issue was jump to the back of the book for my beloved Michael Kupperman!

Don't pretend we didn't play each other. One moment I was reading a breezy celebrity interview, and the next, you'd have me twenty pages deep in a piece about the subtleties of translating seventeenth-century memoirs from Portuguese into Russian (or whatever). Was it manipulation? Who cares! It was heaven.

Eventually, we shacked up. I sold you a tall tale about a singing lumberjack who explained the technical nuances of logging right in his songs. You were intrigued, because of course you were. And then we had that glorious year and a half together in San Francisco. Nights at the Latin American Club? Days at Valencia Pizza & Pasta? Perfection.

I owe so much of myself to you. You let me in. You changed me. I felt old and hardened when I came to you. You cracked me open, helped me find my curiosity again. You introduced me to so many people that I still count among my dearest friends. I know you must get this a lot, but you made me a Believer... in *myself*.

Our time together is tinged with sadness for me, because sometimes I wonder if I was ever really in your league. There were so many nights when you'd be out at a reading or a fundraiser and I'd be home, smoking weed and playing *Spelunky* on my Xbox. Maybe I should have read all those dusty old books you loaned me. Maybe I should have actually learned InDesign, so I could understand you better. (It's just not a very intuitive program.)

I'll stop myself here, though. We all live with regrets. I know I taught you a few things too. You didn't even know about my hometown's famous exploding whale when I met you! You didn't know about the "I like turtles" kid! The interns knew—so many brilliant interns; I miss them too—but you didn't!

It's a testament to you, dear old *Believer*, that you can hold court with astrophysicists, philosophers, comic book nerds, and daytime-TV bingers alike. You really *love* them all. You find humanity and wonder in the strangest places, high and low. I'm so grateful for all that we did share: Tonya Harding, Jason Polan's little giraffes (RIP, you sweet genius), funny words (is a *broomcorn* an actual thing?). We'll always have the Music Issue! We'll always have Schema, and those ridiculous little lists you keep! And, yes, we will always have the Goddamn Sex Blimp.

Long may she sail. Yours always,
Casey Jarman
Portland, OR

Dear Believer,

On the occasion of your 150th issue, I've been thinking a lot about how I spent my formative years as an editor at your publication with some of the cleverest and most dedicated creative people I have had the privilege to know. I first opened a *Believer* magazine in 2006 and leaned in to smell the paper. It's a singular smell. (I believe the paper comes from a special source, or is that just lore?) At that moment, I knew it was something I wanted to be part of. I made contact with Ed Park and Heidi Julavits, and they gave me the formidable task of taking on the slush pile. But I didn't care. I was in.

The magazine opened up the aperture of my world and introduced me to the work of incredible writers, artists, and musicians. It was where I first learned of Robyn O'Neil's profound art, where I first met and befriended Jason Polan, and where I was able to edit the work of some of the literary world's most exciting luminaries, including Rachel Kaadzi Ghansah. I am so grateful that I was able to spend eight years of my life alongside the talented people who worked tirelessly to bring this iconic publication to readers. And I'm even more grateful that it continues today.

I just flipped through a September 2014 issue of the magazine—and smelled the pages, of course—and came upon Chris Kraus's essay about Kathy Acker and was reminded how, to us, it was absolutely imperative that the magazine we built be timeless.

All my best,
Karolina Waclawiak
Los Angeles, CA

NICK HORNBY READS AGAIN!

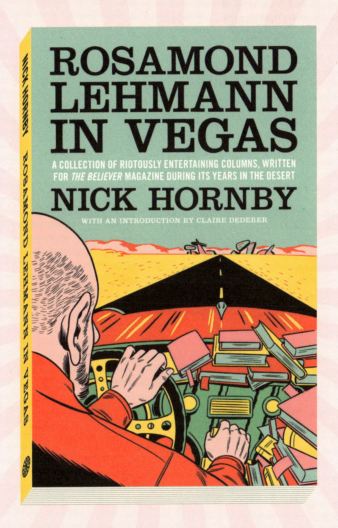

A new volume of Hornby's *Believer* column, "Stuff I've Been Reading," spanning the magazine's Las Vegas era

AVAILABLE NOW
store.mcsweeneys.net

THE INDEX
to issue one hundred fifty

A
	PAGE
Allopathic	51
All-you-can-eat	19
Alphabetical Diaries	66, 71–73
Andrea Settimo	34, 38–39, 98
Andrew McCarthy	15
Annalee Newitz	10
Antigone Kefala	119
Ashram	46, 48, 50, 53, 55,
Automatic Noodle	10

B
Babes	15
Benjamin Tausig	124
Bernie Lomax	16–17
Bill Bright	102–105, 108–109
Billy Rose Theatre	12
Biofeedback: The Yoga of the West	46, 48
Black Humor	111
Blaxploitation	74
Boredom	69, 106–107
Brobdingagian	20
Buddhism	112, 116–118
Byzantine	119

C
Caitlin Van Dusen	126
Campus Crusade for Christ (Cru)	98, 102, 104,

"ADVENTURES IN JESUSLAND"
(page 98)

Cara Blue Adams	66
Cartoonist	75, 110–111, 114–115, 118
Cecily Parks	16
Charles Burns	6, 32–33, 36
Charles Dickens	20
★ Charles Johnson	110–118

Charlotte Gomez	37, 46
Chicago Dojo Wars	111
Childhood	46–47, 50, 53, 55, 62–63, 84, 117
Chinatown	10
Christlike	14
Cocaine	16
Consciousness	47, 112, 119
Corpse	15, 17

D
Daffodil	19
Dallas	104
David Brown	29
David J. Morris	98
David Lynch	11
Diary	65–66, 71–73
Drake	17
Dr. Duke	30–31
Dr. Usharbudh Arya (Swami Veda)	46–49, 51–54, 57–59

E
East River Park	18
Ebony	111
Eczema	52
Edward Albee	12
Elizabeth Taylor	13, 102
Elliptic Bed Spring Company	21
Envy	78–79
Ernest Lehman	13
Erotics	120
Escapism	121
Etel Adnan	119
Evie Shockley	13
Exvangelical	98

F
Fairy tale–like stories	68
Faye Dunaway	11
Florence Marryat	75

Foreclosure Gothic	121
Four Spiritual Laws	101, 104, 106
Frank Sinatra	108
Fredrick Forsyth	14
French fries	26
Friction	73
Fru Dahl	126
Fuel	120

G
Ganja Meda	75
Gemma Marx	32
George Floyd	3, 109
George Mason University	109
George Roberts	20–21, 23
Gish Jen	19
Gonorrhea	105
Grace Byron	120
Grammys	4, 25
Great Decision	19
Guggenheim Fellowship	110
Guru	46–53, 55–60

A BREAKDOWN OF THIS ISSUE'S CONTENTS
(by number of pages)

Essays *(58 pages)*
Interviews *(26 pages)*
Comics *(10 pages)*
Reviews *(3 pages)*

H
"Hagar; Or, the Twin Beauties"	21, 23
Hamburger	24–26, 30–31, 101
Harris Lahti	121
Heather Greener	121
Helen Gurley Brown	29
Hellscape	120
Himalayan Institute	48–29, 58, 61
Holly Brickley	11
Hollywood Presbyterian	103–104
Homer	120
Honesdale	48, 50, 55
How Should a Person Be?	66–70

I
IHOP	24, 27
IMDb	28
Immortality	74–75
Impressionistic	119
India Claudy	123
Inspiration	29
Irene Silt	120
Italo Calvino	119–120
Iyengar	47

J
Jackie Kennedy	13
Jack Kirby	115
Jeffrey Renard Allen	111
Jet-lagged	86
Jet Skiing	63
Joan Silber	18
Joe Gough	38
Joe Orton	65, 71
Johnny Trotter	30
Jomtien	62–64
Jones Beach	15
Jordan Taliha McDonald	75
Josh McDowell	105
Julia Child	11

K
Karachi	77–87
Katharine Webster	54
Kazuo Ishiguoro	69
Kenneth Dillon	121
Koh Samui	64
Korean-Mexican-American	108
Kris Kristofferson	104
Kristian Hammerstad	8, 10–11, 24, 34, 36, 38, 41, 65, 110
Kurosawa	15

L
Labor Day	16
Landline	67
Leviathan	23
Lexapro	120
Los Angeles	28, 72, 74, 102–103, 120, 121
Lower East Side	18
Lula Konner	103, 116
Lydia Sigourney	21
★ Lyle Lovett	24–31

Lyricism	119

M
Madonna	105
Marc Augé	63
Margaux Williamson	66
Maxime Gérin	88
Maya Segal	32

Compiled by Gemma Marx and Dan Gutenberg; portraits by Kristian Hammerstad; hand and burger illustrations by Andrea Settimo

Mayor LaGuardia 18	Pali................................... 46	Sheila Heti 65–73	Tony Millionaire...................
Meara Sharma 119	*Passing*............................ 126		.... 32, 34, 36, 40–41
Melissa Locker 25	Pathologist....................... 65		Tourism 63–64
Metaphysical 120	Pattaya 62–64		Tranquil 63
Mizmaru Kawahara 19	Paul Collins 20		*True Blood* 74
Monopoly 17	Pete Gamlen 119–121		Turds 19
Montreal 66–67	Peter Wolf 11–12		Turkeys 119
"Moon Hoax" 21	Philly Joe Jones 11		*Twilight* 75
Muay Thai 63	Pitchaya Sudbanthad........ 62		
Mustard-gas breath 102	Playwriting 67–68		**U**
	Pompeii............................. 10		University of Iowa............ 15
N	Porn 15, 100, 105		Un-seal-worthy 19
Necrophilia 121	Portrait 119		Urban heat island ....
Nella Larsen 126	Postal Act of 1845 20		.... 80, 86
New Mexico 120	Premarital sex........... 105, 108	Shruti Swamy 45	Uriah Derick D'arcy 74
Nick Hornby 11	Prince Bush...................... 87	*Sinners* 75	Uruk................................ 74
Non-place 63			Usain Bolt........................ 19
Nora Lange 15			Uttar Pradesh 47
			Utopian 120
O			Uzbekistan....................... 18
Octavia Butler................. 110			
Old Dracula..................... 75			**V**
Oliver Wendell Holmes 21			Vampires 74–75
Oregon State University 99, 109			Ved Vyas......................... 47
Ostional 121			Vic Greener 121
Ostracism 102			Video Vault 15, 17
Overconsumption............. 86			Vietnam War ....
Ovid 120			.... 63, 105, 109
Owen Pomery.................. 78			Virginia Woolf 65, 71
Oxherding Tale..... 110, 115–116, 118			Volcanic Repeating Firearms....... 21
			Vulgarity 75
P			
Pakistan 77–78			**W**
			Waiting on the Moon 11–12
			Walla Walla 27
	Psychedelic 47	THE ROUTINE, WITH JOAN SILBER *(page 18)*	Walt Whitman 21
			Wastewater 17, 64, 81
	Q		"Water mafia" 81
	Queen of the Damned........ 74		*Weekend at Bernies* 15
	Quota system................... 47	Skin rashes...................... 64	West Queen West............. 65
		Sogdiana 10	*Who's Afraid of Virginia Woolf?*
	R	Su Ertekin-Taner 17, 56, 69, 113	 11–12
	Raccoons 121	Susan Sontag 65, 72	Widow 78–79
	Rafia Zakaria 77	Swami Rama 46–48, 51–61	Wilhelm Reich 114
	Rheumatoid arthritis......... 85		Woke 109
	R. Hoe & Company 23	**T**	Wyna Liu....................... 124
	Richard Wright............ 113–114	Taj Mahal......................... 19	
	Robert Altman 25, 28–29	Tastemaker 23	**Y**
	Roe v. Wade........... 98, 102, 108	Texas A&M	Yale 66
	Roger Ebert..................... 15	.... 24, 26, 30, 107	Yankee 20–21
	Roman Empire............... 120	Texas Cowboy Hall of Fame ..	YMCA............................. 48
	Rosie Stockton 120	.... 25, 30–31	Yoga 46–49, 51–53, 112
	Russ Kunkel 31	T. C. Boyle 15	*Yoga Journal*..................
		Thailand..................... 63–64	.... 54–57, 59, 61
	S	*The Feminine Mystique* 13	
	Sanskrit................. 46–47, 49	*The Illuminated Quadruple Constellation* 20–23	**Z**
	Semi-vegetarian 18	*The Island* 119	Zeitgeist 11, 109
			Zelig................................ 11
			Zen koan 52
			Zola................................ 69
			Zoom.............................. 27

I FOUND THE MOTHER CHARACTER VERY TOUCHING.

Photo by Joan Silber; comics panel by Maxime Gérin

UNDERWAY

WE ASK WRITERS AND ARTISTS: WHAT'S ON YOUR DESK? WHAT ARE YOU WORKING ON?

by Annalee Newitz

Coffee Cup
My favorite Canadian purchase: a weird maple leaf moose coffee cup from the International Village Mall

Laptop
The trusty laptop is covered in queer stickers and stuffed with PDFs about Sogdiana

Audio Recording Equipment
Podcasting mic and headphones, to record Our Opinions Are Correct *on the road*

Hand Moisturizer
I have a strangely large collection of hand moisturizers.

Dungeons & Dragons Dice
Never travel anywhere without D&D dice.

Serving Tray
My cats are obsessed with this small serving tray, which they occupy constantly for mysterious reasons.

Buckyball Dome
I can see the Science World buckyball dome through the window as I write, often illuminated by rainbow LEDs. It's heartening to be in a city whose most iconic megastructure is dedicated to science.

I spent the first quarter of 2025 living in Vancouver, Canada. I'm writing this from one of those high rises on the edge of Chinatown that glitters like a retro-futurist arcology over the city's coastal parks and cloud-muffled mountains. All my previous novels featured Canadian places, but I just finished copyedits on a forthcoming novella, "Automatic Noodle," which is set entirely in San Francisco. It might be my first and last extended fictional tale of the city where I've spent most of my adult life.

I'm doing early research for my next nonfiction book, which is an ancient history of parties. What can archaeology reveal about how our distant ancestors boogied down together thousands of years ago? I'm finding out. I'm also deep into my next sci-fi novel, about a graduate student from beyond the galaxy, doing research in Roman-era Pompeii. My brain is hiding in the distant past, and my body is hiding in Canada. But every day it feels like the United States of 2025 follows me around, yelling. ✦

Illustration by Kristian Hammerstad

STUFF I'VE BEEN READING

A QUARTERLY COLUMN, STEADY AS EVER

by Nick Hornby

BOOKS READ:
- ★ *Waiting on the Moon: Artists, Poets, Drifters, Grifters, and Goddesses*—Peter Wolf
- ★ *Cocktails with George and Martha: Movies, Marriage, and the Making of "Who's Afraid of Virginia Woolf?"*—Philip Gefter
- ★ *Loved and Missed*—Susie Boyt
- ★ *Deep Cuts*—Holly Brickley

BOOKS BOUGHT:
- ★ *Bitch: On the Female of the Species*—Lucy Cooke
- ★ *Cocktails with George and Martha: Movies, Marriage, and the Making of "Who's Afraid of Virginia Woolf?"*—Philip Gefter
- ★ *Family Happiness*—Laurie Colwin
- ★ *Becoming a Composer*—Errollyn Wallen

Do you remember Steve Morrow, the Arsenal player who fell off his captain's shoulders during a celebration after the 1993 League Cup final and broke his collarbone? I don't think you do. I don't think you've ever heard of him. Well, true story. He once came to one of my book signings with his son. If I were to write a book in the style of Peter Wolf's memoir, *Waiting on the Moon*, that true story would be in there. That's why I shouldn't write it.

Wolf, once a DJ and then the lead singer of the J. Geils Band, is pop culture's Zelig. Woody Allen's character, you may remember, managed to appear alongside Babe Ruth and Al Capone, Charles Lindbergh and Hitler, Hearst, Chaplin, and scores of others. Wolf—who, it's important to stress, is not a fictional character—was put in charge of the mic that Eleanor Roosevelt was to speak into at his high school. He messed it up. When he was a young boy, Marilyn Monroe fell asleep on his shoulder in a movie theatre. Bob Dylan harangued him on the subject of truth outside a restaurant in the Village. He met with Hitchcock to try and get his band on the soundtrack of the great director's last movie, *Family Plot*. Muddy Waters stayed in his apartment. David Lynch was a roommate, and changed the locks when Wolf couldn't pay the rent. Charlie Watts punched him during an argument about who was the greatest drummer of all time. (Wolf, unforgivably, thought Watts was making a case for Jo Jones, Basie's drummer, when actually and predictably he was talking about Philly Joe Jones, who played for Coltrane, Miles Davis, and Bill Evans.)

And Faye Dunaway… Well, Faye Dunaway married him, which is kind of a cheat in the Zelig game. You can't go around *marrying* one of the people who represent the zeitgeist and expect to get a point. You're just supposed to be in a room in the right place at the right time—Dunaway disallowed. Through Dunaway, he met the fashion photographer Terry O'Neill, although that was an example of being in the wrong place at the wrong time: O'Neill was in Dunaway's bedroom at the time, and the meeting ended with Wolf smashing several of O'Neill's lenses. Maybe that one doesn't count either.

He sat next to Tennessee Williams in the theater; they were watching a production of one of Williams's plays, and the playwright annoyed the audience by laughing too hard at his own lines. He went to dinner at Julia Child's

Illustration by Kristian Hammerstad

house, where Child served coleslaw and Pepperidge Farm snacks. George Cukor. Warhol. *Peter Wolf went drinking with Pelé and he didn't recognize him.* And of course there are the musicians—Aretha, John Lee Hooker, the Stones, Van Morrison. After a while you start to laugh at the sheer relentlessness of it. But Wolf is laughing with you. What makes *Waiting on the Moon* such a joy is that Wolf isn't dropping names. He's saying, *What the fuck?* He can't believe it either. The book is organized around these people (the subtitle is *Artists, Poets, Drifters, Grifters, and Goddesses*) rather than around his own career—it's about a wide-eyed fan who can't believe his luck. There's hardly any mention of the J. Geils Band, who meant a great deal to me: the first four or five J. Geils albums, the ones they made before their big 1980s pop hits, were fierce, funny R&B albums that unearthed a whole ton of obscure 1960s singles for me, and their live shows were ferocious. But you don't have to be a devotee of the band to enjoy *Waiting on the Moon.* You just have to be a devotee of *something.*

The star power in *Cocktails with George and Martha*, Philip Gefter's deeply entertaining book about *Who's Afraid of Virginia Woolf?*, the play and the movie, could power a rocket to Mars and back. Nobody, however, is standing around gaping: just about everyone concerned knows—or feels—that he or she is a star. That's too many stars in one place, and one of the possible outcomes of a stellar collision is a black hole. Another is the creation of a brighter star, and nobody involved in the movie version of Albee's play

had their light dimmed by the experience. It was one of only two films in history that was nominated for every single eligible category in the Oscars, and it won five. Irene Sharaff, incidentally, was the very last winner of the Best Costume Design in Black and White award, in 1967.

But it all began with a piece of graffiti: the words of the title, spotted by Edward Albee in a bar in Greenwich Village. Those words went into him, hung around for a few years, and then became a play, which opened on October 13, 1962. Chances are you have already spent some time in that week this year: Bob Dylan played at the Gaslight Café on October 15, a day after the Cuban Missile Crisis began. *A Complete Unknown*, the Oscar-nominated Bob Dylan movie, shows the panic and the ominousness of those few days. Albee's play didn't cause the Cuban Missile Crisis—historians, feel free to quote me—and Albee might not have heard of Bob Dylan, and vice versa. But the three events combined must have created some kind of murky and foreboding atmosphere in New York City that autumn: the end of marriage in the theater, prophesies of doom in the folk clubs, the end of the world live on TV. The Yankees won the World Series that week. It's not often you can rely on your sports team to lift the gloom. The play caused a sensation, despite, or because of, the reviews in some of the New York newspapers: "Three and a half hours long, four characters wide and a cesspool deep," said the *New York Daily News*. "A sick play about sick people," said *The Mirror*. I'd have run all the way to the box office, and a lot of people

did. The *New York Daily News* then decided it wanted to shift a few more tickets by running a follow-up piece a few days later in the weekend section, with the headline FOR DIRTY-MINDED FEMALES ONLY. In 1963 the Billy Rose Theatre could probably have sold the last remaining tickets to dirty-minded females alone. But there must have been a lot of young men thinking to themselves, Well, Tinder hasn't been invented yet…

There was an inevitability about the movie adaptation that was peculiar to its time. As you probably know, the play really is only four characters deep, and it is set in one room, over one night, and it's airless and savage, and it's very hard to imagine twenty-first-century people finding the appetite for it. (What do twenty-first-century people have an appetite for? I'm leaving myself out of this. I'm a twentieth-century person, I suspect. Or at least, I came of age in a time when we did all huddle around a book, or a movie or a TV show we all watched at the same time, like losers.) And of course, plays happen in only one big city per country, initially, at least. One thing that's changed is that people who do not live in that big city no longer give much of a shit about what happens there. The phrase *metropolitan elite* became politicized, mostly by bad people, but let's face it, it was ripe for politicization. Telling newspaper readers in Manchester or Atlanta all about a play they can see in only one theater in London or New York… Well, I suspect those days are nearly gone, not least because those newspaper readers have all stopped reading newspapers,

TRANSITIONS
by Evie Shockley

i.
death descends, in spite of help, in spite
of the one who would help who
is rendered instead—on the sweaty bed, on the cold
bathroom tiles—witness. but what is there
to see. they—we—used to say
the soul would slip like smoke
between parted lips & rise to hover
above its fleshly vehicle, giving up gravity
for air. maybe what falls upon us—each witless
witness, instantly alone—is
insight, that what we cannot stop
or watch we can feel: the *dead
weight* of what someone beloved has discarded
into our arms. maybe what drops into the scene
is not death, but life, the weight
of what we call carrying
on.

ii.
in an uncentral park, maya lin plants
a *ghost forest*, atlantic white cedar from the pine barrens
killed by salt from rising seas, claimed
for art to haunt the city
with the consequences of climate change. we cut
trees down for coffins, they cradle
our remains without audible complaint. lin
installed those bare-branched cedars
amongst the leafy red oaks &
maples so we could keep their corpses
company. close your eyes. lean
first against the pulsing, textured trunks, then
the dry, twisted wood. we startle away
from the absence of sap, feel death's stillness settling
in.   life courses.   even through bark, in the most
rooted of creatures, it moves
us.

---

or died. *WAoVW?*—if I may—opened at a different time, when a local metropolitan event could grab national attention, and therefore the interest of a film studio could be guaranteed. Warner Bros. paid Albee half a million dollars for the film rights.

There are so many fascinating, gossipy tidbits studded throughout *Cocktails with George and Martha* that you want someone to ask you what you're reading just so you can spew some of it back out. Henry Fonda's agent turned down the role of George on his client's behalf without letting him know; when Fonda found out, he fired the agent. Elizabeth Taylor liked to be given very expensive jewelry by… Well, by just about everyone who crossed her path, professionally or personally. If such a gift were not forthcoming, she was likely to turn a bit sulky. (Ernest Lehman, the producer and screenwriter, refused to cough up, on the not-unreasonable grounds that he was paying her enough already.) The movie—surely one of the least complicated ever made—was delivered two months behind schedule and two million dollars over budget. The total cost was seven and a half million—seventy million in today's money. Ernest Lehman received an Oscar nomination for Best Adapted Screenplay, despite having written only a couple of transitional lines—everything else came from the play. And when the movie desperately needed the approval of the National Catholic Office for Motion Pictures, a big deal back then, Mike Nichols arranged for Jackie Kennedy to sit behind two important representatives of the Church and say loudly, "Jack would have *loved* this film" as the credits came up at the end.

But this is a smart book, too, a proper piece of cultural history, placing the play and the film in their time, a time that produced Betty Friedan's *The Feminine Mystique* and Richard Yates's *Revolutionary Road*, as well as *WAoVW?*, all within months of one another. In 1963 only eight states gave stay-at-home wives any claim on their husband's earnings, and rape was defined as "forcible sexual intercourse with a woman other than one's wife." No wonder Martha was angry; no wonder that anger was recognized and then amplified.

The women in *Loved and Missed*, Susie Boyt's painful and lovely novel, have every right to be angry, but they're not, not really. They're sad, and disappointed, and damaged, but that doesn't mean the book has no tension or energy: the central character, Ruth, is determined to do the right thing. The right thing happens to be the thing that gives her life meaning and brings her joy, and that's what makes the book so compelling to read.

Ruth's daughter, Eleanor, is an addict, lost to drugs and squats and squalor, and she lives, or exists, anyway, down the road from her mother, so she is never out of sight or out of mind. When Eleanor gives birth to a daughter, Ruth takes the baby and brings it up as her own child. *Loved and Missed* is a perfectly realized book. It feels true, deeply felt, with a Christlike sympathy for its characters, however flawed and misguided. It has little twists that have the power to shock, and the almost complete absence of men—the ones who hover on the fringes, noticeable only by their absence, are feckless, cruel, irresponsible, hopeless—is actually a strength, because it enables Boyt to create a world that is mostly invisible but very real nonetheless. And it has an ending that kills you.

A friend in London gave me the book; later that same day, another friend, in California, completely unconnected to the first, texted to ask if I had read it. This was slightly unnerving—Boyt is a lovely writer, but she has been unfairly overlooked over the course of a seven-novel, thirty-year career. Her last novel, *Love and Fame*, has received fifty-three reviews on a website we no longer talk about; this one has more than nine hundred. The gift and the text seem to indicate that *Loved and Missed* is finding a readership it deserves.

On the second page of Holly Brickley's new novel, *Deep Cuts*, the narrator has a conversation with a guy in a bar about "Sara Smile," the Hall & Oates song. As they listen to it playing, the guy says the song is perfect. The young woman, Percy, isn't so sure.

"I would call this a perfect track, a perfect recording. Not a perfect song… A perfect song has stronger bones. Lyrics, chords, melody. It can be played differently, produced differently, and it will almost always be great… See? The most beautiful part of the verse is just him riffing. A great song—and I'm talking about the pop-rock world here, obviously—can be improved by riffing, or ruined by riffing. But it cannot *rely* on riffing.'"

The second page! Page two! It is fair to say that I am the target audience for this book. Have you seen *The Day of the Jackal*, the reboot of the 1973 film adapted from the Frederick Forsyth novel? Bear with me. One of the things I learned from the series—actually the *only* thing I learned from the series, which to be fair was not put on Earth to teach me things—is that the world record for a sniper shot is well over two miles. Two miles! (Excuse the exclamation marks in this paragraph, which is becoming unruly.) Anyway, I felt like one of the Jackal's sniper victims. I had no idea where this book came from, or how far away from me the author lives, but she spotted me through some kind of insane telescopic sight, and fired.

I wanted to argue with Percy straightaway, of course, by drawing her attention to the jazz pianist Joe Alterman's cover of "Sara Smile," where he finds the sturdy and clever chords on which the song rests. Or he finds his own, anyway. But I remained in conversation for the book's entire length. I haven't read anything quite like *Deep Cuts* before, because part of its subject matter is a contemplation of the educated, deeply focused music fan's relationship with talent: Percy meets and falls for a songwriter, Joe, and she becomes some part of the process— a cowriter, an arranger, a producer, never quite enough to be able to describe herself as a musician. Meanwhile, Percy makes a living as some kind of influencer-harvester. The subject matter is, in itself, a deep cut. There is love, jealousy, complication, and the world that the book describes is modern, flimsy, baffling. It wasn't around twenty years ago, and it probably won't be around in twenty years' time. Brickley isn't aiming for immortality, which is maybe why it has a chance of lasting. None of the people in it are famous, and they probably won't be, but they are the people who may well come to represent this peculiar, nebulous century. I wish I could remember what Steve Morrow said to me. I think he was working with the youth team at the time, so we probably talked about that. ✩

RESURRECTOR

A ROTATING GUEST COLUMN IN WHICH WRITERS
REEXAMINE CRITICALLY UNACCLAIMED WORKS OF ART

by Nora Lange

★ IN THIS ISSUE: *Weekend at Bernie's*

Weekend at Bernie's is about being wealthy in America: babes, boats, fraud. According to my mother, *Weekend at Bernie's* qualifies as a movie, not a film. In 1989, when the movie hit theaters, it flopped. The critic Roger Ebert said the twist wasn't funny enough to carry the story forward. He hated it. But what he didn't see, may he RIP, was that the one-note, unapologetically crass materialism was worth the rental price of seeing it through to the end.

It was my mom who taught me as a kid to distinguish between a movie and a film: Movies were notoriously more "fun," which was like saying, in other words, "sort of stupid," and notably American. Films were about the mind, which was to say they were art, and they were notably of the high-art type and notably foreign. While she was a student at the University of Iowa, she ran an independent movie theater called the Bijou in Iowa City—a theater where the writer T. C. Boyle took his then girlfriend, now wife of decades, Karen Boyle, on dates to see Kurosawa and Bergman films. In the years since, T. C. and Karen have said they learned everything they know about cinema during those years when my mother was the programmer.

In the mid-'90s, my mom and her partner, Sherry, took over the neighborhood video store in our mini neighborhood shopping center on the west side of Santa Barbara, near Foodland, a Laundromat, and a dollar store. They renamed it the Video Vault and put up a fresh new sign. They added foreign and independent rentals to the mix and kept the porn section in a designated corner. Dusty-rose curtains hung from the ceiling to demarcate that space. When I first asked my mother about *Weekend at Bernie's*, she wrote to me that she didn't remember it. I quickly received a follow-up email: "I just remember laughing at it even though the premise was kind of sick." She was referring to Bernie, a corpse that was being toted around the beach.

In the movie, Larry/"Larr" (Andrew McCarthy) and Richard/"Rich" (Jonathan Silverman) are both low-level employees at an insurance company in New York City. Over the course of an unusually hot summer, the two likable imbeciles—who've been tasked with auditing the company's financials—have been working weekends. Meanwhile, they find what passes as a kind of simulated joy on the rooftop of their corporate office—"This sucks, I'm so unhappy," Larr says. The two substitute their dream of hitting the "real beach" (though Rich notes there are "no more real beaches" and suggests they go to Jones Beach and float around in hospital waste) with a boom box and an inflatable pool: "Sizzle, sizzle, sizzle as the Big Apple becomes the Baked Apple," the radio announcer laments. Their luck shifts when they discover in

Illustration by Kristian Hammerstad

their audit that there's been life insurance fraud at the company: "Hold the phone, buddy—I got it!" Rich tells Larr. Come Monday morning, they report the error to their boss, and he invites them to his beach mansion in the Hamptons for Labor Day weekend. Bernie Lomax (Terry Kiser) is a CEO's CEO: gold watches, a potpourri of ladies, sprawling properties, healthy cocaine and company-embezzlement habits. Later that same day, after Larr and Rich pointed out the discrepancy, over a red-and-white-checkered-tablecloth dinner, Bernie asks his murdering thugs to take out Rich and Larry, but the thugs instead determine that it's Lomax who needs to go.

At the end of the week, Rich and Larry arrive at Bernie's house in the Hamptons, but when they get to the front door, he doesn't show himself to let them in. As legitimate, invited guests, they let themselves into his modernist, rectilinear beach palace. The interior has been dressed in an array of pastel colors, the art and the furniture, like a roll of Smarties. "All of this could be yours if you set your goals and work hard," Rich says to Larry of the sprawl. "My old man worked hard. All they did was give him more work," Larry says about capitalism. The two guys pop champagne and discover that Bernie is dead. But before they can call the cops to report it, people start arriving for Bernie's annual Labor Day weekend party. Nobody notices that Bernie is catatonic on the couch. Bernie is flawlessly lifeless, but he still manages to please his angry girlfriend; pinch a woman's tush; fulfill his promise to give a baggie of cocaine to another woman; and, with his tennis coach,

SEPTEMBER

by Cecily Parks

I was conversing
with the blossomless canes
in the hot fall air
the weak breeze
that briefly jostled
us all gone I guess
I loathe this trellis
said the shrub rose
And we these velvety lettuces
said the munching bunnies
sculpted for maybe
eternity into the stone
bench I sat on and late
I walked away from them
with the no-smell
of leaves blotched brown
and black hypanthia that once
cupped blooms but now
nothing and the piebald moon
sweating in the sky not
knowing if I wanted to run
to the cold river or the cold
river to run to me
—to us, really,
and scour our cages clean.

finagle, barter, and eventually settle on a good selling price for his Porsche; and mostly please his trainer (the trainer notes that Bernie needs to pump more iron but admires his relaxed physique as he rubs his arms). Larr and Rich take note of the fact that nobody seems to notice Bernie is dead. Bernie appears to be himself, fully. How far can Larr and Rich take this? Maybe the doofuses will enjoy a holiday after all.

As the movie progresses, Bernie becomes even more himself, and Larry and Rich get into their new roles puppeteering the body of their slain boss around town. (It must be mentioned that the two learn from Bernie's answering machine, which mistakenly catches Bernie on tape, that *they* had been the intended murder targets.) This is just the self-justifying lubricant the two dudes need to see this thing—their deserved vacation at a real beach sans wastewater—to its completion. The bits like this continue throughout. Rich fumbles over his preposterous fables about Bernie, at one point telling his love interest (a summer intern at the office) that Bernie is too busy to talk. Larry day-drinks and plays Monopoly with Bernie's body, whom he supplies with a lit cigarette in one hand and whose other hand he manipulates with an umbrella cord, so that Bernie's corpse can wave to the friendly girls in bikinis passing by on the beach, and so that the two lovable schmucks can finally relax and maybe even get laid.

Stay in it for the party, when an "authoress" (as she's identified in the credits) says to a mate, "Harvey, you promised me a review on the front page of the *Sunday Times* books section," but is told that the subject matter—some piece suggesting that Sherlock Holmes and Dr. Watson were secretly married—was of no interest to readers. Stay watching for the books on Bernie's desk in his home office: *Crimes and Criminals*, Elmore Leonard's *Glitz* (dubbed "a cat-and-mouse tale with claws"), *What's Next* (not the Drake song). If explicit irony isn't what does it, stay for the boat scene. That was the part in the movie that my mom and I laughed at the hardest: Bernie's body gets tied to a seat on his boat, but when Larry swerves to avoid another boat, his body is thrust overboard. Bernie is then dragged behind the boat, hitting all the channel markers, ringing their bells one by one. Stay to see the delighted buffoons vacuum Bernie's toupee, and then staple it in place to his bald head. Laugh heartily when his limp body falls from a wheeled reclining chair, off the deck, and onto a sandy beach, only to be buried by a spicy toddler with his plastic shovel and bucket. Besides, as *People* magazine pointed out, the actor who played Bernie Lomax was not actually dead. So there's nothing to be ashamed of. We're forgiven.

People say a lot of stuff, like "Money isn't everything," and "Laughter is the best medicine." Bernie Lomax may have been sick-rich, with an enviable roving set of chicks, race cars, and a formidable tan, but he does not end up with the potential of a future—as his employees do—by the movie's end. (Rich finds true love, for one.) Bernie may have had it all, but then look where it got him. I enjoyed where it got me and my mother. My mom had to close the Video Vault in the early aughts. Even our two-for-one weekend deals and my adding weekends to my schedule couldn't salvage the declining number of customers and the introduction of DVDs. People had moved on. Sherry and my mother sold the place and all its contents and barely broke even. Nothing in the store was worth anything, the market dictated. We would never party like the Bernies of America, those decamillionaires who grew in number rapidly in the '80s, those men that could continue celebrating and haunting others even when dead, but we gave ourselves heartburn laughing at their foibles from the comforts of our mediocre living rooms. When I emailed my mom asking how she'd felt then about selling the Video Vault, she wrote: "Sure was fun, though, having it, and the customers loved us. You were our most reliable and best employee."

But the end of the Video Vault would never take away our love of cinema—of its crass or intellectual nature. We lived in America, which was to say, my mother promoted an ethos of embracing the absurd and finding the gems, however small and hidden. When we vacated the building, we left the unframed posters on the walls and the membership punch cards in their little bowl near the cash register. We left the display racks, like a maze woven throughout the store. The heavily fingered recent blockbuster movie releases with their solicitous stickers were there at the entrance, right next to smaller-budget, pristine, deeply adored films from a previous decade, like *Chungking Express*. We unplugged the Video Vault sign and took ourselves home for good. ✱

ACTORS WHO GAVE UP SHOWERING TO PREPARE FOR A ROLE

✱ Halle Berry—*Jungle Fever*
✱ Shia LaBeouf—*Fury*
✱ Robert Pattinson *The Lighthouse*
✱ Viggo Mortensen—
   The Lord of the Rings
✱ Jeff Goldblum—*Death Wish*
✱ Benedict Cumberbatch—
   The Power of the Dog
✱ Russell Crowe—*Gladiator*,
   Cinderella Man, and *Noah*
✱ Marlon Wayans—
   Requiem for a Dream
✱ Daniel Day-Lewis—*The Crucible*
✱ Tom Hanks—*Cast Away*

—list compiled by Su Ertekin-Taner

THE ROUTINE: JOAN SILBER
AN ANNOTATED RAMBLE THROUGH ONE ARTIST'S WORKDAY

7:30 a.m. Took dog, Jolie, out to East River Park to play. Jolie is a rescued street dog from Taiwan who is very social—loves hanging out with other dogs on the Lower East Side.

10:30 a.m. Went to Essex Market for groceries. It's an indoor public market that Mayor LaGuardia originally built (1940) to house vendors with pushcarts. Dog came with me.

1 p.m. Had lunch. I'm a semi-vegetarian, addicted to peanut butter sandwiches.

5 p.m. Took dog for walk. → **5:30 p.m.** Back to desk.

7 p.m. Met friends for dinner in East Village. The waiter, who knew us, had running jokes with my friend Chuck. Much political analysis and deep sorrow.

7:30–11 a.m.

11 a.m.–12:30 p.m.

1–2 p.m.

5–7 p.m.

9–10 p.m.

9 a.m. Read *NY Times* in print over breakfast.

9:15 a.m. Had long phone conversation with dear friend Myra.

11:15 a.m. Read book on Uzbekistan, for a planned trip next month and also maybe for a story I want to write.

12:30 p.m. Midday dog walk to Seward Park.

2 p.m. Thought about story I might want to write and took notes. Wrote a paragraph that has possibilities, which made me happy. Looked up a number of vaguely related things. Getting ideas. Some are dumb, some not.

9:45 p.m. Dog walk.

10 p.m. Listened in bed to audiobook of *Stone Yard Devotional*, nominated for Booker and written by Charlotte Wood, whom I met in Australia in 2020. Loved it and thought about what to write to her in email. ✱

Photos by the author

ANIMAL

WILD TURKEY

by Gish Jen

FEATURES:
* Runs almost as fast as Usain Bolt, albeit in bursts
* Flies faster than most hummingbirds, albeit in bursts
* Gobbles, purrs, yelps, chirps, clicks, and kee-kees

It is a truth, if not universally acknowledged then at least generally believed, that Ben Franklin put forth the turkey as our national bird. This is not true. He did criticize the eagle on a draft of the Great Seal as looking rather like a turkey, and in so doing he did call the turkey, however un-seal-worthy, "a much more respectable Bird" than an eagle. Eagles, he said, did not make their livings honestly, being too lazy to fish for themselves. A turkey, in contrast, besides being "a true original native of America," was, by his lights, "though a little vain and silly," still "a bird of courage."

That was not to praise the turkey to the skies. That was to throw shade on the eagle. But never mind. *Meleagris gallopavo* is indeed just as vain and silly as its name, *gallopavo*—meaning "chicken peacock"—would suggest. What an improbable creature, after all, all puff and strut, with wattles and a snood that change color like a mood ring: going from pale gray-blue when it's feeling chill, to hot chili red when it's, um, not. Notably, the snood also engorges and elongates, especially during mating season, or when its owner is simply in the mood for action. As for which is the "bird of courage," the eagle or the turkey—that is a question beyond the scope of this essay. More important: Is yesterday's bird of courage today's domestic terrorist? At present, up and down the East Coast, we poor plodding humans struggle to protect ourselves against the protected turkeys. Wild turkeys are a conservation success! Large as they figured in the first Thanksgiving, as of 1851 there was nary one to be seen in my home state of Massachusetts. And yet now they once again rival the bunny rabbit in multiplication enthusiasm.

To clarify, wild turkeys are not doomed, domed butterballs perfect for stuffing in late November. They are snood-engorged gang goons focused on street domination. They see three times better than we do, and natural as it may be to claim they all look alike, they would make no such claim about us. If you feel like they remember you, you are correct. They do. That said, it is not always personal when they surround your minivan so you cannot get out. Look at their snoods: it may just be their mood. They will surround your car, too, so you can't get in, or chase your car down the street, or mob your front grills, a.k.a. their all-you-can-eat bug buffet. And only sometimes is this personal (though then it completely is).

Happily, they can be mesmerized, especially by themselves. Savvy car owners realize they should on no account wash their cars in the spring, especially if they have dark cars, as turkeys will fixate on their reflections in the shiny surface of a clean dark car and peck at their alter egos for hours. They also stalk pregnant women and terrorize cats, and though they loiter in front of bookstores, staring into the windows, no one is fooled: in books, as in all things, they seek only their own reflection.

In our neighborhood, they will roost in our neighbor's tree across the street, spending the night in its fair branches—first, so they might fertilize its roots in characteristic fashion, the females depositing delicate spiral turds, while the males dump J-shaped plops. But mostly they rest there so they might rise perfectly situated to dig up our other neighbor's daffodil bulbs. These, as it happens, are not just any daffodil bulbs. These are daffodil bulbs our former neighbors planted to commemorate their great love. They met in Switzerland and chose each other in an era when that was not done; and as their Great Decision was made in a daffodil field, they later filled their whole front yard with daffodils to e'er remember it. That is to say, that yard is their Taj Mahal.

Or, rather, it was. (Daffodil bulbs are, it seems, a great turkey delicacy.) I hold out hope that, discriminating creatures that they are, turkeys can be trained to be mesmerized by their reflections in Teslas. In the meanwhile—dare I say it?—what a bunch of turkeys. ✶

Illustration by Mizmaru Kawahara

THE LAST MASTODON

THE SHORT AND DISASTROUS LIFE OF THE WORLD'S BIGGEST NEWSPAPER

by Paul Collins

I hesitate a moment at Stanford University's Special Collections desk. "I got in touch about seeing the *Constellation*? The newspaper from 1859?" I ask Tim Noakes, the library's head of public services.

"Oh"—he motions toward the front of the room, where a newspaper sprawls over an entire reading table—"the *big* one?"

An act of typographical hubris that long held the title of "world's largest newspaper," the July 4, 1859, special issue of *The Illuminated Quadruple Constellation* survives today in only a handful of libraries. Published in Manhattan and distributed nationally, it was printed on seventy-by-one-hundred-inch sheets—bigger than a king-size bed—and then folded twice to produce eight pages, each fifty inches long and thirty-five inches wide. Its footprint can hold roughly six copies of *The New York Times*. When I lay my phone down next to a copy in Stanford University's rare books room, the effect is of a tugboat bobbing in the water next to a battleship.

One page of *The Illuminated Quadruple Constellation* is the size of 117 iPhone SEs.

"It cannot be excelled in its mammoth dimensions," brags the front page, "because a sheet of any greater length and breadth would be absolutely unmanageable." This is not an idle boast. Upon attempting to read this behemoth, I find myself walking sheepishly back to Noakes at his desk.

"We need two people to turn the pages," I tell him.

You can easily hold one of the first American newspapers in one hand: *Publick Occurrences Both Foreign and Domestick* from 1690 approximates letter-sized paper. But as more modern-looking broadsheets emerged in the 1830s, the magic ingredients of disruptive media also appeared: new technology, IP theft, and a government loophole. The US lacked copyright protection for popular foreign authors like Charles Dickens; what it did have, though, were new steam-driven printing presses, and a far lower postal rate for newspapers than for books or magazines. The trick to steam-powered piracy, then, was somehow to cram a book into a newspaper.

"The Mastodon of American Newspapers" and "The Largest Paper in All Creation," announced the *Universal Yankee Nation* in 1841. At about eleven square feet, it was twice the size of a typical broadsheet. Other piratical behemoths like *The New World*, *Brother Jonathan*, and *The Boston Notion* soon followed. These "mastodon" or "bed-blanket" weeklies could provide a book's worth of reading: Charles Dickens's *American Notes* was gleefully ripped off in its entirety by *The New World* in a twelve-and-a-half-cent issue, days before his usual publisher could issue a book costing twice as much.

Inevitably, the mastodons turned their tusks on one another, each boasting of greater Brobdingnagian proportions than the last; the announcement of a "Double Double Yankee Nation" spurred a competing quadruple version of *The Boston Notion* ("The Mammoth 'SUN-ECLIPSER,' coming at last! Acres of entertainment!"). Not to be outdone, *Brother Jonathan* claimed "upward of 100 engravings" for its Christmas issue. Mastodon papers had a problem, though, and it wasn't just how hard it was to turn their pages. They relied on a business model that could be destroyed with a stroke of a pen. After the Postal Act of 1845 limited the size allowed for the newspaper rate, they could be big, but not sun-eclipsing big.

All the stranger, then, when a baffling announcement by veteran publisher George Roberts appeared fourteen years later, in *The New York Tribune*, on June 30, 1859: "THE GREAT WONDER OF THE AGE! THE MASTODON OF NEWSPAPERS, PUBLISHED ONCE IN A HUNDRED YEARS! The subscriber announces that he will publish, and have for sale everywhere, on SATURDAY July 2, THE LARGEST SHEET OF PAPER EVER MADE AND PRINTED. It will be known as 'THE ILLUMINATED QUADRUPLE CONSTELLATION.' PRINTED ON ONE SHEET 70x100 INCHES… GREAT CURIOSITY OF THE 19TH CENTURY."

It seemed like an incredible promise. Roberts's *Constellation* was a

Images throughout courtesy of the Department of Special Collections, Stanford University Libraries

struggling weekly that hadn't put out an issue in months, and assembling the largest newspaper ever was a tall order even for a thriving publisher.

Even more incredibly—he pulled it off.

"Ready?" Tim asks. We hold opposite edges of a page and turn it in tandem, like we're making a bed.

You don't so much read an *Illuminated Quadruple Constellation* as behold it. When I actually *do* try to read it, I feel like I might be voiding the warranty on my brain. Each page is thirteen columns wide. Even the steel engravings scattered across the front page—a hodgepodge of President James Buchanan, Andrew Jackson, Harvard president Edward Everett, and the like—scarcely alter the overpowering amount of type. The *Constellation* limited its engravings to one side of its massive sheet during printing; because each sheet is folded into eight pages, there are pictures on pages 1, 4 to 5, and 8, while on the paired facing pages of 2 to 3 and 6 to 7, there is only verbiage, sometimes nearly running off the bottom of the page altogether. The effect is of standing under a waterfall of text, amid a ceaseless roar of words.

At a hefty fifty cents, or about nineteen dollars today, the *Constellation* wasn't cheap—unlike its forebearers, it didn't qualify for cheap postage—but in classic mastodon fashion, its content was still more about quantity than quality. Along with newly commissioned shockers like "A Night in the Devil's Den; or, the Gallows Tree!" and the romance novel "Hagar; Or, The Twin Beauties," the *Constellation* ran a celebratory poem whose tetrameter of alternating seven- and eight-syllable lines includes this line-break atrocity:

Then from his pocket he drew
   forth
The—New York
   CONSTELLATION,
The best and largest paper pub-
Lished in our Yankee nation.

Still, to lead his Herculean effort, Roberts hired none other than Park Benjamin—a champion of Nathaniel Hawthorne, mentor to a young Walt Whitman, and a man who, Edgar Allan Poe once marveled, "has exerted an influence scarcely second to that of any editor in the country." So the *Constellation*'s pages include some pointedly literary work as well: an excerpt from Oliver Wendell Holmes's *The Autocrat of the Breakfast-Table*, a poem by Lydia Sigourney, and a rerun of the New York *Sun*'s 1835 "Moon Hoax."

The real entertainment, though, is in the ads, which include notices for Brandreth Pills ("A Medicine Which Often Cures and Cannot Possibly Injure"), Volcanic Repeating Fire Arms ("10,000 men armed with this terrible weapon, would be equal to 300,000 armed in the ordinary way"), and the Elliptic Bed Spring Company ("We now see no room for improvement in this invention").

With their big and ornate typesetting, the ads are blessedly readable. The rest of the paper requires walking around the table and leaning all the way over at a perpendicular angle to browse essays like "Never Marry a Woman Until She's Had the Small Pox." I take more than a hundred photos of *The Illuminated Quadruple Constellation*, roughly gridding out each page. It will be easier, I decide, to read it later on my phone.

Upon the *Constellation*'s nationwide release, *The New Hampshire Patriot and State Gazette* pronounced it a "MONSTER PAPER... [this] could have originated no where but in this go-ahead

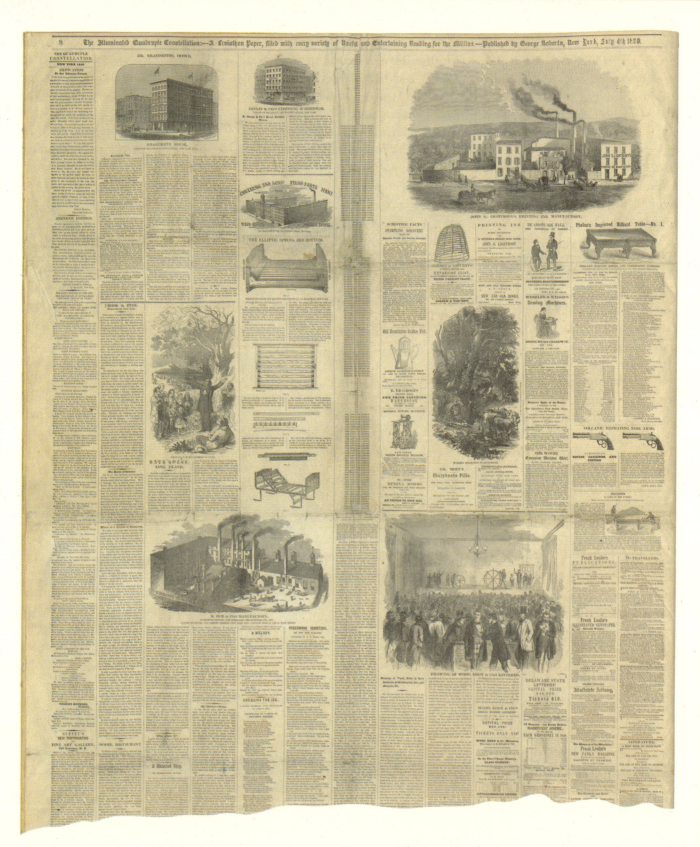

country." The *Weekly Telegraph* of Macon, Georgia, reserved judgment: "When we get a ladder applicable to the purpose, we shall read the paper." Most papers had a response like that of *The Daily Picayune* of New Orleans: "It is a mammoth, a leviathan, a mastodon, a whale of a newspaper."

Close inspection, though, reveals cracks in its mighty edifice. The ostensible July 4 issue of the *Constellation* suspiciously resembles a long-delayed Christmas special: one item reports "Utah news to the 26th of November has been received," while another invites poetry entries for the centenary of Robert Burns's birth, a celebration thrown back in January. Then there's the ad for "Professors Bond and Gein's Skating Academy," an enterprise notably ill suited for July. Even the featured romance novel ("Another instant, and she was in his arms. 'Dearest Raymond!' 'My own Hagar!'") turns out to be a mess. Sharp-eyed readers may have spotted that "Hagar; Or, the Twin Beauties" was in fact a wholesale lifting of E.D.E.N. Southworth's 1850 novel *The Deserted Wife*. But not of *all* of it: it starts on page 7, confusingly jumps back to page 2 to conclude, and reproduces only the second half of the book. To read the first half, you needed to have bought the previous regular issue of the *Constellation* three months earlier.

The mammoth newspaper was, in fact, a mammoth disaster. Months earlier, freelancer Thomas Butler Gunn found publisher George Roberts "really 'cornered' about money": Roberts owed Gunn forty-five dollars, but could pay only ten dollars of it. As Gunn left the office, a printer passed him on his way in, yelling at Roberts about money. And though the newspaper trumpeted the hiring of the literary tastemaker Park Benjamin, a surprise awaited readers on the *Quadruple*'s final page: the venture had lost ten thousand dollars, the famed editor was now the famed former editor, and he was suing the paper. "All association, interest, connection, or friendship… [with] PARK BENJAMIN has ceased," the publisher announced.

The Illuminated Quadruple Constellation was less a tour de force than a Hail Mary pass, a desperate attempt at novelty to recoup mounting losses—and a reminder of how tough, even in its glory days, the newspaper business could be. The irrepressible Roberts couldn't help suggesting that enough customer demand might result in a second edition with, as he bafflingly put it, "mostly, entirely new matter." I've never found a second edition of the paper, perhaps because sales of the first do not seem to have gone well. Stanford's copy has a red stamp of *20* over the initial fifty-cent cover price. A copy in Duke University's library is restamped at fifteen cents. By December 1859, newspaper ads in *The New York Times* tried to unload "A MASTODON PAPER for the HOLIDAYS!" for as little as a dime.

Although George Roberts also hawked keepsake boxes for *The Illuminated Quadruple Constellation* ("so it can be placed upon the centre-table of the parlor… to be looked at with wonder by your children, and your children's children… as the GREAT CURIOSITY OF THE 19TH CENTURY"), these days, Stanford is one of the few places where you can view a copy. But even after seeing it in person, a mystery persists: just *how* Roberts managed to produce it.

He would only hint that "it has taken eight weeks of unceasing labor of nearly forty persons." The secret hid in a private company history at the printing press manufacturer R. Hoe & Company: "Much speculation and discussion were indulged in about their new monster press that could print such a sheet," one printer mused. "As a matter of fact, it was folded to page size and printed on their ordinary press by refolding and running it through eight times." It's no wonder it took months to print.

The Illuminated Quadruple Constellation long held a place in the *Guinness Book of World Records* as the "largest newspaper," but its 134-year reign ended with the June 14, 1993, special issue of *Het Volk*, of Ghent, Belgium. With pages of about fifty-six by thirty-nine inches, it's six inches longer and four inches wider than the *Constellation*. But you can't compare it to a regular issue of *Het Volk* anymore: that paper disappeared in a 2008 merger.

The *Constellation* probably remains the biggest paper ever printed in English, though, and with broadsheets going extinct like, well, mastodons, that record may stand. Occasionally a surviving copy turns up; one sold in 2009 fetched four hundred and eighty dollars, rather higher than its original cover price. Its auction listing remains the best advice ever given for a would-be reader:

"Not recommended," it notes, "for reading on the subway." ✯

LYLE LOVETT

[MUSICIAN]

"I'VE ALWAYS MADE IT A POLICY TO NEVER QUESTION GOOD FORTUNE."

Food items mentioned by Lyle Lovett:
Summer strawberries from the Pacific Northwest
Eggs, bacon, and pancakes from IHOP
Two-thirds-of-a-pound burgers, served with chips and a jar of pickled jalapeños

Lyle Lovett has been a mainstay of the American music scene since he was playing the bars and burger joints around College Station, Texas, in the 1980s. He learned to sing in his Lutheran school choir and started playing guitar while his age was still in the single digits. While Lovett always loved music, he didn't start trying to make a go of it until he was attending college at Texas A&M and began playing around town. Eventually, the legendary Texas troubadour Guy Clark heard a demo tape of Lovett's songs and helped him get a deal with MCA Records.

While Lovett's self-titled debut makes a great country album, it's his later work that's earned him legions of devoted fans and industry accolades. Albums like 1987's *Pontiac* and 1989's *Lyle Lovett and His Large Band* start on a foundation of country and build a world out of blues, Western swing, and rock and roll, all expanded by Lovett's uniquely gimlet-eyed lyrics. Lovett never quite fit into the Nashville mold, but found a home with alt-country listeners and open-minded rock fans.

Illustration by Kristian Hammerstad

He's collected some of the music industry's grandest accolades, including four Grammy Awards and the Americana Music Association's inaugural Trailblazer Award, and he's a member of the Texas Heritage Songwriters' Association Hall of Fame. He also has an impressive list of film credits, after catching the eye of director Robert Altman.

Hollywood isn't Lovett's natural stomping ground, though. He was born and raised in a patch of Texas that is named for his great-great-grandfather who settled the region in the 1840s. He grew up riding horseback, is a proud inductee into the Texas Cowboy Hall of Fame, and is a lifelong member of the Lutheran Church–Missouri Synod, where he still performs with the choir.

Perhaps due to his time on the range, he's learned to be a patient man, a trait that spills over into his songwriting. He's willing to wait for an album to fully coalesce before releasing it into the world. Guy Clark, who is a hero of Lovett's, once told him that he won't release an album until he gets ten songs he likes. "That always stuck with me," Lovett explained. "And that's sort of how I feel." So, after a ten-year hiatus, Lovett eventually came up with enough songs he liked to return with an album. His twelfth studio album, *12th of June*, was released, naturally, on the 13th of May 2022. Lovett kept himself busy during his time away, not only waiting for the muse to appear, but also getting married and becoming the father of twins, whose birth date is memorialized in the album title.

Lovett is a deeply curious person, who, during the course of our conversation, kept attempting to interview the interviewer. ("Where did you grow up, Melissa?," "How many are in your family?," and "How tall are you?" were all asked of me.) Topics discussed include bulls, burgers, and why you should always talk in the elevator.

—Melissa Locker

I. DEAD SOLID PERFECT

LYLE LOVETT: Excuse me, but I'll be right back. I have to get a coaster.

THE BELIEVER: Yes, please. I believe in protecting the furniture at all costs.

LL: I'm really protecting myself from those unsightly rings on the furniture that never go away.

BLVR: Glad we are starting this interview with some furniture safety tips. Feels right.

LL: I looked over the Jim Jarmusch interview you did, and it reminded me a little bit of the old *Interview* magazine interviews they would do. They had one personality interview another personality, and they were kind of all over the place—in a good way.

BLVR: *Interview* magazine is back, and they are doing those interviews again.

LL: Well, that's great. I interviewed Josh Brolin once for that magazine, and, gosh, somebody interviewed me in 1994. I'd have to look that up. I think it was actually my friend Sam Robards. I knew Josh from kind of running into him in an elevator once in Austin, and he came to some of my shows and he put me up for the job.

BLVR: Do you often meet people in elevators?

LL: Yeah, you never know who you're going to meet in an elevator. But there's always that sort of awkward elevator etiquette of: Well, do I speak? Do I not speak? Do I just look at the numbers? Do I look up? Do I look down? All that? But I usually try to break through that and just say hi.

BLVR: Is that a good opening line for you?

LL: It usually starts something, yeah. I met Jack Black and his family once in an elevator. Well, waiting for an elevator. He was pushing a stroller, as I recall—this was years ago. Talking to him was delightful. It was sort of like doing a scene with him, in a way, because he was Jack Black, you know? And as we were talking, the door of the elevator I was waiting for opened, and we talked long enough that the door closed and the elevator went away, and he said, *Oh, man, sorry. I didn't mean to make you miss your 'vator.* Just like that.

BLVR: Gotta love a 'vator reference! So what did you interview Josh Brolin about?

LL: It was a film that he had coming out. I think *No Country for Old Men*? Was he part of that?

25

BLVR: Josh Brolin was in *No Country for Old Men*, so you may have interviewed him about that film. Did you ever want to be a journalist?

LL: Well, I studied journalism in school. I have a degree in journalism from Texas A&M. But there was a point at which I stopped asking myself the question: What do I want to do? And I finally fell to asking myself: What can I do? My first couple of years, I took general studies courses, and I'd fallen in with a student organization through the Student Center that sponsored a coffeehouse. It was mainly a performance space for students, but we had enough of a budget to bring in professionals two or three times a year. I was a freshman when I got involved in this organization, the Basement Coffeehouse. It was built out of what had been the Student Center bicycle shop. They allowed us to build a stage and a balcony and some seats, and it held about a hundred people. We hosted student performances every Friday and Saturday night from eight to midnight, and each act did thirty-minute sets.

In the very first meeting I went to, they said, *You'll be in programming*, and I said, *Well, what's that?* And they handed me a sheet of paper with a list of names and phone numbers, and they said, *You call people and ask them if they want to play.* And so that's what I started doing. As a result, I got to know all the students on campus who were interested in performing. It was what I was trying to do at home in my bedroom. I felt as though immediately I was a part of this community of performers on campus. Texas A&M was not known for its liberal arts in those days, and the only music—formal music education—that existed on campus was the marching band, the Fightin' Texas Aggie Band, a three-hundred-piece military marching band, and a music appreciation course where you learned to pick out, you know, instruments in classical compositions, recordings, and such. So, being a part of the music community there on campus was appealing. It was also a small, specialized group of people who were not like most of the other students on campus, and I enjoyed that distinction. And I really enjoyed getting to know all the people around town, around campus, who wanted to play and sing. It inspired me to practice. It inspired me to try to write songs. I started playing out the next year—I was just obsessed with wanting to play and sing—and was able to book myself two or three or four nights a week somewhere in town for fifty dollars a night. In one case, I had a two-year gig at a hamburger joint on Sunday evenings that paid me in hamburgers instead of money.

BLVR: Do you still order hamburgers? Or are you completely, permanently sick of them?

LL: No, no, I love them. It was really great, because it was a wonderful hamburger place called Dead Solid Perfect, named after the golf book. The owner of the place had a very basic menu. Didn't serve french fries, didn't serve any ice cream or ice cream drinks. It was just bottled beverages, beer, and soda water. And they had a big jar of pickled jalapeños on the counter, and you got either a hamburger or a cheeseburger, served with potato chips. Two-thirds of a pound of meat in each burger. For a two-hour gig, from six to eight, with a break in the middle, on Sunday evenings, he paid me eight burgers a week. I could never eat that many, so I had a tab of burgers built up. I could take anybody to lunch, anytime I wanted, for those two years. It was a great gig, and of course, I didn't ever imagine it would work into something that I could do for a living.

II. REVERSE INTERVIEWING

BLVR: What did you think you were going to do at that age?

LL: I was not the best student, not the most serious student. I tried to do well in the classes I took, but I just didn't know what I wanted to major in. I was a history major for a while, and then I thought, Well, I don't know that I'd make a good professor. So I started thinking, What can I do? I'd always gotten good grades on my papers and writing assignments, and I could type, so I went to the journalism department and took their typing test, which was thirty-five words a minute to pass. I did that and I walked into the newsroom of the school's daily paper and I saw *people*. I saw a community there that reminded me of our Basement Coffeehouse community. I saw people who were as interested as I was in writing and pursuing stories and getting the daily paper out. I saw people working together. I saw how everyone was invested in what they were doing, and it was inspiring, really. So I signed up. I became a journalism major. I was on the city desk, and my beat was the city council in Bryan, Texas, the city right next to College Station. I covered every city council meeting for a couple of years and also wrote some entertainment stories. I was usually able to write about musicians, singers, and songwriters coming to town that I was interested in.

BLVR: Do you remember any artists you covered?

LL: Oh yeah, I remember everybody I covered. I tried to make a point to do in-person interviews, and the very first interview I did was with a singer-songwriter from Houston named Don Sanders, who had been booked by the Coffeehouse. At that point, I had left the Coffeehouse committee, so there was no conflict of interest. I went down to Houston to interview Don Sanders, and Don was lovely. I was supposed to talk with him for about an hour at the IHOP on Memorial Drive in Houston, and we sat there for about three hours on a Saturday afternoon.

BLVR: That is a lot of time in an IHOP.

LL: It was, but it was good. IHOP was sort of home in my student days. I pulled lots of all-nighters in IHOPs.

BLVR: Did you have a go-to IHOP order?

LL: Yeah, I would order eggs, bacon, and pancakes, just the usual. Where did you grow up?

BLVR: Portland, Oregon.

LL: Portland! The Pacific Northwest is a beautiful part of the country. I've always felt as though I'm not at home when I'm there. I feel far away from home—in a good way. I feel like I'm someplace different, which is a wonderful feeling to experience when you travel. So much of the world has shrunk, so many of the places and businesses you see feel the same these days. But when you go to the Pacific Northwest and you're in that beautiful geography, you really do feel like you're somewhere else. And if you're there in the summertime, during the two weeks when the strawberries come in—oh man. I've never tasted better strawberries in the world than those.

BLVR: Oh, you should try to find Hood strawberries. They are really special.

LL: I bet. We usually go in the summertime. I've been to Bend many times. Bend is such an old cowboy town.

BLVR: You would know cowboy towns more than I would!

LL: Well, in terms of Western culture, the eastern parts of Oregon and Washington are more Western-feeling than the western parts. Bend, and some other towns like Walla Walla and Spokane, are in the eastern parts of those states, but you really feel that Western culture there. I've always been interested in Western culture. But anyway, I love Oregon. We always stay at [redacted].

BLVR: Oh, they used to have a café and bakery where you could get a cup of coffee for one dollar and a loaf of bread for about one dollar, and I would spend almost every single afternoon drinking black coffee and eating bread. And you don't know this, because we're on Zoom, but I'm pretty short, and I think it's because I ate just coffee and bread for about four years.

LL: How tall are you?

BLVR: Five foot two.

LL: That's plenty tall.

BLVR: Thank you.

I should not have been surprised that you majored in journalism, because when I was doing research for this interview, almost every interviewer mentioned the fact that you would start interviewing them; I feel like some of that journalism training has lingered.

LL: [*Laughs*] Well, doing an interview is blatantly self-promotional, and if you just do it that way, it's no fun. It's always nice to know who you're talking to. I appreciate any interview that is more of a conversation. I like to sort of feel that out, because it affects what I say and it affects where an interview might go, even though it's a pretense. In a way, an interview really can be a human experience.

I've always felt that way. When I talk to people, interview people, it's nice to try to figure out what it is someone is wanting to put forward. What is their motivation behind it, you know? Why in the world would anybody choose to be onstage and, you know, have a bright light shine upon them?

BLVR: I agree, but I prefer being in the background. I always joke that I became a music journalist because I love music, but I cannot play and would *hate* being onstage. So being able to talk to people who do is fascinating.

LL: Yeah, well, I love music too. I started playing music because I was a fan. And, really, as enjoyable as those Bryan, Texas, city council meetings were… [*Laughs*] It really was fascinating, you know, the heated debates over whether the new McDonald's would get one curb cut or two, that sort of thing.

BLVR: Wait, I'm on the edge of my seat. Did they get one curb cut or two?

LL: Well, ultimately two. It was on a corner and it was only right. But people can be so passionate about what they're trying to accomplish. It's fascinating. I think, in general, people are so much the same. So it's the small differences among us that are what make us interesting to one another. I've always enjoyed engaging people and talking to people and finding out who they are. I have had the good fortune in my career to work with people who are really good at that. Like getting to sort of accidentally fall into working in film with Robert Altman, who—when I got to know him personally—seemed to be endlessly interested in people. Robert Altman had that ability to make you feel special and to zero in on you. In person, he was very much the way his films are, in that his films are always about stripping away the pretense in behavior and getting at someone's real motivation. I appreciated him for that, and I've always been interested in people in that way too. You know, we all present ourselves in ways, so what's real about that and what's the presentation, and where's the authenticity in any situation? The older I get, the easier I think it is to just be myself. I think you see over time that presentation really doesn't make any difference ultimately, and you may as well just be who you are.

III. "MAY I SPEAK TO LYLE?"

BLVR: A lot of musicians want to be actors, and it doesn't seem like you had any plans to become an actor, but you still found a career. How did you make that segue to being on camera?

LL: No, I didn't have any plans—and to refer to it as a career is an overstatement.

BLVR: You have a long IMDb entry, so I think it counts.

LL: Well, I have gotten to do some acting that I'm really proud of and that I've enjoyed. But it really was Altman himself. Altman came to a show we did in 1990 at the Greek Theatre [in Los Angeles]. It was a summer tour with Rickie Lee Jones, a co-bill. So we played first, but we each had, like, seventy-five minutes to play a full set. And Altman and his wife, Kathryn, were there at the invitation of their granddaughter Signi, who brought them along to the show. I didn't meet Altman that night, but he called me the next week and asked me if I wanted to be in a movie. So it was just like that. It really is thanks to him that I've had other opportunities as well.

BLVR: What was that first conversation like? Was he like, *Hey, kid, want to be in pictures?*

LL: Well, yeah. The phone rang and he said, *Hi, it's Bob Altman, may I speak to Lyle?* I said, *This is he, but who is this really?* And he said, *You want to be in a movie?* And I said, *Well, sure, but what should I do? Should I take some acting lessons?* He said, *Heavens, no, they'll just mess you up.* I appreciated how much free rein he gave—as much rope as he let out to great actors in that film, like Tim Robbins. He was very helpful to me. He gave me some great direction that I found reassuring. He knew I needed help or would appreciate his help, and he was perceptive enough to realize that. He was a great judge of character. Altman could just see right through you. He could see right through a lead wall. [*Laughs*] The first day I was on set on *The Player*, I was brand-new and I was just fascinated with everything that was going on. I was sort of shy about it, kind of trying to be discreet, but all of a sudden Altman saw me and I thought, Oh no, oh no. But he put his arm around me and said, *Get in here where you can see.* He was just very inclusive and open about his process. I worked for a couple of days in a row, went to dailies, didn't work for a couple of days, so didn't go to the dailies. The next time I was on set, he walked over to me and said, *Where were you?* And I said, *Well, I didn't work.* He said, *Come to dailies.* So I went to dailies every day, whether I was in the scenes or not. That summer of 1991, doing *The Player*, was a great film school. I got to watch the entire film come together. I got to watch every take of every shot, and Robert Altman was sitting at the back of the screening room with David Brown, and Helen Gurley Brown would be there sometimes as well. And they would watch every take and then we ate pizza—so it was like an end-of-day party every day. Then, in 1994, doing *Prêt-à-Porter—Ready to Wear*, they call it here—he had the entire cast in Paris for twelve weeks. It was such an ensemble cast that nobody worked more than three or four days a week, so there was lots of downtime, and the hotels were near one another. We all had lunch. It was like being in school, but my classmates were people like Tracey Ullman and Richard Grant and, oh gosh, Danny Aiello and Lauren Bacall and Sam Robards, Bacall's son. We all ran around together. It was an extraordinary experience. And so all of that came about for me because of Robert Altman.

BLVR: What do you think he saw in you that made him want to cast you in his movie?

LL: I don't know. I've always made it a policy to never question good fortune. When he called, I just said yes. He was actually working on *Short Cuts*, the film that he did based on Raymond Carver's short stories before he was working on *The Player*, but then *The Player* came up. So it was *Short Cuts* that he had originally called me about. But in the meantime, *The Player* presented itself and he included me in that, as well.

BLVR: You mentioned in passing that Helen Gurley Brown was hanging out on set. What was she like in real life?

LL: David Brown, the producer, was her husband. She would come to the set with him. She was lovely, you know, elegant and lovely. My mom was a forty-year career woman with Exxon. Spent the first twenty years of her career as a secretary and the last twenty years of her career there as a training specialist in HR, and then continued for another twenty-five years after she retired, working for Exxon as a consultant with her own business. She turned ninety-five two weeks ago. She was a great mom and she was always such an inspiration to me. She worked hard, she pursued her interest, and she worked in a world of men as I was growing up in the '60s and '70s. She navigated all that successfully and in a real positive way. So I always appreciated the point of view that Helen Gurley Brown put forward in *Cosmopolitan*. Growing up in that world of, you know, women's lib, as they called it in those days, with a working mom, I felt like I had a front-row seat to a lot of that.

IV. "PANTS IS OVERRATED"

BLVR: How did you celebrate your mom's ninety-fifth birthday?

LL: For about a week, we had different get-togethers with different parts of the family. We just all tried to be together. We went to one of her favorite restaurants and invited anyone in the family and her friends who could come. We just spent time together. Now, my mom's kind of never, never made anything about herself.

BLVR: She sounds like a good mom!

LL: She was and is good to me and her grandchildren. My wife, April, and I have seven-year-old twins, a boy and a girl. My mom had given up on me so long ago in terms of providing grandchildren for her, so these last several years have been particularly joyful for all of us.

BLVR: Yes, you had kids later in life, and in almost every interview about your most recent album, you seem to talk more about your twins than the songs on your album. Most musicians would hate that, but you seem to love it.

LL: Yeah, I've never been more enthusiastic about anything and I've never enjoyed anything more in my life than being their dad. Of all the many things that I've gotten to do that I enjoy, there's just nothing that compares. They have been my main focus since they were born.

BLVR: Do you think you're going to end up making a children's album?

LL: I know a lot of people do that, but it really is hard to resist. I appreciate how people are motivated to do children's music because of having children—or to write a book or to start drawing, which I'll never do. But, yeah, maybe. Probably some of the songs that have been inspired by them should be children's songs. I've turned them into songs that we play onstage in the large band, songs like "Pants Is Overrated."

BLVR: I like that song a lot, because pants are overrated. Would you want your kids to go into the music industry? I feel like it's changed so much since, well, certainly since you started in the industry.

LL: Gosh, yeah, it has, hasn't it? How long have you been writing about music?

BLVR: Since I was about fifteen.

LL: You're twenty-five now [*Editor's note: I am not, in fact, twenty-five*], so you would have seen it change quite a bit in these last ten years. It really is different, and I kind of feel like I'm outside the music business at this point. To answer your question, I would support them if they wanted to try to play music. I mean, they are taking piano lessons now. They seem to like music, but I would encourage them to do anything they wanted to do. I don't require them to share my taste in anything, and I wouldn't impose anything on them. But to see them kind of naturally be interested in some of the things that I'm interested in is really fun.

BLVR: You've been in the industry a long time, and a new generation may really appreciate what you have to tell them.

LL: I don't know that they would. [*Laughs*] Do you have a TikTok account?

BLVR: I do. It's fun because my algorithm has been perfectly trained to serve me cooking videos, dog rescue videos, book recommendations, and almost nothing else.

LL: I don't have TikTok. I have Instagram and Facebook and the former Twitter, but I usually post to Instagram because it's easiest for me to navigate. But everything that comes across my Instagram is usually parenting advice and health advice, at this point.

BLVR: Well, if you want to change the videos and posts you're being served, may I suggest dog chiropractic videos? There are people out there who do chiropractic treatments on animals, and it is fascinating.

LL: That sounds worth watching, I'm sure. I've been involved with horses my whole life, and there are horse chiropractors that are very effective.

V. THE COWBOY HALL OF FAME

BLVR: I did notice you are a member of the Texas Cowboy Hall of Fame. That's a pretty big honor.

LL: Thank you very much. You know, it really is an honor. I grew up in the '60s, watching Western television programs. I can't remember ever not wanting to be a cowboy. So, years later, to be inducted into the Texas Cowboy Hall of Fame was a big deal to me. Johnny Trotter, who was inducted around the same time—a great horseman from out in West Texas—said in his induction acceptance speech something that was just absolutely true. *You don't call yourself a cowboy. You're not a cowboy until somebody else says you're one.* So being called a cowboy, being referred to as a cowboy by the Hall of Fame, by other people—it truly is a real compliment because it speaks not just to skills you might have in working on a farm or a ranch, but also to character and to a way of life, to values.

BLVR: How did you find out you were going to be inducted?

LL: They called me. It was actually a former inductee who put me forward, Dr. "Red" Duke from Houston. And Dr. Duke was very helpful to me in my life on many occasions. But he was a real character. He had gone to Texas A&M University and then went to medical school in the UT system. His daughter worked at a local hamburger joint in College Station. I had just graduated, but she was still an undergrad, and I got to know her and got to know him through her. He was important in the Medical Center in

Houston, head of trauma at Hermann hospital for years, and he started the Life Flight program in Houston, which is a helicopter rescue ambulance system. He was important to me, and he was the one who put me up for the Texas Cowboy Hall of Fame.

BLVR: Further proof that you are a cowboy is that you were hurt by a bull at some point.

LL: Yes, in 2002. I got in a wreck with one of the bulls that we owned. Most cattle have the instinct to get away from people, but he was one that was orphaned by his mother and we bottle-raised him, so he was tame, really. We needed to figure out if a pecan tree in his pen needed to come out, and my uncle said, *Let's go look at it*. I knew for a fact that a "tame" two-thousand-pound animal is something to be wary of, so I was always really careful with him and didn't get in the pen. But I was with my uncle, a cattleman all his life, and so I thought, Well, it'll be OK. Unc wouldn't be going in here if it weren't safe. And the bull was over on the other side of the pen, way away from us. But he came wandering up and got after us. I was lucky. I made it to the fence. He got my uncle down first, and then he came after me and I ran for the fence. My friend James Gilmer, who I started playing music with in 1978, and who has since passed away, had come over that day to go to lunch. So he was out there while we were in the pen, and I don't quite remember how, but I made it to the fence, and I remember feeling James's arm across my back. He grabbed me by my belt and lifted me with one arm over the fence to safety. It was a pretty bad deal, and could have turned out a lot worse. My uncle was banged up pretty good and had some broken ribs. And they got me to the hospital right away. And they brought me to Dr. Duke in the emergency room. I remember Dr. Duke asking somebody, *How much morphine has he had?* I had been keeping up with the amount of morphine, and when Dr. Duke asked, I said the number of milligrams of morphine I'd had, and he got real close to me, and he said, *Shut. Up.* Just like that. And that's the last thing I remember.

BLVR: Do you think that experience kind of put you over the edge to be in the Cowboy Hall of Fame?

LL: Yeah, maybe.

BLVR: I want to be mindful of your time, but also to talk about your incredibly long and impressive music career, which we're going to cram into the next five minutes. I'm sure it's hard to tell, when you're in the middle of it, but do you feel like your music has evolved over the years? Do you go back and listen to some of your earlier stuff and think, Oh, I would do that differently.

LL: I appreciate my recordings and my songs for what they are, but, yeah, I do think about how much fun it might be to go back and re-record things. I'd love to have a chance. The thing that moves work forward over the years is the people you meet and the people you get to associate with. They make it possible for your imagination to go places it might not have gone otherwise. I have been so fortunate to work with people in the business who are so deep in their experience and their knowledge and so accomplished. Like working with my first producer, Billy Williams, who was a part of all my records until he decided to retire, after my record *Natural Forces*. And to be signed by Tony Brown at MCA Records in Nashville, who played piano with Elvis and produced so many great gospel records and became one of the in-house producers at MCA Records. He, along with Billy Williams, produced my first three records. To work with people with that sort of knowledge and experience, to play, to record with great musicians like Matt Rollings and Leland Sklar and Russ Kunkel and Jim Cox and Stuart Duncan and Mark O'Connor and Paul Franklin. To be able to record with an A-team of studio musicians, who then would go out on the road with me and be part of my band. Wow. You know, it doesn't get any better than that. I've been fortunate to be able to work with people that I was already a fan of from their previous work. So I guess the thing that's helped me—or the thing that makes me still enjoy playing and singing after all these years—is that I get to do it with people that I have ultimate respect and admiration for.

BLVR: Do you pay your band in hamburgers?

LL: Well, hamburgers are definitely part of the deal. ✱

A SPECIAL ANNIVERSARY INDEX
cataloging 150 issues of this magazine

INDEXING 150 ISSUES OF THE BELIEVER MAGAZINE

INTERVIEWS

A — ISSUE

- Chris Abani — 12
- Fatima Abdelrahman — 54
- Marina Abramović — 127
- Vito Acconci — 40
- Joey Lauren Adams — 42
- Chimamanda Ngozi Adichie — 59
- Renata Adler — 97
- César Aira — 114
- Kaveh Akbar — 147
- Damon Albarn — 48
- Edward Albee — 101
- Alan Alda — 140
- Sherman Alexie — 87
- Laylah Ali — 30
- Monica Ali — 44
- Moreshin Allahyari — 131
- Mark Allen — 37
- Robert Alter — 59
- David Altmejd — 85
- Jonathan Ames — 66
- Trey Anastasio — 82
- Laurie Anderson — 86
- Gina Apostol — 139
- ★ Fred Armisen — 106

- Karen Armstrong — 90
- Miguel Arteta — 140
- The Art Guys — 93
- John Ashbery — 60
- Shuvinai Ashoona — 85
- Paul Auster — 21

B — ISSUE

- Bun B — 35
- Lil B — 114
- Judy Baca — 148
- Angelo Badalamenti — 126
- Matt Bai — 55
- Jacques Bailly — 23
- John Baldessari — 76
- Jesse Ball — 81
- Roger Ballen — 102
- Devendra Banhart — 29
- John Banville — 7
- Ilisa Barbash — 70
- Kevin Barnes — 45
- Matthew Barney — 40
- Andrea Barrett — 63
- Lynda Barry — 58
- Julianna Barwick — 82
- Rostam Batmanglij — 120
- Noah Baumbach — 98
- Panda Bear — 48
- Paul Beatty — 119
- Beck — 25
- Michael Bell — 18
- Pat Benatar — 2
- Silvia Benso — 13
- Rose Levy Beranbaum — 19
- Amy Berkowitz — 132
- David Berman — 129
- Jane Birkin — 120
- Alan Bishop — 55
- Eula Biss — 141
- Björk — 26
- Jack Black — 8
- Black Thought — 138
- B-Boy Blakk — 102
- Peter Blegvad — 67
- David Blei — 119
- Judy Blume — 104
- Eric Bogosian — 42
- Ian Bogost — 87
- Christian Bök — 63
- Sissela Bok — 8
- Eavan Boland — 110
- Deborah Borda — 114
- Wes Borland — 91
- Lizzi Bougatsos — 100
- Anne Boyer — 127
- Megan Boyle — 125
- Arthur Bradford — 61
- Joe Bradley — 94
- Sarah Braman — 108
- Glenn Branca — 109
- Creed Bratton — 146
- Breyten Breytenbach — 39
- Isaac Brock — 33
- Jericho Brown — 132
- Jessica Bruder — 119
- Bebe Buell — 114
- Stephen Harrod Buhner — 130
- Hannibal Buress — 123
- Charles Burns — 50
- Ishmael Butler — 100
- Judith Butler — 2
- David Byrne — 41, 82, 126

C — ISSUE

- Tia Cabral — 147
- John Cale — 116
- Sophie Calle — 90
- Steve Carell — 84
- Leonora Carrington — 94
- Anne Carson — 119
- Bianca Casady — 77
- Lucien Castaing-Taylor — 70
- Nick Cave — 65
- Paul Chan — 94
- Wo Chan — 141
- Dan Chaon — 14
- Heather Chaplin — 60
- Roz Chast — 111
- Ted Chiang — 128
- Brian Chippendale — 91
- Margaret Cho — 101
- Heather Christle — 92
- Sandra Cisneros — 127
- John Cooper Clarke — 133
- Daniel Clowes — 71
- Betsy Cohen — 86
- Bojana Coklyat — 138
- William Connolly — 89
- Marianne Constable — 75
- T Cooper — 33
- Robert Coover — 112
- Francis Ford Coppola — 68
- Jane Corrigan — 128
- Ronald Cotton — 113
- Wayne Coyne — 35
- Jim Crace — 9
- Stanley Crawford — 69
- Simon Critchley — 5
- David Cross — 53
- John Crowley — 62
- Robert Crumb — 111
- John Currence — 75

D — ISSUE

- Chuck D — 137
- Jeff Daniels — 143
- Nikki Darling — 121
- John Darnielle — 15
- Rameshwar Das — 115
- Julie Dash — 133
- N. Dash — 111
- Ram Dass — 115
- Arnold Davidson — 34
- Jenny Davidson — 80
- Lydia Davis — 50
- Mike Davis — 10
- Richard Dawkins — 56
- Colin Dayan — 96
- Alain de Botton — 117
- Josephine Decker — 136
- Brian Degraw — 87
- Don DeLillo — 35
- Julie Delpy — 61
- Daniel Dennett — 11
- Frans de Waal — 47
- Helen DeWitt — 93
- Hernan Diaz — 145
- Dale Dickey — 141
- Joan Didion — 87
- Ani DiFranco — 14
- Daveed Diggs — 117
- Angela Dimayuga — 118
- Christina Dimitriadis — 127
- DJ Shadow — 39
- Peter Doig — 88
- Nathaniel Dorsky — 143
- Doseone — 57

Compiled by Maya Segal and Gemma Marx; Fred Armisen portrait by Tony Millionaire

Sir Arthur Conan Doyle	22
Margaret Drabble	111
David Duchovny	136
Tom Dumm	59
Carroll Dunham	76, 110
Grace Simonoff Dunham	116
Brenda Dunne	43
Geoff Dyer	88
Marcel Dzama	109

E	ISSUE
Jennifer Egan	36
John Ehle	77
Deborah Eisenberg	125
Phil Elverum	64
Tracey Emin	12
Brian Eno	82
Will Eno	57
Anne Enright	104
Enya	114
Nora Ephron	88
Steve Erickson	123
Jeffrey Eugenides	96
Percival Everett	138

F	ISSUE
Sam Farber	87
Usama Fayyad	6
Silvia Federici	125
Feiffer	113
Leslie Feist	100
Tina Fey	8
Thalia Field	77

David Fincher	75
Amy Finkel	88
Shannon Finnegan	138
Nikky Finney	132
Eric Fischl	20
Dorian Fitzgerald	81
Peter Fitzpatrick	28
Flavor Flav	141
Robert Forster	73
Paula Fox	47
Gary Francione	78
James Franco	85
Joe Frank	97
Thomas Frank	16
Ian Frazier	17
Valentine Freeman	121
Bruce Jay Friedman	57

G	ISSUE
Jenny Gage	6
Mary Gaitskill	60
Jackson Galaxy	139
Peter Galison	81
Kristen Gallerneaux	131
Merrill Garbus	109
Andrew Garfield	139
Bryan Garner	71
William H. Gass	29
David Gates	45
Jeremy Gaudet	144
Paul Giamatti	33
Ben Gibbard	35
Joe Gibbons	135

ISSUE 1!

JOAN DIDION
(Issue 87)

CELEBRATING OUR 150TH ISSUE

33

Joan Didion portrait by Charles Burns

"THE JOY OF PERSONA" *by Ross Simonini (Issue 148)*

Rhiannon Giddens	144	Bob Gluck	99	Julian Gough	84
Terry Gilliam	1	Jonathan Gold	92*	Temple Grandin	123
Dawit Giorgis	13	Francisco Goldman	16	Grass Widow	90
Renee Gladman	123	Kenneth Goldsmith	84	David Gordon Green	39
Milton Glaser	6	Adam Goldstein	101	Garth Greenwell	131
Phoebe Gloeckner	72	Mira Gonzalez	117	Marjorie Grene	22
				Bear Grylls	116
				Sarah Gubbons	136
				Lisa Guenther	99
				Alexis Pauline Gumbs	137
				Myriam Gurba	121

BOOTS RILEY
(Issue 147)

H	ISSUE
Jonathan Haidt	26
Donald Hall	118
Trenton Doyle Hancock	99
Kathleen Hanna	147
Barry Hannah	75
Dian Hanson	111
Hilary Harkness	83
Dan Harmon	81
Mary Harron	106
PJ Harvey	144
Noah Hawley	149
Todd Haynes	52
Shirley Hazzard	15
Brooks Headley	130
Matt Healy	135
Julie Hecht	53
Kati Heck	97
Antony Hegarty	100
Tim Heidecker	125
Steven Heller	40
Aleksandar Hemon	68
Amy Hempel	48
Joe Henry	38
Don Hertzfeldt	51
Lena Herzog	81

Werner Herzog	52
Cheryl Hines	41
Robyn Hitchcock	32
Philip Seymour Hoffman	10
Paul Holdengräber	112
Tanja Hollander	110
Nicole Holofcener	34
Christian Holstad	84
Maureen Howard	71
Tehching Hsieh	124
Alana Hunt	138
Gary Hustwit	70

I	ISSUE
Ice Cube	9
Michael Imperioli	141
Bjarke Ingels	95
Samantha Irby	130

J	ISSUE
Arthur Jafa	131
Japanese Breakfast	126
Jim Jarmusch	142
Ricky Jay	89
Margo Jefferson	122
★ Barry Jenkins	122

Matthew Jeon	138
Tyehimba Jess	125
Chris Johanson	87
Rashida Jones	98
Rickie Lee Jones	140
Sarah Jones	23
S. T. Joshi	78
★ Miranda July	25, 113

K	ISSUE
Mindy Kaling	85

"The Joy of Persona" illustration by Andrea Settimo; Boots Riley portrait by Kristian Hammerstad; portraits of Barry Jenkins and Miranda July by Tony Millionaire

KATHLEEN HANNA
(Issue 147)

Maira Kalman	85
Sandor Ellix Katz	124
Tim Kehoe	44
William Kennedy	38
William Kentridge	142
Etgar Keret	33
John Kerry	18
Angélique Kidjo	31
Ed Kienholz	20
Killer Mike	109
Ashida Kim	2
Robin Wall Kimmerer	134
Jamaica Kincaid	4
Jemima Kirke	107
Lola Kirke	119
Ragnar Kjartansson	76
Keith Knight	58
Ezra Koenig	114
Wayne Koestenbaum	90
Kogonada	119
Terence Koh	85
Aline Kominsky-Crumb	67
Rem Koolhaas	129
Harmony Korine	70
Chris Kraus	101
James Howard Kunstler	29
Hari Kunzru	128

L	ISSUE
Neil LaBute	110
Suzanne Lacy	103
Lady Saw	73
Dany Laferriere	95
Ingrid LaFleur	132
George Lakoff	18
Jaron Lanier	132
Victor LaValle	80
Rev. James Lawson	97
An-My Lê	148
Fran Lebowitz	121
Elizabeth LeCompte	112
Leigh Ledare	106
Min Jin Lee	127
Young Jean Lee	92
Victoria Legrand	126
Annie Leibovitz	148
Mike Leigh	61
Kasi Lemmons	128
Felicia Luna Lemus	5
Arnold Leo	94
Ben Lerner	82, 110
Jonathan Lethem	89
David Levine	60
Micah Lexier	102
Yan Lianke	134
Jamie Lidell	35
Michael Light	76
Delroy Lindo	149
Alphonso Lingis	133
Gordon Lish	59
Paul Lisicky	135
Liso	53
Margot Livesey	3
Kenneth Lonergan	107
Barry Lopez	128
Carolina López	108
Nick Lowe	62
Robert Lowell	57
Lisa Lucas	149
Eileen Luhr	68
Garielle Lutz	31

M	ISSUE
Ling Ma	140
Ian MacKaye	55
Guy Maddin	77
Sananda Maitreya	45
Janet Malcolm	18
Stephen Malkmus	7
Aimee Mann	25
Khaela Maricich	45
Mary Ann Marino	122
Marc Maron	90
Lucrecia Martel	121
Chris Martin	103
Demetri Martin	31
Steve Martin	24
Eddie Martinez	90
Patrick Martinez	142
Pat Martino	64
Harry Mathews	86
Adrianne Mathiowetz	134
Matmos	19
Peter Matthiessen	108
Tim Maughan	132
Maxwell	129
Wong May	107
Richard McCann	56
Tom McCarthy	54
Scott McCloud	43
Ian McEwan	26
Harold McGee	60
Ryan McGinley	51
Mark McGurl	62
Keegan McHargue	76
Joyce Meadows	134
Suketu Mehta	51
Colin Meloy	14
Sam Mendes	61
Natalie Merchant	144
Stephin Merritt	111
Pat Metheny	139
George Meyer	17
Linda Ross Meyer	101
MIA	73
Mary Midgley	51
China Miéville	23
Lydia Millet	105
Mike Mills	106
Aleksandra Mir	9
Pankaj Mishra	42
★ Moby	91

Juana Molina	35
Pharoahe Monch	77
Meredith Monk	109
Kent Monkman	145
Alan Moore	99
Lorrie Moore	28
Jason Moran	120
Jerry Moriarty	67
Errol Morris	12, 33
Anna Moschovakis	123
Ottessa Moshfegh	133
Mark Mothersbaugh	27
Bob Mould	28
Simone Muench	74
Ismail Muhammad	132
Nico Muhly	57
Matt Mullican	92
Walter Murch	79
Eileen Myles	146

N	ISSUE
Noor Naga	143
Robin Nagle	74
Mira Nair	43
Laurel Nakadate	38
Kumail Nanjiani	111
Vi Khi Nao	139
Mick Napier	23
Navi	102
Meshell Ndegeocello	110
Brad Neely	65

Photograph of Kathleen Hanna by Rachel Bright; Moby portrait by Tony Millionaire

Name	Issue
Alondra Nelson	129
Maggie Nelson	137
Shirin Neshat	5
Sheila Nevins	113
Griffin Newman	119
Joanna Newsom	14
Viet Thanh Nguyen	119
Guy Nordenson	66
Jockum Nordström	30
Sigrid Nunez	33
Alissa Nutting	118
Diana Nyad	95

O — ISSUE

Name	Issue
Karen O	25
Joyce Carol Oates	99
Darren O'Donnell	80
Steve & Mark O'Donnell	16
★ Nick Offerman	93

Name	Issue
Victor Oladipo	144
Angel Olsen	140
Stephen O'Malley	35
Michael Ondaatje	46
Robyn O'Neil	58
Niela Orr	132
Beth Orton	1
Julie Otsuka	142
Christopher Owens	84
Laura Owens	2
Ruth Ozeki	42

P — ISSUE

Name	Issue
Monica Padman	145
Chuck Palahniuk	107
Kumar Pallana	1
Orhan Pamuk	34
Panda Bear	48
Gary Panter	63
Polixeni Papapetrou	95
Mary-Louise Parker	115
Annie-B Parson	143
Mike Patton	95
Alexander Payne	22
Dustin Payseur	149
Mario Van Peebles	22
Sean Penn	134
Elise R. Peterson	120
Raymond Pettibon	20
Elizabeth Peyton	103
Liz Phair	3
Danica Phelps	15
Rasheedah Phillips	132
Melissa Holbrook Pierson	54
Alison Pill	96
Lido Pimienta	121
Aubrey Plaza	140
Martha Plimpton	97
Judit Polgár	107
Michael Pollan	43
Robert Pollard	16
Pope.L	116
Genesis Breyer P-Orridge	82
Padgett Powell	37
Richard Powers	41
Devon Price	146
Richard Price	53
Seth Price	98
Brontez Purnell	126

Q — ISSUE

Name	Issue
Q-Tip	14
Nii Quarcoopome	115
Alice Quinn	32

R — ISSUE

Name	Issue
Mary Lynn Rajskub	17
Rakim	130
Harold Ramis	32
Tejal Rao	129
Megan Rapinoe	113
Jessi Reaves	123
David Rees	3
Diana Reiss	105
Sandy Reynolds-Wasco	52
Trent Reznor	69
Simon Rich	90
Andy Richter	6
Boots Riley	147
Jimmy Robert	112
John Roderick	25
Richard Rodriguez	100
Kirstine Roepstorff	119
Matthew Rohrer	90
Clare Rojas	76
Matthew Ronay	30

RESURRECTOR: AMERICAN PSYCHO by Susan Steinberg
(Issue 145)

Name	Issue
Richard Rorty	3
Caroline Rose	146
Mika Rottenberg	93
Maya Rudolph	29
Ed Ruscha	32
Michael Ruse	4
Douglas Rushkoff	82
David O. Russel	19

S — ISSUE

Name	Issue
Raphael Saadiq	120
Joe Sacco	81
Laetitia Sadier	126
Zainab Salbi	111
Paul Salopek	127
Mark Salzman	7
Dyveke Sanne	58
Lucy Sante	15
Marjane Satrapi	36
George Saunders	11
John Sayles	61
Suzanne Scanlon	149
Kristen Schaal	54
Tom Scharpling	45
Lawrence Schiller	71
Peter Schjeldahl	108
Shawn Nelson Schmitt	90
Carolee Schneemann	130
Sarah Schulman	96
Michael Schur	113
Christine Schutt	62
David Schutter	121
Casey Schwartz	138
Jason Schwartzman	83, 149
Gail Scott	142
Mike Scott	47

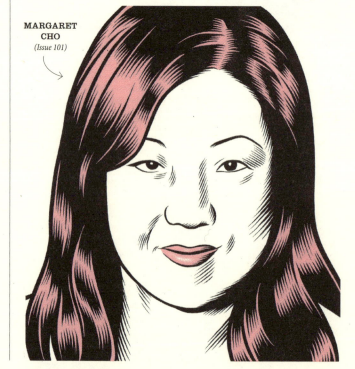

MARGARET CHO
(Issue 101)

36

Nick Offerman portrait by Tony Millionaire; Resurrector illustration by Kristian Hammerstad; Margaret Cho portrait by Charles Burns

Katerina Seda	89
Amy Sedaris	11
David Sedaris	28
Will Self	63
★ Maurice Sendak	94

Elif Shafak	108
Steve Sharp	136
Wallace Shawn	74
Will Sheff	44
David Shields	72
Martin Short	4
David Shrigley	84
Joan Silber	20
Michael Silverblatt	72
Sarah Silverman	27
Charles Simic	63
David Simon	46
Paul Simonon	48
Helen Simpson	47
Mona Simpson	145
Nancy Sinatra	109
Peter Singer	31
Jenny Slate	129
Robert Smigel	62
Anna Deavere Smith	84
Imogen Sara Smith	102
Kiki Smith	13
Michael Smith	148
Tracy K. Smith	122
Smoosh	25
Steven Soderbergh	36
Rebecca Solnit	65
Todd Solondz	21
Kate Soper	120
Alec Soth	104
Dana Spiotta	39
Jerry Stahl	113
Starlito	104
Ilan Stavans	36
Edward Steed	124
Kari Steffanson M.D.	4
Frank Stella	58
Tom Stoppard	27
Allyson Strafella	96
Jack Stratton	147
Galen Strawson	1
Eve Sussman	21
Anthony Swofford	41
Wanda Sykes	37
Martine Syms	148

T	ISSUE
Olúfẹ́mi O. Táíwò	146
Amber Tamblyn	112
Astra Taylor	125
Timothy Taylor	3
Tegan and Sara	131
Irma Thomas	55
Ahmir Thompson (Questlove)	5
Linda Thompson	50
Marcus Thompson II	145
Heba Thorisdottir	106
Robert Thurman	132
Lynne Tillman	116
Tim & Eric	56
Lol Tolhurst	144
Fred Tomaselli	86
Adrian Tomine	48
Justin Torres	121
Natasha Trethewey	124
Jeff Tweedy	136

U	ISSUE
Mierle Laderman Ukeles	117

V	ISSUE
Christine Vachon	122
Liliana Valenzuela	127
Jeannie Vanasco	132
Gus Van Sant	54
Agnès Varda	66

"WHY CAN'T MY SON VOTE?" *by Paul Collins*
(Issue 146)

Maurice Sendak portrait by Tony Millionaire; "Why Can't My Son Vote?" illustration by Charlotte Gomez

Eddie Vedder	14
Craig Venter	24
Paul Verhoeven	79
Vladimir	52
Margarethe von Trotta	97

W	ISSUE
David Wain	79
Martha Wainwright	82
Scott Walker	100
Jeff Wall	117
David Foster Wallace	8
Ryan H. Walsh	144
Eric Wareheim	121
Warp Records	73
Elissa Washuta	135
John Waters	122
Sarah Waters	69
Mike Watt	114
Reggie Watts	120
Lauren Weinstein	44
Eyal Weizman	80
Irvine Welsh	39
Margaret & Christine Wertheim	78
Edmund White	102
Jack White	2
Jim White	34
Mike White	106
Vanna White	118
Alex Whybrow	68
Benjamin Wiessman	22
Diane Williams	57
Lucinda Williams	91
Gordon Willis	106
August Wilson	19
Nancy Wilson	46
Patrice Wilson	105
Debra Winger	79
Jeanette Winterson	97
Tobias Wolff	24
Winnie Wong	103
Denis Wood	86
Roy Wood Jr.	137
Jim Woodring	87
Jeffrey Wright	88
Rudy Wurlitzer	98

Y	ISSUE
Hanya Yanagihara	115
Gene Luen Yang	143
Weird Al Yankovic	74
Charlyne Yi	70
Yo La Tengo	24
Thom Yorke	64
Alison Young	38
Charles Yu	112

Z	ISSUE
Pamela Z	120
Kate Zambreno	147
Brad Zellar	104

Zhuang Zhou	98
Philip Zimbardo	65
Andrea Zittel	67
Slavoj Žižek	15
Rob Zombie	115

ESSAYS

A	ISSUE
Megan Abbott	65
★ Hanif Abdurraqib	126

John Adamian	55, 62
Skylaire Alfvegren	73
Sandy Ernest Allen	147
Michael Almereyda	33, 51
Steve Almond	55
Hilton Als	70, 148
David Amsden	10
Lili Anolik	88, 106
Zaina Arafat	119
Sasha Archibald	103
Mario Alejandro Ariza	122
Chris Feliciano Arnold	139
Colin Asher	95
Michael Atkinson	2, 4, 9, 29, 30, 52, 61, 79, 88, 96
Rachel Aviv	32, 41, 48

B	ISSUE
Chris Bachelder	17, 18, 41, 68, 78
Blake Bailey	54
Andrea Bajani	141
Anika Banister	143
Zach Baron	75
John Barth	30
Chris Baty	37
Charles Baxter	8, 51
Daniel Baxter	51
David Beal	91
Thomas Beard	79
Joshuah Bearman	12, 13
Ann Beattie	145
Graham T. Beck	70
Daniel Levin Becker	87
Christopher R. Beha	20, 37, 60, 62
Amy Benfer	9
David Berman	14
Judy Berman	64

"ARISTOCRAT INC" *by Natalie So*
(Issue 140)

Sven Birkerts	2, 10
Eula Biss	51, 110, 145
Tom Bissell	3, 4, 9, 12, 22, 39
Tom Bligh	22
Aaron Bobrow-Strain	87
Charles Bock	123
Lorraine Boissoneault	130
Jason Boog	47, 57, 74
Katie Booth	126
Greg Bottoms	27

Victor Brand	46
Oliver Broudy	25, 60
Marshall Brown	82
Petra Browne	134
James Browning	6, 27, 43, 57
Scott Browning	43
Bliss Broyard	117
Franklin Bruno	20, 56
Stephanie Burt	13, 23, 24
Ashley Butler	75

"SUCH PERFECTION" *by Chloé Cooper Jones*
(Issue 125)

Hanif Abdurraqib portrait by Kristian Hammerstad; "Aristocrat Inc" illustration by Andrea Settimo; "Such Perfection" illustration by Joe Gough

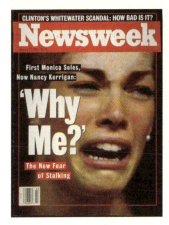 

"REMOTE CONTROL" by Sarah Marshall
(Issue 104)

	ISSUE
Blake Butler	55
Jeff Byles	3

C	ISSUE
David Cairns	52, 79
Pablo Calvi	113, 146
Frances Cha	82
Jeff Chang	67
Julio Villanueva Chang	69
Pari Chang	118
Kyle Chayka	138
Dan Chiasson	9
Robert Christgau	10, 31
Louis Chude-Sokei	108
Arthur C. Clarke	7
Brock Clarke	17, 60, 91
Joshua Clover	59
Chris Cobb	58
Joshua Cohen	58
Rachel Cohen	94
Rich Cohen	35, 65, 101
Robert Cohen	46, 69, 95
Damaris Colhoun	103
Paul Collins	4, 7, 11, 19, 28, 30, 35, 39, 43, 45, 49, 55, 56, 64, 82, 144, 146
Andrew Lewis Conn	40, 146
Jon Cotner	85
Bill Cotter	90
Peter Coviello	91
Sara Crosby	37
Sloane Crosley	90
Rob Curran	116, 144
Ron Currie Jr.	93
Aaron Cutler	61

D	ISSUE
John D'Agata	7, 68
Trinie Dalton	36
Lisa Darms	93
Meghan Daum	19, 86

	ISSUE
Jenny Davidson	36
Avi Davis	50, 66, 76, 94
Shea Dean	7
Christopher DeLaurenti	55
Matthew Derby	1, 14, 21, 23
Helen DeWitt	52
Colin Dickey	95, 105, 129
Millicent G. Dillon	81
Chinnie Ding	85
Katrina Dodson	119
John Domini	68
Elisabeth Donnelly	112
Charles Duhigg	18
Lena Dunham	115
Geoff Dyer	74, 90

E	ISSUE
Scott Eden	39
Brian T. Edwards	54, 70, 108
Dave Eggers	11, 12, 13, 141
Ben Ehrenreich	2, 16, 29
Jordan Ellenberg	8
Carl Elliott	9
Michael A. Elliott	67
Stephen Elliott	6, 12, 17, 38, 42, 65
Lee Ellis	108
Álvaro Enrigue	112
Matthew Erickson	102
Leyla Ertegun	70
Brian Evenson	3

F	ISSUE
Abou Farman	58
Melissa Febos	114
Susana Ferreira	116, 127
Monica Ferrell	18
Eric Fischl	30, 33
Fernando A. Flores	144
Jeff Fort	32
Amanda Fortini	129

	ISSUE
Catherine Foulkrod	112
Karen Joy Fowler	11
Porter Fox	40, 72
Hannah Frank	62
John Freeman	41
Rodrigo Fresán	42
Andrew Friedman	36
Amy Fusselman	122, 142

G	ISSUE
Elisa Gabbert	146
Rivka Ricky Galchen	44
Joe Galván	120
Scott Geiger	80
Hafizah Geter	138
Tavi Gevinson	100
Rachel Kaadzi Ghansah	102, 111, 140
Bianca Giaever	125
Amelie Gillette	69
Gina Gionfriddo	14, 45
Gregory Gipson	22
William Giraldi	18, 61
Anne Gisleson	74

	ISSUE
John Giuffo	3, 5
David Givens	52
John Glassie	30, 40
Misha Glouberman	81
Elizabeth Isadora Gold	46
Ben Goldfarb	132
Francisco Goldman	92
Manuel Gonzales	16
Alena Graedon	59
Sara Gran	65
Jen Graves	40
Gary Greenberg	112
Lavinia Greenlaw	55
Elizabeth Greenspan	137
Elizabeth Greenwood	87
Stephanie Elizondo Griest	85, 114
Izzy Grinspan	31
Lev Grossman	71
Arnon Grunberg	101
Elizabeth Gumport	72

H	ISSUE
Joe Hagan	64, 73
Shuja Haider	126

"SISYPHUS IN THE CAPITAL" by Eskor David Johnson
(Issue 149)

"Sisyphus in the Capital" illustration by Andrea Settimo

"WHAT HAPPENS THERE" by John D'Agata
(Issue 68)

J.C. Hallman	66
Ed Halter	37
Howard Hampton	5, 6, 14, 16, 35
Robert Hass	72
Christopher Heaney	98
Anthony Heilbut	91
Marc Herman	1
David Hockney	20
John Hodgman	6
Mark Holcomb	4, 70
Nick Hornby	87
Stu Horvath	144
Michel Houellebecq	18
Ken Howe	143
Hua Hsu	82, 114
Hillery Hugg	42
Maria Hummel	48
Joshua Hunt	142
Samantha Hunt	28
Amber Husain	139
Asti Hustvedt	80

I	ISSUE
International Necronautical Society	76
Robert Ito	30, 46, 68, 81

J	ISSUE
Lauren Michele Jackson	138
Leslie Jamison	80, 105
Casey Jarman	100, 120, 126
Margo Jefferson	97
Joshua Jelly-Schapiro	100, 109
Eskor David Johnson	149
R. Kikuo Johnson	31
Robert R. Johnson	74
Caitlin Jones	30
Chloé Cooper Jones	125
Tayari Jones	51
Rozalia Jovanovic	63, 82
Heidi Julavits	1, 4

K	ISSUE
Jennifer Kabat	116
Mark Kamine	7, 29, 47
Marc Katz	83
Alexander Kauffman	49
Adalena Kavanagh	149
Kristin Keane	149
Steven G. Kellman	61
Adam Kempa	73
Dimiter Kenarov	80
Dorna Khazeni	24
Jordan Kisner	127
B. Kite	7, 8, 28
Alex Kitnick	61, 76
August Kleinzahler	66

Joe Kloc	110
Chuck Klosterman	52
Saki Knafo	73
Alan Koenig	16
Wayne Koestenbaum	110
Dan Kois	40
Chris Kraus	110
Kea Krause	113
Lawrence Krauser	21
Benjamin Kunkel	2, 5
Rachel Kushner	98

L	ISSUE
Catherine Lacey	121
Paul La Farge	1, 17, 24, 97, 37, 62
Nick Laird	5
Jessica Lamb-Shapiro	27
Andy Lamey	13
Mark Lane	103
Reif Larsen	77
Nicole Lavelle	148
Amy Leach	121
Michelle Legro	98
C. S. Leigh	61, 76
Jonathan Lethem	1, 63, 84, 97
Alan Levinovitz	78
Lisa Levy	33, 53, 84
Gideon Lewis-Kraus	15
Dennis Lim	30
Ed Lin	76
François Le Lionnais	99
Sam Lipsyte	6, 38

Zefyr Lisowski	145
Mimi Lok	144
Andrew Losowsky	32
Bess Lovejoy	79
Ana Puente Flores & Valeria Luiselli	127
Erik Lundegaard	52
Peter Lunenfeld	54, 79
Garielle Lutz	59
Benjamin Lytal	19

M	ISSUE
Guy Maddin	14
Rachael Maddux	91
David Mamet	28
Sarah Manguso	11, 53
Mary Mann	112
Alex Mar	99, 113
Michael Marcinkowski	58
Ben Marcus	4
Lauren Markham	143
Sarah Marshall	104, 117, 140
Clancy Martin	115
Alexandra Marvar	132
Michael Paul Mason	67
Ben Mauk	127
Jason McBride	26
Tom McCarthy	89
Kailyn McCord	73
Ted McDermott	40, 55, 88, 142
Garrett McDonough	63
Tim McGirk	96

"IF HE HOLLERS LET HIM GO"
by Rachel Kaadzi Ghansah
(Issue 102)

"What Happens There" photo by JR; "If He Hollers Let Him Go" illustration by Tony Millionaire

	ISSUE
Will McGrath	147
Devin McKinney	32, 52
James McManus	29
John McMillian	25, 45
Morgan Meis	58
John Menick	131, 137
Margot Mifflin	30
Ange Mlinko	55
Kevin Moffett	13, 19
Alexandra Molotkow	109
Rachel Monroe	92, 115
Ander Monson	47, 56
Jon Mooallem	28
Rick Moody	2, 23, 25, 35, 44, 55, 63, 73
Adam Morris	112
✱ Haruki Murakami	55

	ISSUE
Eileen Myles	50

N

	ISSUE
Ahmed Naji	134, 146
William Nakabayashi	119
H. M. Naqvi	131
Victoria Nelson	39, 61, 84, 93
Francis M. Nevins	8
Annalee Newitz	24
David Ng	13, 26
Don Novello	5

O

	ISSUE
Rod O'Connor	43
Meghan O'Gieblyn	125
David K. O'Hara	75
Philip Oltermann	48
Mark Oppenheimer	21, 79
David Orr	23
Clarence Harlan Orsi	88

P

	ISSUE
Kyle Paoletta	133
Ken Parille	64
Ed Park	1, 25, 40, 97
Alan Michael Parker	49, 67, 94
Nicole Pasulka	92, 100
Annie Murphy Paul	16
Nate Pedersen	83
Gustav Peebles	8
Jack Pendarvis	27, 31, 41, 60, 84
Mark Peranson	5

	ISSUE
Georges Perec	37
Tony Perrottet	6, 26
Anne Helen Petersen	107
Per Petterson	53
Larissa Pham	135
Stephen Phelan	71
Adam Philips	62
Mike Plante	70
James Pogue	124
Rachel Poliquin	49, 57, 92
Jenelle Porter	40
Rolf Potts	38, 39, 52, 56

"THE MAKING OF THE BURU QUARTET" by Joel Whitney
(Issue 149)

	ISSUE
William Poundstone	17, 37
Michael G. Powell	72
Matthew Power	15
Laura Preston	130
Jenny Price	33, 34
Jana Prikryl	22
Alexander Provan	49, 53
Todd Pruzan	60

Q

	ISSUE
Lauren Quinn	107

R

	ISSUE
Emily Raboteau	93
Heather Radke	123
Sandi Rankaduwa	114

	ISSUE
Mallika Rao	139
Katie Arnold Ratliff	106
Vladic Ravich	107
Shruti Ravindran	132, 137
Monte Reel	84
Eileen Reynolds	82
Nathaniel Rich	80
Andrea Richards	69
Zandria Felice Robinson	120
Keir Roper-Caldbeck	104
Alex Rose	70
Carlo Rotella	43
Davy Rothbart	27, 38, 42, 55
Rebecca Rukeyser	141
Jim Ruland	14, 20, 34, 41
Milana Vuković Runjić	29
Kent Russell	99
Katie Ryder	104, 110

S

	ISSUE
Katie Gee Salisbury	143
Britt Salvesen	58
Livia Manera Sambuy	111
Ash Sanders	128
Lucy Sante	19
Strawberry Saroyan	33
Steven Boyd Saum	111
Ross Scarano	141
Theo Schell-Lambert	59, 77
Stephen Schenkenberg	31
Tony Scherman	100
Robert Schneider	111
Michael Schulman	63, 86, 105, 111
Ghita Schwarz	41
Amber Scorah	96
Ronnie Scott	82
Damion Searls	65, 74, 95
John Sellers	45, 46
Andy Selsberg	34, 46, 77
Namwali Serpell	71
Leanne Shapton	49
Meara Sharma	145
Jim Shepard	1, 3, 6, 9, 17, 21, 24, 28, 52
Zander Sherman	113
Kristina Shevory	112
David Shields	9, 32
Aaron Shulman	113
Steve Silberman	120
Matthew Simmons	55
Ross Simonini	64, 138, 148
Will Sloan	102
Mychal Denzel Smith	147
✱ Zadie Smith	54

	ISSUE
Noah Sneider	94
Suzanne Snider	2, 23
Michael Snyder	114, 121, 128
Natalie So	140
Dalia Sofer	101
Alexis Soloski	7
Billy Sothern	84
Matthew Specktor	96
Eric Spitznagel	47
Angela Starita	11
Sam Stark	51
Bijan Stephen	136
Will Stephenson	124
Pepper Stetler	148
Brandon Stosuy	55
Susan Straight	75, 97
Ginger Strand	21, 31, 50, 66, 89
Benjamin Strong	7, 18
David Suisman	14
Mark Sundeen	36, 48
Barrett Swanson	117
Fritz Swanson	85
Mark Swartz	4, 21, 58
R. Emmet Sweeney	52, 147
B. Alexandra Szerlip	89

41

"The Making of the Buru Quartet" illustration by Kristian Hammerstad; portraits of Haruki Murakami and Zadie Smith by Tony Millionaire

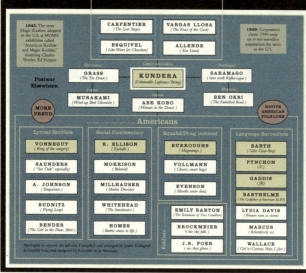
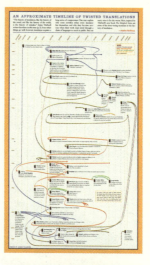

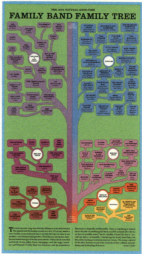
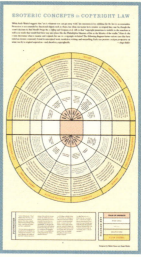

T	ISSUE
Stephanie Tam	135
Greg Tate	114
Ben Tausig	37
Barbara Taylor	62
Jonathan Taylor	43, 58
Justin Taylor	44, 64
Rebecca Taylor	79
Michelle Tea	8, 34, 64, 67, 118
Tori Telfer	122
Adam Thirlwell	57, 92
J. T. Thomas	65
Jyoti Thottam	3
Dave Tompkins	45
Samantha Topol	40
Anne Trubek	38
Ken Tucker	73
J. M. Tyree	23, 26

U	ISSUE
David L. Ulin	64
Deb Olin Unferth	77

V	ISSUE
Marcela Valdes	10
Anne Valente	111
Jeannie Vanasco	86, 112
Adrian Van Young	75, 88
Santiago Vaquera-Vásquez	69
Vauhini Vara	123
Chloe Veltman	16
Vendela Vida	5
Elisabeth Vincentelli	35

42

Schemas from issues 2, 57, 5, 144, 78, 67, and 75

Charity Vogel	81
William T. Vollmann	2
Deenah Vollmer	107
Sasha von Oldershausen	134

W	ISSUE
Karolina Waclawiak	76
Justin Wadland	97
Casey Walker	69
James Wallenstein	66
Ryan H. Walsh	140
Esmé Weijun Wang	113
David Warshofsky	15
Madeleine Watts	124
Donald Weber	39
Sarah Weinman	68
Benjamin Weissman	20, 86
Joe Wenderoth	37
Dan Werb	113
Lawrence Weschler	7, 42, 58, 76, 98
Joel Whitney	149
Alec Wilkinson	31
Mary Williams	62
Natasha Wimmer	15
Meaghan Winter	83
Tana Wojczuk	89
Douglas Wolk	11, 25, 27, 35, 55, 109
Frederick Woolverton	35
Alex Wright	39
C. D. Wright	43
Annie Julia Wyman	71, 111

Y	ISSUE
Molly Young	74

Z	ISSUE
Alexander Zaitchik	36
Rafia Zakaria	125, 140
Alejandro Zambra	128
Lindsay Zoladz	91

SCHEMAS

A	ISSUE
Shoshana Akabas	104, 112
Aku Ammah-Tagoe	144

B	ISSUE
Chris Bachelder	48
Elizabeth Baird	47, 58
Mac Barnett	22
Michael Barron	105
Landon Bates	126
Daniel Levin Becker	77
Andy Beta	55
Blair Braverman	125
Alyse Burnside	134
Nick Buttrick	51
Kylie Byrd	95

C	ISSUE

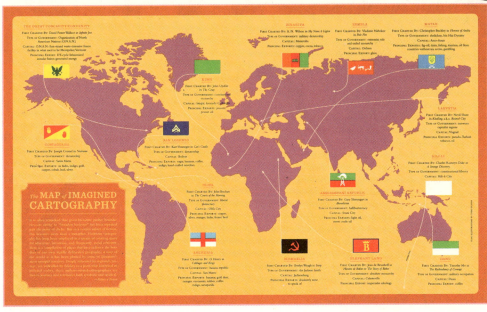

Lina Maria Ferreira Cabeza-Vanegas	116, 127
Justin Carder	142, 144
Sylvia Christie	113
Emily Clancy	115
Joshua Cohen	67
Simon Critchley	60

D	ISSUE
Meagan Day	82
Jon DeRosa	100
Jason Diamond	93
Brian Dillon	69
Cem Dinlenmiş	120
Larissa Dooley	54
Tyler Doyle	110
Louisa Dunnigan	103

E	ISSUE
Toph Eggers	79

F	ISSUE
Josh Fischel	87
Dylan Fisher	130
Sarah Bean Freed	99
Neil Freeman	12, 17

G	ISSUE
Rebecca Giordano	85
Ginger Greene	141
Ben Greenman	7, 11, 46, 64, 73
Jennie Gruber	40
Karen Gu	135

H	ISSUE
Moze Halperin	72

Doogie Horner	81
Vanessa Hua	119
Naomi Huffman	131
James Hughes	88, 94

K	ISSUE
Nina Katchadourian	20
Alex Kitnick	8

L	ISSUE
Catherine Lacey	96
Tim Lane	90, 101
Greg Larson	41, 43
Gideon Lewis-Kraus	2, 3, 4, 9
Eric Lidji	15

M	ISSUE
Dave Mandl	91
Lucas Mann	123
J.W. McCormack	149
Jordan Taliha McDonald	137
Jess McHugh	102
Brian McMullen	5, 6, 31, 37, 97
Kevin Moffett	19
James Morrison	76

N	ISSUE
Jesse Nathan	53, 59
Dina Nayeri	129
Peter Owen Nelson	26

O	ISSUE
Koye Oyedeji	117

P	ISSUE
Yasmin Patel	140

Claire Vaye Watkins & Derek Palacio	110
Rebecca Power	83

R	ISSUE
Megan Reid	133
Megan Roberts	89
Nicholas Russell	124, 128

S	ISSUE
Ben Schott	107
Steve Seid	70
Bob Solotaroff	98
Mairead Small Staid	108, 147
Jude Stewart	36, 65, 68, 71, 75, 80, 92, 146

T	ISSUE
Tony Tulathimutte	122
Gustavo Turner	33, 47

V	ISSUE
Nick Valvo	13
Vendela Vida	2
Alvaro Villanueva	14

W	ISSUE
Angie Waller	78
Zaria Ware	148
Zeynab Warsame	136
Brady Welch	86
Shawn Wen	118
Bryce Woodcock	145

Y	ISSUE
Chris Ying	49, 56
Yeonjae Yuk	74

Schema from issue 83

HEART STOPPER

CELEBRATING OUR 150TH ISSUE

HER GURU WAS STRONG ENOUGH TO STOP HIS OWN HEART—
BUT WAS THERE A MORE FRIGHTENING ASPECT OF HIS POWER?
by **SHRUTI SWAMY**

DISCUSSED: *Swami Rama, Living with the Himalayan Masters, Biofeedback, The Menninger Foundation, Exquisite Control, Sanskrit, Guru-hood, Child-Memory, The Smell of Cigarettes and Cologne, Palo Alto, Ayurveda, A Fucked-Up Zen Koan, Yoga Journal, Katharine Webster, Sexual Violence, Shiva, Logical Contortions, Pandits, The Rubric of Desirability*

ILLUSTRATIONS BY:
Charlotte Gomez

Baba didn't want it known where his ashes were scattered when he died—he didn't want anyone to make a shrine to him. But when he died we didn't call it that: we said "left his body." He had done it before, when he was younger: had changed bodies while keeping his soul intact. "When you tear your shirt, do you cry? Get a new shirt," he said. He didn't worry about mending it. He wore a white T-shirt under the rough maroon robe of an enlightened one; the robe smelled like cigarettes because he could control every aspect of his body and could choose not to die of cancer. He died—left his body—in India, because he did not want to return to America. Of the allegations that surrounded him, one had led to a lawsuit against his organization, and he refused to heed the summons to appear in court. In exile, he maintained his silence around the subject, into death.

I have no memory of meeting Baba for the first time, of not knowing him. Likely because I was so little—only five—and because I grew up hearing and believing stories about

him that elevated him to the level of myth, the times I actually spent with him stretched over the times I didn't. Baba, we all called him, which means "father." When I was nine, he initiated me in India at his ashram. In my family, the honor of becoming my guru was one he bestowed only on me. On the balcony of his suite I offered him fruits and flowers that my parents had bought for the occasion. In Sanskrit I repeated back the words he offered to me, promising in my heart to be obedient to him, to follow his teachings, to trust him with the care of my soul. He gave me a mantra in my ear. He wrote it down for me but it was secret, and I told it to no one. I still remember it, though it has been at least a decade since I reached for it.

Baba visited me in my dreams, could read my thoughts, wanted only what was best for me. He was the symbol of a world that made sense, one in which our family was chosen, special, protected. But there was another side to Baba, or there was another world, one less magical, at once more dangerous and mundane. For years, I lived joyously in the first world, until slowly, then all at once, I arrived in the second.

In the spring of 1989, my father had a spiritual revelation. He had been in the Santa Cruz Mountains attending a talk by Dr. Usharbudh Arya, the founder of the Meditation Center in Minneapolis, who was on a national lecture circuit to spread his knowledge about yoga. Dr. Arya was a serious scholar, fluent in not one but two ancient languages—Pali, the language

of the Buddha, as well as Sanskrit—and was a former professor of South Asian studies at the University of Minnesota. An autodidact, he received no formal schooling until enrolling at the University of London, where he earned his BA and also an MA; he then earned a LittD from Utrecht University, in the Netherlands. To me, he always looked a little like a brown Robin Williams, with a square, friendly face bedecked with '80s dad-glasses, and, for much of my childhood, a white beard that also reminded me of Santa Claus's. When my dad approached Dr. Arya after the lecture was finished, they looked at each other. My father, deeply moved by the power of this gaze, vibrating with the distress from the conflicts that had driven him to seek spiritual solace, laid his head on the shoulder of his future guru, and began to cry.

This encounter, of two souls meeting in a state of immediate, profound knowing, is reserved for romantic love in Western culture. In our spiritual tradition, however, the instant connection felt between guru and future disciple pointed to a spiritual certainty: that the two had known each other in different lifetimes, and that they had work to do together in this one. Dr. Arya was a disciple of Baba—Swami[1] Rama—whom he had met years earlier in a similarly dramatic encounter. Already an accomplished scholar of Sanskrit and a meditation teacher, Dr. Arya took Baba immediately as his guru when they met in 1969.

---

1. *Swami* is a spiritual title, meaning "master of himself," and also a common South Indian surname. My last name bears no connection to Swami Rama, or to any swami.

The guru–disciple relationship is a bond of intense spiritual significance, formalized by the initiation ceremony, after which the disciple is "their guru's responsibility," says my mother. "You make this resolve that this is the person who will guide you, and you will follow him unquestioningly. And the guru will do whatever is necessary for your *spiritual* well-being, which might involve putting you through difficulties and pain. Just like parents, who might ground you for your own good, which you might not like." The guru figure can be both parent and trickster, someone whose antics would disturb their disciple's complacency with the illusion of the material world, their attachments, or their self-conception. My mother remembers this aspect of Baba and Dr. Arya's relationship: times when Baba would belittle Dr. Arya in front of their disciples, cut him down to size—acts that Dr. Arya always took with good humor, my mother reports, accepting them as lessons in shrinking the ego. No matter what: the disciple owes her guru absolute obedience. The guru owes his disciple nothing less than the safeguarding and the development of their soul.

When Dr. Arya took Baba as his guru, he joined the ancient lineage Baba represented, and began to see himself as a vessel for its knowledge. In the dedication to a book about the *Yoga Sutras*, Dr. Arya writes, in Sanskrit (as translated by my mother): "The tradition that started with the golden source of the creation, continued by Ved Vyas and other sages, and ending at the feet of Sri Swami Ram[a], I bow to that unbroken guru lineage." When my parents were initiated by Dr. Arya, he echoed this idea: "It is not me who is initiating you. This is the lineage of Swami Rama that comes straight through me," my mom reports him saying. If my parents' guru was the most significant spiritual leader in their lives, then the guru of my parents' guru, Swami Rama, was ever more powerful, almost unimaginably so. Even in absence, even before we met him, he was a constant presence in our lives. I didn't dream then that the honor of initiation that had been bestowed on Dr. Arya by Swami Rama could also be given to a child—to me.

Who was this man—the leader who would become my guru—who had the power of a god? When I was a child, my understanding of Baba blurred fact with magic. As an adult, I'm both surprised and validated to learn that Baba's reputation reached far beyond our community, and that, for a time, he played on the national stage.

Baba has many names: Swami Rama of the Himalayas, Brijkishor Kumar, Brij Kishore Dhasmana. His autobiography, *Living with the Himalayan Masters*, and the biography written by his disciple and successor Pandit Rajmani Tigunait, *At the Eleventh Hour*, are both filled with mythic origin stories, and vanishingly few dates. Born to a Brahmin family in Uttar Pradesh, Northern India, in 1925, Swami Rama lyrically describes a childhood in the Himalayas spent under the tutelage of his guru, Bengali Baba, in *Living with the Himalayan Masters*. Alongside his yogic accomplishments, his educational claims included study at Oxford University, though this is contested by some of his former disciples. The fabrication would be in line with his ambition: not content to remain in India, the Swami had set his sights on making his mark on the West.

And America, at that moment, was particularly primed for his teachings. Yoga had arrived in this country decades before Swami Rama did, but the '60s brought an explosion of interest in some aspects of Indian culture: sitar music, spirituality, and textiles. The psychedelic explorations of the era had also led to an openness toward other consciousness-expanding practices like meditation (Paul McCartney, speaking to reporters after a weeklong meditation retreat: "We don't need [drugs] anymore. We think we're finding other ways of getting there"). Swami Rama landed in the States in 1969, during a moment of spiritual yearning at the closing of a decade of social upheaval and free love. At the same time, the Immigration and Nationality Act of 1965 had removed the quota system that had limited immigration from Asian countries, resulting in an influx of Indian engineers, and many swamis. With some exceptions, yoga had, up until then, been popularized and taught mostly by white people in America. From the transcendental meditation taught by the Beatles' Maharishi, to the asanas of Bikram and Iyengar, Swami Rama's teachings were part of a wave of Indian yogis looking to build their American legacy.

As a yogi, Baba practiced what we in the West now solely think of as yoga—asana, the postures that can increase strength and flexibility—as well as pranayama, meditation, and yogic philosophies deriving from Hindu scriptures.

He came to America with a mandate from his guru: "All the spiritual practices should be verified scientifically, if science has the capacity to do so." After teaching yoga at YMCAs around the country, he received an invitation from the husband-and-wife research team Dr. Elmer and Alyce Green to join their research at the Menninger Foundation, an influential hospital and research facility in Topeka, Kansas.[2] Their research focused on what we might now call wellness, the mind–body connection, and Eastern spiritual practices that could promote physical health. In 1970, Swami Rama became their "Swami in residence," a position that went beyond research subject, as he also proposed experiments and spent time outside the lab with the Greens.

In the documentary *Biofeedback: The Yoga of the West*, which the Greens later made about their research, Baba is younger than I ever saw him, all dark curls and coppery skin. In striking contrast to the other jolly-faced gurus and ash-smeared freakshows, Swami Rama "was forty-five years of age, tall and well-built," as Dr. Green writes in his 1977 book, *Beyond Biofeedback*, recalling their first meeting. "He reminded me of an Italian Renaissance nobleman.… With a lot of energy for debate and persuasion, he was a formidable figure." In Swami Rama the Greens had found a perfect ambassador for the alien East: he was fluent in English, dignified, Italian-adjacent, charismatic, and, yes, handsome.

---

2. The Foundation will sound familiar if you've read Ben Lerner's *The Topeka School*.

At the Menninger Foundation, Baba awed the researchers with the power of his control over various aspects of his autonomic nervous system. In one experiment, he voluntarily constricted an artery, which resulted in an eleven-degree temperature differential between the left and right sides of one of his hands, a feat that stunned Dr. Green. He writes, "The Swami's demonstration showed exquisite… control over this normally uncontrolled piece of the neural apparatus." In a later experiment, he demonstrated a feat that Western science had deemed impossible: by causing his heart to beat at five times the normal rate, he suspended the organ's primary function of moving blood through the body without even "[twitching] an eyelash" in the process, observed Alyce Green, a phenomenon known as "arterial flutter." Afterward, he removed the wires and went off to deliver a lecture.

Baba had, in effect, stopped his own heart.

I am still dazzled to discover that Baba's canny connection with the Menninger Foundation generated national media coverage in 1971—this was the man upon whose lap I had sat as a child! *The New York Times Magazine* and *Esquire* both ran articles about Baba's work, and I found a surprisingly in-depth report in *Playboy*, whose reporter even tried out meditation himself: "I loved it. After the extended session I felt very relaxed, very good. I would recommend the experience to anyone."

I was not the only one to be dazzled. The research and the subsequent coverage gave Baba the legitimacy and

the exposure to build a following in America and raise money to create the sprawling organization that would be his legacy: the Himalayan Institute of Yoga Science and Philosophy. The Institute's American headquarters were in Honesdale, Pennsylvania, an ashram situated in the Poconos, where we visited Baba in the summer, but it had centers all over America and in India as well. The Institute was officially under the governance of a board of directors, which comprised Baba's most vigorous disciples (excluding Dr. Arya, who led his own organization)—but really, it was Baba's show. It was his home, his shelter, his community, his world—the world he created from his teaching and his desires, and from his ability to bend the reality of those around him.

In some respects, my parents were typical of their demographic: Indian immigrants who had arrived in America for graduate school in the late '70s, my mother to study aerospace engineering, my father, computer science. Both had been raised in Brahmin households, my mother's lower- and my father's upper middle class. My mother, by choice, quit her aerospace engineering job soon after she gave birth, and stayed at home to raise me. My dad, who arrived in Silicon Valley in the gold rush days of the '80s, worked long hours at various start-ups, making good money, but never making it big. But in other ways, they were very different from their peers. They came from different communities in India and had refused arranged marriages to love-marry against the wishes of my father's

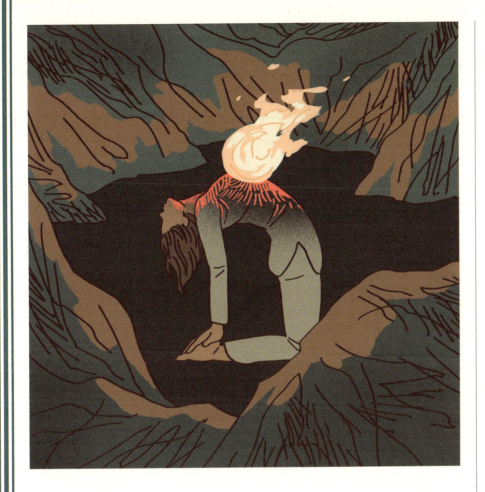

well-to-do Tamilian parents. Both had graduated from the top engineering school in the country—my mother was one of about a dozen women among hundreds of men, a fact that made it hard for her to find a job in India, where employers were nakedly dismissive of female candidates. They were also artists: my mother a kathak dancer, my father a musician—both were lovers of North and South Indian classical dance and music. And both, caught in cycles of generational trauma and a troubled marriage, were actively looking for a spiritual path that would lead them through it. Despite their training as engineers, they were interested in the unseen, subtle world that yoga described, deeply curious about the ways the millennia of yogic knowledge could offer guidance and even peace to people living profoundly modern, complicated lives.

The Himalayan Institute, therefore, was not the first—or the last—of the spiritual communities my parents participated in. Restless, seeking, my parents were an uncommon if not fully rare sight in these communities, each headed by an Indian guru, but mostly composed of white disciples. While some Indian immigrants were drawn to these organizations, most were not, preferring to find their spiritual community at Bay Area temples whose members were almost all Indian: fledgling in the '80s, and flourishing today. We did visit these temples occasionally, but for my parents these spaces did nothing to address the enduring spiritual need they felt, and reminded them, my mother especially, of the religious conservatism they had fled. They preferred the wilder, freer flavor of American yoga.

But they were also discerning. What might have made these groups intriguing to their white members was in part the escape they appeared to offer from American culture and American life. Having little prior knowledge of yoga, Sanskrit, Hinduism, or even Indian culture, these white seekers could have been dazzled simply by the exotic nature of the offerings. My parents, both raised in Hindu households, were well versed in the scriptures. My mother knows Sanskrit. She was skeptical when she first met Dr. Arya, based on previous experiences she'd had with gurus, but was won over by a lecture she attended in which he offered an unconventional—even feminist—reading of the female saints of India. She was moved by the purity of his knowledge and his seeming lack of interest in the trappings of guru-hood, like the shows of obsequiousness from his devotees insisted on by other gurus my mom had encountered. The bond my parents had with Dr. Arya, the deep trust and love they felt for him, was solidified in these years—and by extension, the regard they felt for Baba. Their lives, and, for a time, their marriage, improved under their spiritual care.

49

These are my parents' memories— what of my own? Writing this, I'm frustrated with the holes in my child-memory, which blur real events and dreams: what I have are flashes of image and vivid feeling. An adult's capacity for creating and retaining memories is a power I've become conscious of while parenting my daughter, who, at six, has entered the age when some memories of these days might actually survive into adulthood. Still, mine, the mother's, will always be more authoritative. My parents have said, "But we didn't even meet Baba that often!" News to me, for my visits with him feel long and numerous in memory. All told, though we never made an official break with the community and continued our practices and relationships long after our drift away, my parents were active there for just a handful of years, from 1989 to 1996. Consequential years, no doubt, but a blip in the life of an adult. That span of time feels different to a child. In my memories—dreams—images— feelings—my guru was a vibrant and constant presence. I was a child and he was a grown adult, but he seemed bigger than the difference between the sizes of our bodies. I could tell right away that he was important; I could see that he was able to hold a room full of adults in rapt silence; I knew that he had magical powers, stories of which were sometimes told to me at bedtime. But my relationship with him had a more approachable quality than the ones I observed with his adult devotees. In some ways, it was not unlike the relationship I had with my grandparents in India, whom I did not see very often, but who doted on

me. There were many moments with my family "backstage"—intimate, spontaneous meetings when Baba was relaxed and playful, affectionate, far from the sometimes-ferocious guru persona he wore out in the world. With me, he could be teasing, even a little silly.

I was a people-pleasing, attention-hungry kid, and Baba gave me beautiful attention. Once, in the Honesdale ashram, walking by the tennis courts, I was called over by Baba and kissed, which I complained about later, far out of earshot: "It was not a real kiss," I claimed. "It didn't make a sound." Baba called me back a second time and kissed me loudly, while my parents looked at each other, astonished. I was five and don't remember this: it's family lore. But I remember the pleasurable scratchiness of other kisses from him, being wrapped in his smell of cigarettes and cologne. I knew I was special to him: even if he was talking to someone else, he would allow me to climb up onto his lap, even during a lecture—his attention made visible to everyone my inherent worth and potential. Somehow there was never another kid around to compete with: no kid was as beloved as me. Though I was an undisciplined child, I would have done anything to please him.

With their black-and-white thinking, children make the best believers. I believed that through his actions, his care, and his attention, Baba proved that my family was exceptional, that if we followed the rules—and we did— we would be rewarded with his special protection; that we would be protected against illness, misfortune,

and even death. No one told me this, at least not explicitly: no one needed to. I had everything I needed to construct these beliefs from the clues the adults around me offered. In Palo Alto, where we lived until I was ten, I led a double life: Indian at home, and as white as possible at school. As the only Indian kid in my school, I had a painful sense of my difference without the language for it: I wanted only to be rid of it, to be like Jennifer and Maggie, with their old-money families, their perfect soccer ponytails, and their normal school lunches. I remember starting to find my social life difficult when I was in fourth grade, but my mom reports that the bullying and exclusion had begun years earlier. Normally, my differences made me feel ashamed, but Baba's love made me proud. It was a secret I had, a bulwark against the isolating pain of racial assimilation, against the pain of a home life laced with tension. In a place where I was beginning to feel worthless, Baba's love showed me my worth. The trick was to keep that love.

The truth was, I didn't *like* to meditate. I loved the idea of magic, but the process of attaining it was too boring, the rewards too distant to ever motivate me to join my parents in their practice. Perhaps, then, I wasn't so special after all, a realization that made me feel uneasy. I had made a promise to Baba to lead a spiritual life simply to earn praise from him and my parents—but the promise was weighty. I dreamed of Baba and told my mother: she replied that he was visiting me to remind me to meditate more. I felt guilty, but I didn't meditate. The window of my childhood was closing: I was aware that whatever special dispensation and indulgence I was receiving would fade. How, then, would I be able to realize the spiritual expectation that had been placed on my shoulders? More worryingly, how would I earn Baba's and my parents' love?

Here was the greatest magic: We had been chosen. Our family was special. Not only had I been initiated by Swami Rama, which was an act radiant with meaning for all of us. He was the reason my brother was born.

In 1990, my father made a fateful visit to India to meet Dr. Arya and Swami Rama. Swami Rama told him that they had to have a long conversation, but every night of my father's trip, when he showed up at Swami Rama's office as instructed, he was told to come back the next night. Finally, on the last night of the trip, he and Swami Rama did talk, but it wasn't a long conversation. "You need to have another child," Swami Rama told him.

"I'd like to," my dad said, "but I don't think my wife would go for it."

"I'll take care of that," said Swami Rama. "Call her tonight." In *Living with the Himalayan Masters*, Baba tells a similar story about his own birth: His father and mother, a childless couple of "advanced age," were instructed by Baba's future guru, Bengali Baba, to have a child. Baba's mother was in her forties when her only son was born. Mine was thirty-nine. When my dad called my mom that night, he was surprised to hear her say yes.

This is my father's story, anyway. When I ask my mother about it, she tells a different one. Prior to my mother's meeting with Baba, another disciple had told her that Baba "had a lot of souls in his pocket waiting to take human form," she remembers. If he asked you to have a child, it meant he believed you were a highly spiritual person and a good parent.

When my mother first met Baba in the fall of 1990, she was struck not only by the power of his presence—the conversation she had with him was also uncanny. He repeated his request for her to have another child, a request that my dad had relayed, but that had not changed her mind on the subject. *Easy for you to say*, she thought, during this meeting with Baba—she thought but did not say. *You don't have to carry and give birth to the child*. Aloud, Baba replied: "I know it's easier for me to say than for you to do."

"It was as though he was reading my thoughts, responding to every objection I had internally but had not voiced, as soon as it came into my mind," says my mother. At the conclusion of this spooky one-sided conversation, Baba had changed her mind, not only ensuring the birth of my brother, but also convincing my mother of Baba's supernatural ability to read people's thoughts, a phenomenon echoed by many other disciples. The magic of this story rhymed with that of countless other stories people told about Baba: about his clairvoyance, a magical act involving an ever-full thermos of chai, and his ability to shrink tumors within his body and change bodies at will. Even now, it is hard to understand where the line is between reality, manipulation, fiction, and magic when it comes to the stories I know about Baba, the man who stopped his own heart.

My brother—BY, we called him in utero, for Bala Yogi, because of all the yoga poses we were sure he was doing in there—was born in 1992, on Guru Purnima. That the yearly festival day in which people honor their teachers with offerings and praise was my brother's birthday simply could not have been a coincidence. Rather, it was proof that he was the great soul Baba had meant to call into this world. It was Baba who named him Bharatendu—"moon of India"—a beautiful if fully unpronounceable name in the West.

Early on, my parents could tell that something was wrong. Large patches of itchy rash bloomed on my brother's face and little body—he was so uncomfortable he was unable to sleep through the night. After months of tests, doctors determined he was allergic to nearly every imaginable food, and lethally allergic to nuts. My parents, at Baba's guidance, treated him with homeopathy and Ayurveda instead of the allopathic medicine that might have offered my brother more immediate relief from his constant suffering. They were dedicated, researching in medical journals at the library, traveling to meet respected practitioners of Ayurveda for treatment, dutifully administering oils and medicines to try to cure him, staying up nights with him: for the first two years of his life, they barely slept more than two hours at a time. Baba said that my brother was a great soul burning off bad karma through this suffering, which may have comforted them through the anguish of seeing their toddler hospitalized for asthma, unable to breathe.

But maybe not. In a box of pictures I find a series of photographs of my brother's body, close-ups of the weeping eczema sores, purply gray, the images wincingly painful to look at. Those images instantly conjure the smell of my brother's sick skin: a vivid, animal scent. They took those pictures to send to Baba. They wanted answers. But they received no reply.

Baba died—left his body—in 1996, while in India. We had seen him there a few months before, a visit of which I have only a dim memory. A long white hallway, Baba is at the end of it, waiting for us, though he has not been alerted to our presence. The crush of closeness: incense. But perhaps I am inventing this memory from the story my mother told me about the visit.

At that point we had moved from Palo Alto to a rural area of Northern California to be close to another spiritual community of white devotees and headed by another Indian guru. This guru had taken a vow of silence and spoke through his curly writing on a chalkboard. He was many people's guru, but not *ours*, a distinction we reserved for Dr. Arya and for Swami Rama, even as we began to drift away from their communities and drift into this one. Despite this, my parents hosted the old Bay Area group of devotees to meditate and honor Baba's passing. The adults spoke ardently of his life and work, both of which, they knew, would continue in different forms. I watched as the story of him

leaving his body began to acquire new, slightly fantastical details, and when I made a joke about it ("Next we'll be saying he sprouted wings and flew through the ceiling!"), I was chided by the horrified adults.

Baba was starting to fade from my life. No one in the new community had ever heard of the old one: the aura of specialness imparted on my family by Baba had no cachet here, where specialness was derived from proximity to a different guru. My parents were disillusioned and exhausted, their marriage strained to a breaking point. When they spoke of Baba, it was with familiar reverence, but over time they spoke of him less and less. I was growing up. My waking life was consumed by the task of escaping my waking life; I was surrounded by the disdainful white children of the white hippies who made up the community, and I escaped not by practicing yoga and meditation, but through the intense and devoted reading of fantasy novels. I still believed in the world that Baba had taught me to believe in, the subtle, energetic world of unseen forces, and of magic. But I was dreaming forwards in time, not backwards, to the prospect of college, an intellectual life, boyfriends—escape.

And—there was something else. I had heard a rumor, or if not a rumor, then a shard of impossible information. There's no one who could have told this to me except my parents, and in all likelihood it was my father. I understood that there had been an accusation against Baba, and from that I constructed a narrative that had no basis in fact: that a young woman had

been pushed into a closet against her will and kissed—I could see it clearly in my mind: a supply closet. Either this had happened, even though that was impossible, or she had claimed that it had happened. Did I believe that it had?

My father and I were close at that time, unusually so. I looked up to him, wanted nothing more than to be in his favor and earn his attention and his love, much as I felt toward Baba. In the past, when we had discussed another account of sexual violence, I had gotten the sense that my dad didn't really believe the survivor, that he felt that she might have been exaggerating, or else, if it was true, that it was icky, something she never should have brought up. This attitude fit the late-'90s stance toward sexual violence: these years were sandwiched between the Anita Hill hearings and the Clinton scandal, which we talked about both in my family and in the culture at large as though a twenty-two-year-old intern had just as much power as the president of the United States. (My father does not recall these conversations.) When I look back now, I know that not a flicker of fear or doubt crossed my mind. I trusted my dad, and he trusted his guru, who trusted Swami Rama.

My position, which was my parents' position, which was their guru's position, was the impossible: that the woman was not lying *and* that Baba had not done it, that the event had happened and it simultaneously had not happened. It was a strange, abstract intellectual puzzle—a paradox—that had no solution, like a fucked-up Zen koan. The accusation was so distant, and the accused was now dead. It stuck like a splinter in my finger, occasionally annoying, but easy to forget.

So easy to forget that after I graduated from college, as my first act of adult independence, I returned to the world I remembered from childhood. I lived for several months in the ashram in Rishikesh, India, run by Dr. Arya, who had, in 1992, ascended to Swamihood by renouncing his householder's life, his family, and his possessions, and taking on the guru-given name of Swami Veda Bharati. At his ashram, I took meditation classes, did data entry in the office, and developed several intense and (mostly) chaste crushes on the young resident monks. Later, I volunteered at the Rural Development Institute in Dehradun and lived in the sprawling hospital-school-institute complex that Swami Rama had built there, in part through donations from my parents. There, surrounded by Swami Rama's legacy and the buildings, organizations, and teachings he had left for us, the paradox that had been handed down to me became a little more troublesome. I'd been through women's studies courses in college; I had been raised by a feminist mother; I knew that false accusations of sexual abuse are vanishingly rare. Yet daily I was surrounded by true believers, people whose lives, they said, had been changed for the better by Swami Rama, and who spoke of him without any caveats, in glowing terms. Their belief strengthened mine. "I'm not sure if I believe in god yet, but I am getting a lot more spiritual these days," I wrote in an email to my skeptical best friend in 2007. "I've started getting used to meditating in the mornings, though for me it feels more like praying, or setting the intention of my day. I say (in my head), 'Baba, please give me patience and strength. Please help me be kind and loving and unselfish. And please send me a boyfriend.'" One of my jobs when I was volunteering was to edit devotees' stories of Baba's miracles, in the style of *Miracle of Love* by Ram Dass—a loving tribute to the guru from the people whose lives he'd touched. My story, contributed anonymously, described a dream of walking into a room where Baba is lecturing: "Immediately, I feel my body fill up with spiraling energy and I can't move. After a while, must have only been seconds, but feels like much longer, it passes. Of its own accord, my hand writes on a piece of paper: *Don't you know I will always be with you?*" As far as I know, the project was abandoned.

In the hospital complex, Baba's apartment had been preserved, and visitors were permitted to look into the room where he died. It had the aura of a shrine. I knelt there and prayed. Though I was beginning to doubt, I kept a picture of Baba in my vest pocket, right above my heart.

Was it idle curiosity or a more urgent desire that pushed me to search online for information about Baba? I returned from India and started my adult life, moving to San Francisco to attend graduate school, doing weird jobs on the side to make rent. I kept up an intermittent yoga practice: in India I had essentially gone through a yoga teacher-training program, and sometimes I wondered if I should get certified so I could teach the yoga class I was always looking for but could never find here, one that was rooted in cultural knowledge and respect and that incorporated aspects of yoga beyond the asanas. I had lost my childhood aversion to sitting still. The subtle world, which I had created an understanding of through practice, scriptures, and stories, had begun to feel rich and mysterious, and formed the basis of my writing. Baba had had deep knowledge of this world, of this I was sure. But my discomfort with my vague knowledge of his transgression was also growing.

It had been a couple years since my father was hospitalized for a heart attack so severe that the sonographer had had to run the echocardiogram twice to believe what he was seeing. When I saw my powerful father reduced to a frail man near death in the hospital, I felt my belief in Baba unexpectedly breaking: the idea that my family was special, chosen, protected was belied by my father's grave illness. What had I thought, that our family would be spared such ordinary suffering? Everyone dies, I remembered suddenly, and as soon as I thought it, I noticed how childish, how absurd it was that I had believed anything different. At that moment, it was irrelevant to me that Baba had likely never made the obviously impossible promise to protect my father against death. If anything, the fact of my father's survival and almost-miraculous return to health could easily have proved to me that Baba's protection held strong. But the belief in my family's exemption from illness and death was one that needed to break. It was a child's way

of thinking, and I was now twenty-five. Perhaps it was this event that cleared the way for my next step into knowledge—knowledge that proved to be stunningly easy to obtain.

A moment of what felt like idle curiosity on Google turned up a long-form investigative article published in *Yoga Journal* in December of 1990, and the ease of finding it still astounds me: it had been there all along. "The Case Against Swami Rama of the Himalayas" by Katharine Webster details decades of alleged abuse. The article was itself years in the making: Swami Veda Bharati (then Dr. Arya), for example, is quoted from an interview at a conference center in Napa, California, in 1989—the same year he had that fateful meeting with my father. The article had been published when my parents were disciples of Swami Veda Bharati's and before I was initiated by Swami Rama.

More than twelve thousand words long, Webster's article gives a meticulous overview of the depth and breadth of the alleged abuse occurring at the hands of Swami Rama, quoting multiple survivors of assault under pseudonyms, as well as former community members and people in leadership positions at the Institute. In the article, many women report similar, sickening experiences of being pressured into unwanted sex (there is a more accurate word for this, which is *rape*) with the idea that intercourse was part of their spiritual journey. Startled to be thrust into a sexual context with a person they believed to be celibate, many women were made to believe that theirs was a special connection to Swami Rama, and were confused and humiliated to discover the existence of other women in similar circumstances. "Because I'd rationalized that he was teaching me a lesson," a former disciple, Carolyn, reports, "I believed he must be teaching other women the same lesson, and I shouldn't begrudge his attention to other students."

But the article is also filled with disturbing accusations that extend beyond sex. Megan describes Swami Rama humiliating a shy female resident, noting that he "bragged to a crowd of disciples that the woman would do whatever he told her, then put his dog's collar and leash around her neck and walked her back and forth, while the others laughed." Other abuses she says she witnessed included Swami Rama instructing female disciples to weed poison ivy bare-handed and kicking a kneeling woman in the buttocks. Unlike sexual assault, which usually happens behind closed doors, these abuses happened in the open, under the gaze of the community.

If I were writing this story as fiction, it would be the discovery of this article that changed everything for me. Strangely, it passed through me without even a shiver. Though I had never witnessed this aspect of him, I could recognize Baba in the horrible stories I read. His mercurial face, powerful and limber, could communicate so much with a single glance. By summoning his powers, I imagined, he could strike one dead with one fearsome glance, like Shiva felling poor Kama out of annoyance—though of course, that was the old way of thinking, mythic and magical. A new way of thinking offered itself to me too: a moment of betrayal in private, when the mask of holiness slipped and the ugly face of power revealed itself, banal and ordinary in its evil.

A wave of bad feeling passed through me—passed. There was a disconnection between myself and this information; I could not incorporate it into my childhood narrative. I didn't know any of the women in the article. As far as I could tell, they had joined the community of their own volition, as adults; from their pseudonyms, and the racial makeup of the community, I could guess that they were all white. This mattered to me, because it separated me from them. It even gave me a prickle of discomfort along racial lines: white women were, according to various stereotypes, both more sexual and more desirable than Indian women; the disgust the white women expressed when talking about their Indian guru likewise touched a nerve, though rationally I knew their disgust stemmed from their horror at the situation, not from Swami Rama's race.

That is all to say that I was already practiced in the art of holding two conflicting narratives in my mind. Even when I added more information to the information I already possessed, I could still hold it away from

me, like a crazy story, like a curiosity. I didn't call my parents or try to talk to anyone about what I had learned. Instead, I did what I do when I can't figure something out: I tried to write about it, in a short story I worked on for years without success. I had been connected with a man who had grown up at the Honesdale ashram— an Indian American man—and I let him take me out to dinner in San Francisco. Knowing that he, too, had been a child in the community gave me hope that as an adult he might be similarly struggling to make sense of the allegations against Baba, that he might uniquely understand my unease. But his memories of Baba were beautiful. Baba was with him still; he had felt his real presence when his father had been in a health crisis and he had sat down to meditate. I didn't—couldn't—bring it up. That night, walking home through the dark city, I had a strange feeling, as though I were traveling not across distance, but across time. By the time I stepped into my bright apartment, it was as though I had left the story behind in the restaurant, like a lost hat. There was no room in my mind, in my life, for this knowledge. I tucked it away.

Maybe another person would have let that be the end of it. Maybe some people don't want to know the truth. I didn't—and I did. Over the years, I would return to the *Yoga Journal* article two or three more times, always with a curiosity that felt casual, but that left me feeling a little nauseated. Did it sink in? It was like taking small sips of poison. A little more each time.

Have you ever broken a taboo from your childhood? Something you were told never to do, never to think? The first time you cross the forbidden line, you do so with your eyes closed, waiting for punishment to strike. But it doesn't come. Still, the belief might not break right away. You might have to cross the line again and again before the thrill dulls and the forbidden thing on the other side becomes plainly true and ordinary. There was a point two years ago when I finally wanted to learn more: I was ready for my belief to break. I broadened my search online, reading everything I could find. In this way, I came across an account tucked inside a legal document that finally changed everything.

I was shivering as I read, I noticed, as though in fear. Because there were some broad but potent similarities between this story and my own, I felt as though I were looking at a flight map of a journey that had been interrupted, watching the trajectory of my relationship with Baba as it could have been. Like me, the disciple had been brought as a child into the community and had been initiated by Swami Rama as a young girl. Like me, she was Indian. But our stories were different too. She was a decade older than me and had known Baba in her early adulthood. She had been abused by the person she had been taught to revere and obey.

What had once been safely abstract suddenly flooded my body with feeling.

My parents and an entire community of people I trusted had placed me in the arms of a predator. It was luck, not their protection, that had kept me from direct harm.

Why did my parents—and later I, myself—fail to make sense of the information we had about the danger the community posed? And why did my parents fail to act? It was a question that included my parents, but was ultimately even bigger than them: How had so many people I loved and who loved me never disavowed this man—against whom there was a mountain of credible evidence—thus allowing him to further harm others? How did they allow me to remain in harm's way?

Here's what I know: Baba could bend reality. But aside from his seeming ability to mind-read and his other yogic powers, there were less-than-supernatural methods he employed. The Institute's leadership, under his direction, used every mode available to them to suppress dissent, including the law. They were viciously litigious in the '90s, filing defamation and fraud lawsuits against people who had alleged abuse at the hands of Swami Rama, and people who supported those people. The very act of seeking *internal* accountability was offensive: letters to the board seeking acknowledgment and institutional change were met with contemptuous dismissal and became grounds for these lawsuits. According to a memo sent to the "Institute Community," its leadership had explored "all possible legal courses of action" against *Yoga Journal* after the "deplorable and misguided" article came out, but decided against them, citing the difficulty of making a case against a publication with First Amendment protections in place. Instead, they urged their community to trust what they knew of their guru: "Don't put much energy into such negative things." They also withdrew all their advertising from *Yoga Journal*, and founded another publication, *Yoga International*, in 1991. (In recent years, a truce seems to have formed between the Institute and *Yoga Journal*: in January 2025, the magazine published a friendly online Q&A with Pandit Rajmani Tigunait, the Institute's current board chair and spiritual head, in which he speaks glowingly of his teacher, Swami Rama.)

Ironically, while the 1990 *Yoga Journal* article had raised awareness—to those who were ready to hear it—about the potential danger Swami Rama posed, the article and other efforts to hold him and the Institute accountable might have had another effect: of serving as a loyalty test for the true believers, ensuring that those who stayed in leadership positions would be vigorously faithful to Swami Rama, even in the face of credible evidence of harm. Indeed, for years, if not decades, allegations of abuse had been brought to the board, all of them dismissed without further investigation. This was costly: with each new allegation the community lost supporters, donors, and board members, who resigned in disgust. Those who remained in leadership positions were

---

A NONEXHAUSTIVE LIST OF BOOKS AND STORIES COMPOSED DURING COMMUTES

✶ *Beautiful Country* by Qian Julie Wang—written on the subway
✶ *Elmet* by Fiona Mozley—written on the subway
✶ *No. 91/92: Notes on a Parisian Commute* by Lauren Elkin—written on the subway
✶ The *Harry Potter* series by J. K. Rowling—written on the train
✶ *The Stranger* by Harlan Coben—written in the backs of Ubers
✶ *The Great American Bus Ride* by Irma Kurtz—written on Greyhound buses
✶ *Call for the Dead* by John le Carré—written on the train
✶ *Falling* by T. J. Newman—written on an airplane
✶ *Barchester Towers* by Anthony Trollope—written on the train
✶ *The Queen of the Night* by Alexander Chee—written on the train
✶ *Station Eleven* by Emily St. John Mandel—written on the train
✶ *Presumed Innocent* by Scott Turow—written on the train
✶ *The Warded Man* by Peter V. Brett—written on the subway
✶ *The Negro Speaks of Rivers* by Langston Hughes—written on the train
✶ *The Brief Wondrous Life of Oscar Wao* by Junot Diaz—written on the subway
✶ *The Nickel Boys* by Colson Whitehead—written on planes and trains
✶ Various works by Lydia Davis—written on planes and trains
✶ *The Old Drift* by Namwali Serpell—written on planes and trains

—list compiled by Su Ertekin-Taner

people who were committed to furthering the narrative of their guru's benevolence at any cost—and were willing to clean up his messes.

Pursuing legal means, expensive and time-intensive for both parties, was only one of the ways the leadership sought to control the narrative of Swami Rama for his devotees. Direct criticism, concern, and dissent were met head-on. Here's Dr. Rudolph Ballentine, then president of the board and a licensed physician, in a letter to Robert Hughes, a board member from 1978 to 1980 and a longtime devotee: "I will not tolerate anyone's malicious stories about the Institute," he writes. "If you really wonder why there are so many stories about Swamiji and why they are so similar, then your knowledge of psychology must be very limited indeed and you must be blind to this society's obviously confused attitudes toward sexuality and its apparent compulsion to discredit those in position[s] of leadership… Get your priorities straight and your head clear." Dr. Ballentine also told others at the Institute that Hughes was spreading rumors about Swami Rama because Hughes was gay and was angry that Swami Rama had refused to arrange a marriage between himself and another man. "When Hughes openly asked questions about Swami Rama's sexual activities during a weekend workshop [put on by the Institute], where he was the featured guest lecturer, he was escorted off the premises and driven to the airport," writes Webster in her *Yoga Journal* article.

Like Robert Hughes, dissenters—both people who raised concerns on behalf of another and the victims themselves—were routinely shunned by the community. Megan, the former community member quoted in the *Yoga Journal* article, occupied both these roles at once, as a witness to the public harassment of others, and as a victim of sexual harassment herself. A graduate student in the Institute's Eastern Studies program, she had decided not to pursue a PhD in clinical psychology and was finishing her first year when she began openly discussing her experience and observations with others. During this time, she was offered a position as the registrar and a tuition-free second year, an act she saw as buying her silence. She left, as loudly as she could.

In the accounts I read, I noticed a pattern: most of the dissenters were people who were either close to alleged victims or alleged victims themselves. It's easier to discount a secondhand story, even a vitally researched article, in the face of pressure from the organization, harder to turn away from your daughter, or your friend. But even the proximity to a woman who had been sexually exploited was not enough to sway the heart of a true believer. When Dr. Ballentine learned that two women close to him had had sexual relations with Swami Rama, he did not disbelieve it; however, he expressed "difficulty in seeing the experiences that the women [had] talked about with Swami Rama as abusive… because that's not what I saw. I saw these women mature and grow and blossom." His belief in his guru was so strong that his thinking could remain flexible enough to justify any troubling scenario. In fact, leaders at the Institute both denied that any sexual impropriety had occurred and simultaneously suggested that *if* such a thing had occurred, it would have been for the women's benefit, and not at all troubling. Speaking to the *Yoga Journal* reporter, Pandit Tigunait encapsulates the kind of logical contortions undertaken by the leadership of the Institute to make sense of the sheer volume and similarity of the accusations, a series of thoughts so amazingly illustrative that I cannot stop myself from quoting them in full:

> Even if it happened, what's the big deal?… People say that Mahatma Gandhi… slept with women. God knows whether it was true or not, and even if it was true, this is a normal phenomenon. And that did not undermine Mahatma Gandhi's work!… No, this would not be shattering, certainly not. My father certainly had sex, and that's why I was born, so will I lose my faith in my father?
>
> Even if I found out—how can I find out? Because I do not want to find out. There's no need for finding out, if I know it is completely wrong.

I look up pictures of these men now, trying to jog my memory of them—a prickle at the back of my neck. They look familiar to me: I crossed paths with them; likely they saw me with Baba. Ballentine's gentle, pious look unnerves me, as does Tigunait's jolly smile. I remember the people who passed through our lives because of our connection to Swami Veda: pandits visiting from India, particularly

57

insufferable community members with touchy egos. But our guru had said to accept them, help them, feed them—so my mother did. It was a part of our spiritual journey to be in community, in part, with jerks. In practice, the fact that we were united by shared beliefs gave cover to all manner of bad behavior. Still, I am stunned not only by the lengths that these men went to suppress allegations of wrongdoing, but by the ways their minds warped around their belief. Their reasoning here, though disgusting to me, does not seem cynical. I believe they are telling the truth when they say they believed that their guru could do no wrong.

A charismatic authority figure who can do no wrong is a hallmark of a high-control group, and groups with unhealthy belief systems will often employ tactics like shunning to suppress dissent, as outlined in *Escaping Utopia*, by sociologists Janja Lalich and Karla McLaren. "Toxic charismatic authority can be difficult to escape (as many of us may have experienced in our own dramatic and unhealthy love relationships) because it engages a powerful need for belonging that keeps followers entrapped by the intense and urgent demands of the leader," they write. Swami Rama's organization was structured around his compelling presence: guru and organization worked in concert to exert exquisite control over his disciples.

This explains why community members who lived and worked at the Institute continued to support Swami Rama and gave little weight to the allegations, but it does not explain—or not directly—the actions, or rather the passivity, of my parents. As they both said to me, "We hardly saw Baba!" But from there, their memories and understandings diverge: they are divorced, and don't need to make their narratives match anymore. When I called my mother about this story for the first time in 2022, she was shaken, driven to answer the question I laid out for her: How could she have missed the signs of danger? For my dad, the story could be held at a more abstract remove. "The bigger question is worthy of research," he wrote to me, when I told him I was writing this article. "Why do so many popular gurus become psychopathic predators?" This is the question asked by a man, in full innocence: a request for another story to be told about the powerful man and not about the people he harmed.

It's true that Swami Rama held some power over my parents, despite the fact that he was not their guru. But I think the reason why they— as people who were only adjacent to the Himalayan Institute and its influence—were not alarmed by the disturbing stories that surrounded him has to do with another person's complicated power over them: Swami Veda's. In many ways the opposite of his guru, Swami Veda invited dissent and questioning of his own teachings. He won my mother over, remember, not by a display of psychic abilities, but by his command of the scriptures, his humility, and his kindness. My mother cites those early years with him as some of the most peaceful of her life. Without close ties to the Himalayan Institute community, my parents turned to their guru.

"We didn't know a lot about the world," my dad says, by way of explanation. "We were stupid, we were so naive," says my mom, in a voice heavy with regret. My mother is a trained aerospace engineer who later became a math and science teacher, and is currently a lawyer. Her sharp mathematical mind makes her impossible to play Scrabble with—she's the kind of person who studied for and aced the LSAT *for fun*. But in this case, once she trusted Swami Veda, she began to get the sense that in order to really commit to her spiritual betterment, she needed to "turn that critical part of [her] brain off, and be in the moment, and surrender" to gain the full benefits of the teachings—something I'd never heard her say before, and that moves me maybe because it speaks to a kind of tenderness involved in spiritual life, the vulnerability that surrender requires. It moves me, too, because it speaks to the hope my mother had, the belief that she could change her life. Baba and the Institute had, in so many ways, created a culture—a reality—in which it was *possible* to believe that there was more to the situation than met the eye. In other words, that there was a reason for these allegations— whether as a test of belief, as a trick of the illusory nature of the world, or as a spiritual lesson—that was not apparent to people at a lower spiritual level than Baba (which was, of course, everybody). His public silence on the matter deepened this impression; it read to my mother like the dignified silence of a man who knows so deeply he is innocent that he does not need to convince anyone else. My mother— who was trying to save her marriage, who was trying to change her life, and who had had a child, now very sick, at the behest of Swami Rama—had a lot invested in maintaining a connection with her guru, his guru, and the communities they led. She looked to the people she trusted, all of whom continued to place their trust in Swami Rama.

Despite many conversations with my dad over the course of writing this article, I still struggle to understand how much he knew, when he knew it, and why it never alarmed him. Partly this is mechanical: after surviving a massive stroke two years ago, my father has made a valiant recovery, but his memory has been altered. I do know he was aware of the *Yoga Journal* article at some point after its publication: my dad remembers when he and a group of devotees confronted Swami Veda about it, and Swami Veda went into silence, a yogic practice conveniently timed. Swami Veda later told my father that he had met with one of the alleged victims and believed her. And yet my dad recalls him saying, "There is a warp in the cosmic mind"—that all is not as it seems, even as no one is lying—a position echoed by the one Swami Veda expressed publicly in the *Yoga Journal* article:

> When I ask Pandit Arya about the allegations of sexual abuse, he admits that he was very disturbed when he first heard them. He also has the integrity to admit that if they were true, it would be very terrible, a violation of the teaching that says one should treat all women as daughters. But for a man of Pandit Arya's background and beliefs, the relationship with one's guru is more momentous than any merely temporal bond. He cannot disbelieve his guru.

"It is a bleak statement on humanity that pretty much all the popular gurus have scandals around them," wrote my dad in response to an email I sent him in the fall of 2022, outlining my distress about what I was learning, a distress he seemed puzzled by. Over the years he had begun to reconsider his relationship with Swami Veda and Swami Rama, a "long, difficult journey" that he considers himself at the end of. He found Swami Veda to be an "inspiring teacher" in the first few years of their relationship. But Swami Veda seemed, to my parents, to change in later years. My mother remembers that at some point, Swami Veda came to expect the shows of obsequiousness he had earlier scorned. She also remembers being assigned tedious, time-consuming tasks, like one that required hours of photocopying, and overhearing Swami Veda explaining, "You have to keep them busy." My father writes, "I found a lot of troubling things as well, just not of a sexual nature. Gurus are human beings too, so one can expect flaws." For his part, he has come to see the relationships with both gurus as ultimately exploitative, while maintaining a belief in the subtle beauty of the teachings themselves, for which both men claimed they were merely vessels.

"Thank god nothing happened to you," my father wrote. That struck me as incorrect. Something *did* happen, I wrote back—but what? "If a parent drives drunk with their kids in the car, but makes it to the destination without an accident," my friend Rhea St. Julien, a therapist, hypothesizes, "is that the same as not taking the risk?" My parents were under the influence, but not of alcohol: the intersection between their manipulation by their gurus and their agency as parents and choice-makers makes things muddy for me. Ultimately, I have no memory of a single inappropriate moment with Swami Rama, and whatever might have happened in an alternate future when he lived into my adulthood will always be an unknown: there is a strange kind of vanity in believing that my guru would have tried to rape me if he'd had the chance.

The curious, overwhelming cold that I feel every time I research, talk about, or write this essay tells me that my body now knows something it didn't before. At first I thought it was like the delayed shaking of a person who has climbed out of a wrecked car without a scratch. But now I think it is something else. I have moved through this world in a female body: it goes without saying that I have been catcalled, harassed, spoken to inappropriately, fondled, and touched without consent an uncountable number of times since I was a girl. But because

I am not white, and because I had always seen myself as existing outside the rubric of desirability, I had thought these experiences were punishment for my desire to be seen as beautiful, instead of as a sign of my vulnerability. Now my body, which is that of a daughter and that of a mother, is catching up to what my mind knew all along: that abuse is about power, not desirability, and that there is little I can do to keep myself safe, keep my daughter safe, in a society that does not value the safety and autonomy of women and girls. And here something clarifies for me: I think the gap between my mother's response and my father's might be due, in part, to their lived experiences, especially when it comes to their vulnerability to sexual violence.

Nearly three years of painful conversations with my parents undergird this essay, conversations that have taken this time in our lives as a starting point but have ranged up and down the family tree, backwards and backwards in time. I might never understand the particular circumstances that drove them to make the decisions they did: I might simply be unable to formulate the correct questions to deepen my understanding, as I lack the correct words to explain my distress to my father, who cannot understand it. My parents were being manipulated by their guru as well as loved by him, given teachings that improved their lives and guidance that harmed them. They were free adults who had choices—not only in what to do but also in what to believe—but because they were believers, their choices were constrained. They chose to believe in their guru,

even as they were losing faith in him. They told me Baba was as powerful as a god, and they believed he could read minds, but still they rarely saw him, and did not think about him much. They wanted what was best for me, but ignored the evidence that Baba harmed people. These powerful and dizzying contradictions both make sense and defy it. But I think I can get a glimpse of the trusting, hopeful, unhappy people my parents were when they first met their guru. They were about the same age, in fact, as I am now. I wonder if the forces that drove me to write this story—the feeling of unease, the thirst for truth, the desire to more deeply understand, and thereby to change my life—are the same ones they felt in their early middle age, and that led them down this path. Spiritual seekers often find their most beautiful qualities and desires exploited. Like my parents, I, too, want to be a part of something larger, a force for good in this world. I, too, have found peace in the act of surrender. As much as I struggle to make sense of their choices, their impulses are as familiar as my own.

Long ago, a structure of belief was planted in my child self: only I and never my guru was considered fallible, capable of making mistakes and practicing ill judgment; even things he did that felt or seemed wrong were in the service of spiritual betterment; submission, surrender, and obedience were moral qualities a good girl possessed. I was accountable to a guru who was accountable to no one. Even as their own doubts began to form, my parents allowed this structure to remain in place.

I am writing this essay to dismantle it.

Sentence by painful sentence.

Though I was able to talk to several people about their experiences with the Institute, none would go on the record for this essay—only, to their immense credit, my parents. The Institute leadership may now be wary of writers asking questions about Swami Rama, even those who spent formative years as his disciple: my repeated queries, even to confirm basic factual information, were politely rebuffed. Others have a concrete reason to stay out of this article: the flurry of lawsuits the Institute filed in the '90s makes speaking out still feel like a tangible risk. Like someone who has fallen asleep for three decades, I'm waking up to a truth that many people have been living with all this time. Some want urgently—whether for the sake of their own healing or to protect the reputation of their brand—to leave this unfinished story in the past.

But I cannot. Simply put, many people have put their reputations, relationships, livelihoods, and finances on the line in order to seek accountability from the Institute and from Swami Rama for the harm they caused, and to prevent future harm. Their courageous actions had a real impact: they inspired others to leave the organization and sent Swami Rama into exile in India in the last years of his life: they protected me. In 1997, a lawsuit was decided in the plaintiff's favor, legally acknowledging the harm and holding the Institute financially liable. But over those years the call for the Institute to take internal accountability went again and again unheeded. In the *Yoga Journal* article, Pandit Rajmani Tigunait suggests that the women were lying either because they had been rebuffed by Swami Rama ("The person wanted something, and the other person did not agree to fulfill their desires… This sudden animosity indicates that there is something fishy in the statement of this person"), or because they were attempting to blackmail him ("Anyone who lives a public life can go through such remarks;… you have heard about all that blackmailing [of famous, rich athletes]"). Tigunait repeatedly declined to investigate the claims brought to the board in the '90s, and continues to be the spiritual head and leader of the Himalayan Institute to this day. It is under his guidance, and his conception of harassment, that the Institute hosts residents, classes, teacher-training programs, and even retreats for women healing from sexual trauma. On the Institute's website, alongside a series of vigorous denouncements of sexual harassment and a nondiscrimination policy, Swami Rama is celebrated as "one of the greatest adepts, teachers, writers, and humanitarians of the 20th century." Without a formal reckoning, how will this community prevent abuse from happening again?

I am aware that the specifics of this story are unique to my family, to the meeting of Indian and American cultures, and to the wild, unregulated space of spiritual life, but the contours are almost frighteningly universal. Someone's father, someone's pastor, someone's uncle, the beloved fantasy writer, your favorite comedian, the lefty journalist, the Supreme Court justice, an American president: whether in the tiny society of a family or at the highest levels of our government and culture, men with power are abusing it, and their organizations are closing ranks to protect them. Learning the truth about Baba led me to other truths buried in my family history, things I had similarly known without knowing. Now, it seems, I am surrounded by stories that have been buried in subtext: offhand remarks, a flinch at a name, a change of subject.

The trick of holding a story— a rumor, a shard of information—in the corner of one's mind instead of letting it influence one's body, actions, and beliefs is not unique to Baba's disciples.

What do you know without knowing? From whose story have you turned away?

Baba had a particular quirk when being photographed: he refused to look directly at the camera. This had to do with power, a devotee told my dad. When he looked at the camera, he gave it something of his essence, so those few pictures in which his eyes met the camera were to be treated with reverence, as though they were sacred objects. Once, when I was sitting in his lap, he said to my dad, "Take a picture of me," meeting the camera's gaze. For years, I would avert my eyes when presented with this rare picture, even when my belief was starting to unravel, deferent to the power he claimed was there.

But I am no longer deferent.

Baba, I am looking back. ✷

SACRIFICE ZONE

A SEMI-REGULAR GUEST COLUMN ABOUT REGULARLY IGNORED PLACES.

by Pitchaya Sudbanthad

✶ IN THIS ISSUE: Pattaya

The villagers called the area Palmyra Beach; it was later renamed Jomtien for a princess from the mythical kingdom said to exist there in a hidden realm.

Each year, as many as twenty-five million people visit the sacrificial landscape of Pattaya, Thailand. If visitors don't arrive by air, then they likely take the eight-lane motorway that zips them along the eastern Thai seaboard from Bangkok to the shores of Chonburi province.

They come for rest and relaxation, purportedly. Frantic development over the decades has put Pattaya at a far remove from its past as a pristine, natural coastline. It's a place made to concede itself. Disuse does not define the area's state of wild abandonment, but rather the hedonistic exploitation and exhaustion of land and sea in a bargain for economic prosperity.

In my 1980s childhood, my family often enjoyed weekend stays on the

Images throughout courtesy of Creative Commons

In recent years, viral photos and videos on social media have shown viscous wastewater gushing from culverts, and Pattaya and Jomtien beaches covered in sewage.

shores of nearby Bang Saen—at the time a tranquil beach, with tall coconut trees and beach morning glories that grew between small bungalows and seafood eateries catering to Thai vacationers—and we'd also usually drive a little farther south on Sukhumvit Road to Pattaya. The beaches by then had already been given over to unfettered tourism, and each visit offered something new to ooh and aah about: barely finished high-rise condominiums casting shadows across the sand; newly constructed luxury hotels looking out over wide blue pools lined with sunbathing, bare-chested foreign guests; and down by the waves, shacks that had popped up to rent rigs and offer boats for recently introduced beach activities, like windsurfing, parasailing, scuba diving, and, most noisomely, Jet Skiing.

Nights in Pattaya were eye-openers for a child. Thoroughfares along the beaches came alive with bar girls dancing under pink neon lights and sunburned Europeans cheering live muay Thai matches. Nightclubs, cabarets, and sex shows welcomed all who carried cash. In this human-made paradise, entertainment reigned supreme, and all forms of leisure had their whispered, rum-breathed price.

The philosopher Marc Augé coined the term *non-place* to describe geographies interrupted by supermodernity and cleansed of their anthropological relationships, histories, and identities to function as conduits of globalized systems. For me, the term *non-place* also describes an entire ecological locale that has been reset, its natural history and diversity turned over and remade to serve outside demands—in Pattaya, the transient touristic populations that flow through daily.

Pattaya used to be a little-known seaside village, inhabited by a few hundred people split into two small fishing communities. Historical records describe an almost-two-mile sandy beach where villagers kept their boats during severe monsoons, protected by the islands of Koh Larn and Koh Sak. Marine life thrived, with abundant coral reefs and undisturbed nesting beaches for sea turtles. Palms grew thick along the southernmost shores, and the villagers called the area Palmyra Beach, later renamed Jomtien for a princess from the mythical kingdom said to exist there in a hidden realm.

Then came violent change as war escalated in Southeast Asia. In the 1960s, with the Vietnam War buildup, US soldiers stationed at military bases around the country came looking for a good time. Pattaya's lore describes an initial truck convoy of a few hundred GIs descending on the village to rent beach houses. The drunken, sordid revelries shattered the tranquility, and Pattaya found itself rocking-and-rolling to accommodate the influx of American military personnel (almost fifty thousand at the peak of the war, with many others from elsewhere).

The ensuing highway construction in the 1970s turned Sukhumvit Road into Highway 3, and many new hotels opened to welcome the visitors now arriving from seemingly everywhere in the world. Around the time of my childhood visits, the tourism-industrial complex in Pattaya was ramping up, securing investment to build nearly 850 vacation properties by 2015; that figure has more than doubled since then,

growing outward and upward from the restless beaches.

The effects are palpable—and smellable. Wherever overwhelming numbers of people gather to feast and frolic, they also foul up the place. In Bangkok, I often heard cautions about visiting Pattaya unless one wanted skin rashes. A 2016 study by the Regional Environmental Office said that the waters at Pattaya's central beach could endanger human life, a warning apparently unheard by beachgoers who still leaped into the frothy waves. In recent years, viral photos and videos on social media have shown viscous wastewater gushing from culverts, and Pattaya and Jomtien beaches covered in sewage. Officials claimed the situation was under control, after expensive treatment plants were built, but at some point later, the sewage-dark sea returned.

Meanwhile, environmental externalities have been so distantly externalized that they keep washing back ashore. Careless boat operators, staffers and guests at nearby island venues, and beach tourists routinely get caught throwing garbage into the sea, with litter appearing on beaches, and ecologically sensitive islands declared off-limits by the navy, to protect wildlife. Almost a hundred thousand tons of garbage piled up on the popular island of Koh Larn before being buried, against the wishes of residents who fear seepage. In Pattaya, a walk along the sand to collect seashells could net diverse specimens of plastic containers, strips of fishing nets, car tires, discarded foam, broken beer bottles, and medical waste, among other delightful finds.

This is not exactly a tragic commons; both governmental regulations and high levels of investment in beach real estate and tourist operations have so far proved insufficient to compel better environmental practices. There's no commons to be sustainably managed, because the here and now is a fluctuating, destabilized locus of transactions with a sunny beachfront. All-consuming activity reigns supreme when the continuity of a fragile marine ecosystem becomes secondary to the unrestricted fun of a global party city.

And come the wild bunch have from all over, not just for good times but also for illicit freedoms. The homegrown seediness that first attracted American GIs has deteriorated into a cosmopolitan free-for-all in the city's underworld. Russian organized crime arrived after the collapse of the Soviet Union. Their unlawful presence in Pattaya, often denied by Thai officials, was confirmed by leaked US embassy cables mentioning Russian mob involvement in the "commission of numerous crimes, including extortion, money laundering, narcotics trafficking, real estate fraud, financial fraud, human smuggling, pandering, counterfeiting, document fraud, cybercrime, and illegal importation of cars." They've since been joined by Chinese gangsters known for online gambling operations and investment scams in this anything-goes city.

In Pattaya, an unnatural paradise has arisen out of the marine idyll. External funding and top-down placemaking have meant the cultivation of any permissible earthly delight to lure an international target clientele to the region. This lucrative model has been re-created in Thailand's other seaside tourism hubs, such as the islands of Phuket and Koh Samui, both of which have seen similar effects from natural degradation and socio-cultural erasure.

Pattaya's tourism operators now say they're done with the "sin city" image. They want to rebrand Pattaya as a cleaner, more enriching, family-friendly destination. The proposed solution: a casino. ✱

SHEILA HETI

[WRITER]

"IT FEELS LIKE THERE'S THIS RIVER RUNNING UNDERNEATH MY WHOLE LIFE. IT'S ALWAYS THERE; I JUST HAVE TO STEP INTO IT."

Diarists mentioned in this interview:
Bertolt Brecht
Joe Orton
Sophya Tolstoy
Virginia Woolf
Anaïs Nin
Susan Sontag

Sheila Heti and I met at the Gladstone, a beautiful old hotel in the West Queen West neighborhood of Toronto, on a cold, snowy January weekend. She was warm, friendly, and generous; on her way to the hotel, she offered to bring me coffee and a croissant, and when she spilled some coffee on her new white pants, she sent me a string of charmingly self-deprecating texts about her attempts to remedy the situation, so that by the time she arrived, I felt that we were friends. In my hotel room, we drank our coffees, and later cocktails, and joked about the handprints on a rose-colored panel in the room, which we'd both attempted to push open, believing it to be a door. At some point early in our discussion, she told me that she once stayed at the Gladstone for several weeks after one of her previous residences caught fire. It was also where she held her first book-launch party, twenty-four years ago.

Heti was born in Toronto in 1976 to Hungarian Jewish immigrant parents. Her mother was a pathologist and her father an electrical engineer; her younger brother

Illustration by Kristian Hammerstad

is a stand-up comic. She has lived in the city for most of her life, though she briefly studied playwriting at the National Theatre School of Canada in Montreal, before completing a bachelor's degree in art history and philosophy at the University of Toronto. Now she shares an apartment, not far from the Gladstone, with her longtime boyfriend and dog. She is the author of eleven books, starting with a collection of contemporary fables called The Middle Stories, *which features stories with titles like "The Moon Monologue" and "Mermaid in the Jar," published when she was twenty-four. Though she has written nonfiction and children's books, Heti is best known for her novels, which include* How Should a Person Be?, Motherhood, Pure Colour, *and, most recently,* Alphabetical Diaries. *Her accolades are many:* How Should a Person Be? *was named one of the "12 New Classics" of the 2000s by* New York *magazine;* Motherhood *was a* New York Times *"Critics' Top Books of 2018" and was shortlisted for the Giller Prize; and* Pure Colour *won Canada's Governor General's Literary Award. She is the former interviews editor of this magazine, for which she interviewed numerous writers and artists, including Joan Didion, Agnès Varda, Mary Gaitskill, and Sophie Calle. Her work has been translated into twenty-seven languages.*

Many of Heti's books are formed through conversation and collaboration. How Should a Person Be?, *about a group of young artists in Toronto and narrated by a playwright named Sheila, incorporates dialogue culled from recordings of Heti's conversations with her friends, most centrally the painter and filmmaker Margaux Williamson.* Women in Clothes, *a* New York Times–*bestselling anthology coedited with Heidi Julavits and Leanne Shapton, collects work from hundreds of women on the theme of what they wear.* Motherhood, *a novel in which the narrator sets out to understand whether she wants to have a child, stages a conversation between herself and either chance or fate, depending on one's perspective, which speaks through the mechanism of a coin toss.* Alphabetical Diaries, *comprising sentences drawn from ten years of Heti's diaries and presented alphabetically, with the original chronology abandoned, becomes a conversation with the self across time.*

Heti's writing often directly tackles big philosophical questions about topics like art, selfhood, desire, our relationships to others, grief, and how a person should live. It is playful, probing, tender, and, in the words of Alexandra Kleeman, adept at capturing "the subtle expansiveness of an individual life." Her work is also formally innovative and boundary-crossing:

How Should a Person Be?, *first published in 2010, is now considered an early example of autofiction. In* The New York Times, *David Haglund wrote of the book: "Sheila Heti [knows] something about how many of us, right now, experience the world, and she has gotten that knowledge down on paper, in a form unlike any other novel I have read." In 2018,* The New York Times *named her part of "The New Vanguard," its list of writers "shaping the way we read and write fiction in the twenty-first century." Her fearlessness and propensity to follow her own curiosity make her a perennially fascinating writer.*
—*Cara Blue Adams*

I. "MY WORLD WAS VERY SMALL"

THE BELIEVER: Since we're in Toronto, I wanted to start by asking you about the city. You were born here. You've lived here most of your life. How has your relationship to Toronto changed?

SHEILA HETI: I loved growing up here. I don't think that when you're a kid, you really fantasize about other places where you might be growing up. Your home is just the only possible place, or at least that's how I felt. But then in my twenties, I had a lot of angst about staying, and then I stayed. And in my forties again it's become this *of course* sort of place, like, where else would I live?

Now we have a place a couple hours north of the city, so we're here half the time and in the country half the time. I'm much less involved in the various art scenes, but in my twenties it was such a huge part of my life to go to people's events and have my own events, to be interested in the cultural life of the city and how to make it better. Ultimately, I'm very happy I stayed. I don't think I could have written in the same way if I'd been in another place.

BLVR: Did you ever live anywhere else for an extended period of time, and if so, did that have an effect on your work?

SH: I've done residencies, so that's a month here and a month there. And I was in Montreal in my early twenties for about a year for school. I lived in New York for three months with a boyfriend who had a summer job there, and recently I spent a semester in New Haven, teaching at Yale. I travel a lot as a writer, too, to do readings and so on, so I feel like I'm always traveling in some way.

I went to Montreal for a few months around the time that I started to write *How Should a Person Be?* I think it was good to be able to be away from my friends and focus and read the Bible and feel lonely and rethink how I wanted to write. But I'm not sure if it was the city that changed me or just going anywhere, you know? Just getting out of my world for a little while.

BLVR: There's something helpful about leaving your life behind.

SH: You're not playing the same part that you're usually playing in your life, which can keep you thinking in the same way and then writing in the same way.

BLVR: You studied playwriting at the National Theatre School of Canada in Montreal, left that program, worked at a magazine for several years, and then went to the University of Toronto to study art and philosophy. What were your student days like?

SH: Theater school was a ball. It was my first time away from Toronto. I was eighteen. I got engaged within two months of being there. I just went crazy, you know? I guess getting engaged can be the opposite of going crazy, but for me, it was going crazy. It was totally wild to do that. I started doing drugs. I smoked pot every day. I'd never done drugs before. It was this program with three other writers, one of whom I'm still quite good friends with, Claudia Dey, and we just had so much time, so much freedom. There were very few classes. The school focused on the actors, and the playwrights were an afterthought. I was writing this weird adaptation of Faust and talking nonstop about art to my boyfriend, who was in the directing program. It was so great. I had no landline, so I wasn't in touch with my family much.

BLVR: You had no landline?

SH: Yeah, for the first few months. I remember writing letters to friends back home, and it just feels like a whole other period in history.

The University of Toronto was different again. I was very isolated. I came back to Toronto with my boyfriend, and we broke up after a couple years, and then I went to university. I didn't have any friends at that point—he had kept our theater friends. But it was also really wonderful. I spent all my time in this big university library called Robarts, thinking about art and artists. I remember thinking a lot about Jackson Pollock for some reason, just the way he used his body, how the art was like a record, a signature, of his body's movements in space. I was really, really into school. I learned so much and thought so much about writing, and now I guess I romanticize how alone I felt. That's when I was writing *The Middle Stories* and trying to figure out what my voice sounded like on the page, or what kind of rhythm my sentences made. I don't know if I have ever since worked quite as intensely as I did then.

BLVR: It's such a special time in life, when you're young and you don't have responsibilities, and you can be alone.

SH: Yes. I wasn't on the internet. I had no phone… I was really profoundly alone. Even if I were just as free from responsibilities now, I wouldn't be able to be that alone.

BLVR: I think sometimes about what it means for our culture to have lost that, for that to have slipped into history.

SH: Yeah. I'm amazed at how quickly culture changes. Even if I went totally offline and threw out my phone, I couldn't recapture that time, for I would still know that this whole world of conversation was going on without me, whereas back then I didn't feel like I was missing out on anything. My world was very small.

II. "I WAS WALKING THROUGH THE GATES OF HEAVEN"

BLVR: When you were in university and writing *The Middle Stories*, you made a rule for yourself that if you had the impulse to write, you had to write.

SH: That's still the way I think about it: that there's a particular feeling in you that tells you that you want to write, and if you don't catch it, that thing that would have been written in that moment will never be written. It's not like you can save it for tomorrow. That feeling, or that awareness, was kind of sacred to me—it felt like the most important thing to honor. That seemed like the point of life, to follow that feeling and get down whatever wanted to come out. It felt very fleeting.

BLVR: Does it still feel that way?

SH: I find now that it doesn't come if I'm in the midst of other activities. It might come in the middle of the night, but rarely in such an insistent way. Now it feels like it comes more from working: if I start working, then after half an hour or an hour or fifteen minutes of work, I'll be in that same space that I used to be able to catch only from the air.

BLVR: Has your process changed in other ways? Has it become more routinized?

SH: There's no routine, but now I can work anytime, anywhere. There are no conditions that I need. I can sit down beside my boyfriend when he's playing video games with his headphones on and just start working. It feels like there's this river running underneath my whole life. It's always there; I just have to step into it. It's not quite as elusive.

It's partly because now I always have so many projects on the go that there's always something my brain can apply itself to. When I was younger, I didn't have even one project. I didn't know what was going to come out, or in what way, or what it meant, or what it was for. It was just pure writing, writing with no sense of publication or a grander form. No sense of: Is it a short story? Is it a novel? It was just writing. So now I have those structures in my head, like, OK, this is this novel I'm working on. This is the other book I'm working on. This is an essay. Having those containers somehow makes it easier to step in. It's easier to step into a container than into the void. Although I still do sometimes step into the void.

BLVR: When you moved from writing short stories to writing your first novel, *Ticknor*, a postmodern novel set in Boston in the nineteenth century and narrated by the biographer of a famous historian, what was most challenging and what was most exciting?

SH: Well, after *The Middle Stories* came out, there was a lot of criticism of me and my writing in Canada. I don't think it got reviewed in the States hardly at all. But here there was a lot of hostility toward me because I was so young, I guess, and sort of cute, and the stories were strange, and I'd had a bit of success already in the States, being published in McSweeney's, and I think all that stuff together irritated people. I felt very pigeonholed, like, *Here's the quirky girl who writes fairy tale–like stories*, which didn't feel at all right or true. I thought I had been unfairly cast in some role.

So I wanted the next book to be the complete opposite, to show the people who had thought that I could only write like that, that I was able to do something completely different. And so *Ticknor* was not at all in my voice. I chose a man as the character, an older man, a Boston Brahmin, just the complete opposite of me in a way. And it was painstaking. It was hard. It wasn't fun. Most of what I wrote could not be put in the book, because it didn't feel like it was in his voice. I was proud that I could do it, that I could work for four or five years on something that was so unpleasant, and that I did manage to make something so different from *The Middle Stories*. And I guess in some ways it turned me into a writer, in the sense of following through on a project when it's not a pleasure. With *The Middle Stories*, I didn't have a vision. With this one, I had a really specific vision, and I fulfilled it. And then FSG bought it, which was the most incredible moment of my life. I remember getting the call at my secretarial job, and walking home, and just feeling like suddenly I wasn't walking on the sidewalk, I was walking through the gates of heaven. It was so meaningful to me. Of course, then they rejected my next book, *How Should a Person Be?* But at the time I thought, This is it, you know? I've been acknowledged by the world in a way that felt so, so meaningful. It was very exciting. I thought I'd have no problems from then on.

III. A SUBTLE, SLOW SENSE OF GROWTH

BLVR: Your subsequent novels tend to be formally innovative. How do you think about plot?

SH: I don't know if I know what plot is. I think you just have to get someone to the end of the book. There are many ways of doing that. It doesn't have to be plot. It can be the switching of moods that a person becomes addicted to experiencing, or a train of thought they become curious about, or a tone they want to stay in. There are so many ways to keep somebody inside a book and to make them interested in what's going on.

BLVR: What are other techniques you use to draw a reader through a book? I'd love to hear you talk more about how you accomplish that, because you do so in unconventional and interesting ways.

SH: Rhythm is something I think about a lot. Breaking things up—like with *Motherhood*, breaking up the rhythm of the coin tosses with monologues and scenes. And knowing where people are going to get tired; I'm very sensitive to boredom, my own boredom and the potential reader's boredom, and I never want to overstay my welcome. That creates a certain momentum that can propel you through a book. A subtle accumulation of details, like in the case of *The Middle Stories*. Or in the case of *Motherhood*, a really subtle, slow sense of growth, as if maybe the narrator's vision is getting gradually wider, deeper. It's a problem with every book: How am I going to get a reader to the end if there's not really a plot?

With *Pure Colour*, there was a kind of narrative, actually, I think. It follows the main character, Mira, as she grieves her father's death, and at some point, Mira and her father are in a leaf. I was particularly concerned in the final third of the book with having Mira try to bring the things she discovered in the leaf into the real world. I wanted her to fail at that, the way one tends to fail when trying to convey a spiritual experience to someone else. That felt like a plot to me. *How Should a Person Be?* had a kind of narrative. And even with *Motherhood*, the narrative was: She's posed herself a question: "Should I have a child?" How is she going to answer it? So maybe I haven't discovered any radically new ways to draw a reader to the end.

I do try to rely on plot as little as possible. I think employing plot makes a lot of sense if you believe that life proceeds by plot—by cause and effect—but I think there's so much more to the path of life than cause and effect. Or maybe it's the case that stories with plot are so satisfying because life actually *doesn't* have a plot, and it's gratifying to be reassured otherwise. I just don't think I can make the mechanics of plot work. You have to manipulate your characters and your reader, in a way, and I don't like to do that. It doesn't feel like it comes from the deepest place.

BLVR: I agree.

SH: Though I love when other writers do it! I was just reading Kazuo Ishiguro and E. M. Forster, for example, and obviously there are all the great nineteenth-century novelists—Tolstoy, Zola. I think it's one of the most incredible things to be able to do in the whole world. If I could do it, I would; I just can't. But those are the books that I really like reading, you know? It's very strange that you end up writing books that aren't necessarily the books you would most like to read. Why is that? Why can't we write the books we most like to read? You have your limitations, and maybe you're interested in reading the things you can't write, because you can't write them.

BLVR: I'm always struck by how often writers' influences are not whom you would guess.

SH: Yeah, people always say, *You should read so-and-so. What they do is so much like your books*. But I don't want to read anything like my books. I'm trying to get away from my books when I read.

IV. THE ONLY WAY TO FIND THE ANSWERS WAS TO GO INSIDE

BLVR: With *Motherhood*, you began with much more material than you needed, and whittled it down from there. It's

---

THE PREFERRED WORKDAY SNACKS OF NOTABLE ARTISTS AND WRITERS

★ Apples in the bathtub—Agatha Christie
★ Vanilla wafers—Flannery O'Connor
★ Cheesecake—Stephen King
★ Pea soup—Jack Kerouac
★ Cake—Walt Whitman
★ Fritos—Neil Simon
★ Raw eggs—Victor Hugo
★ Roast beef—J. D. Salinger
★ Canned meat and apples—F. Scott Fitzgerald
★ Lime Popsicles—Joyce Maynard
★ Raw carrots—Daniel Handler
★ Boiled milk and croissants—Marcel Proust
★ Gelatin, orange juice, and bananas—Agnes Martin
★ Carrot juice—Andy Warhol
★ Lentils and rice—Marina Abramović
★ Homemade yogurt and wheat germ bars—Georgia O'Keeffe
★ Salted herring—Rembrandt

—list compiled by Su Ertekin-Taner

69

a process you often use: you generate a lot of material and then edit. Can you talk about what it's like to see the structure once you have accrued a large mass of words? When what you've called "the engineering mind" steps forward and you can see what it is you want to make?

SH: There's not really a moment. It's more like a structure accumulates. Gradually, every passage has found its place and can't be moved anywhere else. It's like a puzzle: You're constantly moving passages and paragraphs and sentences around, and then one will lock in somewhere. And then you keep doing that until everything's locked in and there are no pieces that are waiting to be put in. All the pieces that are meant to be in the book are in the book and are locked in, and there's nothing in the book that can be taken out without upsetting the whole. It finds its only form.

BLVR: In writing *Motherhood*, at what point did you decide to use the coin toss as a method for driving the conversation?

SH: I flipped coins and asked questions of the coins for over a year and a half before I thought I would write a book about motherhood. The coins were an interim process after *How Should a Person Be?*, where I wanted to be in dialogue but also wanted to be alone. At one point I thought it was going to be its own book, "Talking to Coins." Then, in 2013, I started to think that I wanted to write a book about this question of whether or not to have children, and also time and motherhood and femaleness. So I started looking at all the writing that I'd done in the previous few years, and I was looking at my journals, and I saw, Oh, there's all this writing about that question in there. I was thinking about this question of motherhood before I realized that it was a book I would want to write. Then, looking through the coin stuff, it was the same thing. So I pulled together sixty thousand words from "Talking to Coins," and the relevant stuff from my journals, and I started a new folder. I think I'm always writing the book before I realize I'm writing it.

BLVR: Whoa, interesting. I would not have guessed that the coin tosses preceded the idea of the book.

SH: Every time I finish a book, I don't know how to write again. So I think the "Talking to Coins" stuff was a way of

teaching myself how to write again, or figuring out how to write alone again, because *How Should a Person Be?* was so much written in the world and among other people, and I just forgot how to write, how to be alone in a room and write.

BLVR: And from there, was it a process of writing a lot of new material before shaping the book?

SH: Yes. I originally thought *Motherhood* was going to be a book of interviews. It slipped into becoming what it became after I finally accepted that the answers to my questions would not come from outside myself, but only by going inside. I didn't want to look inside myself, though. I felt very resistant to that idea. But that was the only way this book was going to work.

BLVR: Where did that resistance come from?

SH: It just felt so much more solipsistic than interviewing other people. And it felt like it was not an important question. I felt embarrassed. I felt ashamed. I felt like no one would care. I felt like *I* shouldn't care. I remember when we were trying to sell the book in Canada, talking to this editor about the proposal, and she said, *Instead of writing this book, thinking about whether or not to have a child, you should just have a child.* So I felt like I wasn't getting a lot of support from the world.

BLVR: And yet it's one of the most profound questions a person can ask.

SH: I know, but it didn't feel like that at the time. When I was writing the book, I could not find a single other book that dealt with this question. Not a single book in the history of literature! So I really felt like this was a topic below literature. Now that seems insane, but that's in part why it was hard to write.

BLVR: When I read *Motherhood*, I had the same thought: Here is this profound question, this question of whether to call another person into existence and incur responsibility to them, to change your life and to create and shape their life. How has no one ever written about it?

SH: Women's literature is really relatively recent.

BLVR: It's true.

SH: It makes you realize how recent women's literature is. And reliable birth control is even more recent, which helps make motherhood more of a choice.

BLVR: When you arrived at the ending of *Motherhood*, were you surprised?

SH: I wrote that last page earlier than I wrote some of the other parts. I always knew I wanted that passage to be the end. I do still sometimes wonder: Was *Motherhood* the right title for the book? Because I think it suggests that the book is something different than it is. I once went to a famous bookstore in New York to sign some books, and the owner welcomed me in, and she was a mother, and she said, *Well, you know what it's like to have a child*, and I said, *No*. And she said, *But you wrote a book called* Motherhood. I didn't want to embarrass her by saying, *Actually, the book is about* not *having a child*. So sometimes I feel sad that the book has that title. But it had to be the title, because the last line had to be the line it was, and the last line is something like "And I called this wrestling place Motherhood."

BLVR: Well, I think it's a perfect title.

SH: Really?

BLVR: Yeah. To me that's the genius of the title: that it's about the wrestling, as well as the various ways in which you might create something, including writing books.

SH: Thank you. That's reassuring. I think in the long term, it *is* the right title. But maybe not in the short term. In the short term, it maybe doesn't attract some of the people who would be interested in it. But in the long term, it had to be *Motherhood*. Even when it was going to be a collection of interviews, I was calling it *Motherhood*. Sometimes the working title becomes the title, and then the whole book shapes itself around the title.

BLVR: And it's also about your relationship with your own mother. So it's apt in that way, too.

SH: Yeah. It is the title, but sometimes I rue that it is the title. But I don't know what else it could have been. I'm actually kind of glad that a book called *Motherhood* is about not having children. I'm glad I got to the title first, before anyone else.

V. AN UNFAITHFUL DIARIST

BLVR: Both *Alphabetical Diaries* and *Motherhood* emerged in part from your process of keeping a diary. What have you tried to capture when you've kept a diary? How faithful have you been as a diarist?

SH: I've not been faithful. I write in my diary—on my computer—when I feel like it, and that's not often. I don't really do it anymore, but it was a place I would go when I had a lot of thoughts I wanted to sort through. I think of it as like combing hair: you are trying to get a knot out, and you keep brushing and brushing until the knot is out. Writing in my diary felt like that—like brushing and brushing until the knot was out. I wasn't often recording what happened, unless there was something really special that I wanted to remember. I had dinner with Lena Dunham in 2013 in New York. It was around the height of *Girls*, and after that dinner, I thought, I want to write down everything we said. But that was very rare. I wish I had had that impulse more. But I was right. That was the only time we had dinner, ever. And I'm glad I wrote that all down. I wish I had done more of that.

BLVR: Who were some diarists you read as you developed your practice?

SH: [Bertolt] Brecht's was one of the first writers' diaries I read. Joe Orton's. I had this collection of excerpts of diaries from women writers, and I owned a large hardcover copy of Sophya Tolstoy's diaries. And I read Virginia Woolf's diaries, and Anaïs Nin's, obviously. There are a lot of diaries I've read, I guess. I mean, you don't read them from beginning to end. You dip in and out.

BLVR: What was the pleasure there for you?

SH: I think it was just wondering, What is the writer's life like? At a time before I knew any writers or knew what my life might be, I wanted to see inside their lives. I wondered, What do they think about? I remember reading Susan Sontag's diaries more recently, and they were very interesting. I think I don't have a 100 percent interest in the diary form. I have like a 50 percent interest. It's not like a novel, where I have a 100 percent interest. You're half-interested because it's just clues.

BLVR: Are there any passages you remember vividly? Any clues that you came across that stayed with you?

SH: No, more just a general sense of: Oh, they're preoccupied with love, you know, in a way that most grown-ups do not continue to be so long into their lives. There are preoccupations with politics in certain ways, obviously, art-making and friendships and productivity and travel, money, you know—maybe these are the preoccupations of everybody. But most people don't keep a diary unless they're a writer, and generally you don't get it published unless you're a writer. Or perhaps a political figure.

BLVR: True, except for Kathryn Scanlan's *Aug 9–Fog*.

SH: Oh, I don't know about this project.

BLVR: She found a diary at an estate sale written by an elderly woman from the Midwest, and she spent years playing with it, cutting and rearranging. It's really beautiful. It's this very ordinary life but it's condensed, and it has a kind of mundanity, but a kind of poetry as well.

SH: When did this come out?

BLVR: Maybe five years ago?

SH: I'll look it up.

BLVR: You can read it in an afternoon. Reading it made me wish that would happen more.

SH: You can just look on the internet, I suppose! Although it sounds different when a diary is written just for the person who is writing it, versus when it's written for the audience of the internet.

BLVR: To me, the writer's diary is interesting because it feels like it's written for both private reasons and for a public.

SH: Yes. Maybe that's what gives it a kind of shimmer.

VI. "THE JOY OF BEING ALIVE"

BLVR: I'd love to talk more about *Alphabetical Diaries*. You began with about five hundred thousand words from your diary, written over a decade. You then alphabetized the material by sentence, and cut it to roughly a tenth of that. The resulting book conveys the texture and sweep of a life without the chronology: preoccupations, daily routines, professional concerns, love interests, friendships. I read the serialized excerpt in *The New York Times* when I was in Los Angeles and had a few months off to write and think. As I read, I was sitting outside in Silver Lake, looking over the city.

SH: Oh, beautiful.

BLVR: It was the perfect experience.

SH: You read it online?

BLVR: Yes. I prefer to read on paper, but the serialized version came to me in the form of a digital newsletter, so I read it on my phone. I found it exhilarating, poetic, funny, and moving. This was a time when I was thinking about diaries myself a lot, and it was so interesting to see something sculpted from a diary that felt like it existed in the worlds of poetry and the novel and nonfiction and conceptual art all at once. I admired the way that it made use of daily life to engage much bigger concerns: love, time, selfhood, how a person does or doesn't change. I wonder if you could talk about juxtaposition and how that began to lead you through the book. What were you looking for as you were cutting?

SH: Just some sense, really. The book makes sense now, but it doesn't if you don't cut. So many of the sentences don't work out of context, for example, and for the book to work, every sentence must work out of its context. But many of them didn't. Many of them had no beauty or tone or feeling. And if you don't cut, it can get way too repetitive; you don't want the same thought expressed six hundred times.

BLVR: That can be the crushing thing about re-reading a diary.

SH: Yeah, you think, I'm so limited. It's really humbling. And playing with juxtaposition was just so fun. Like when you realize, Oh, if I cut these three sentences, then sentence one and sentence five come together and they have this frisson, this friction that makes them sparkle, and that makes sentence one and sentence five both have more meaning, which is delightful. It was hard—that book took ten years to figure out. I didn't know how long it should be. I didn't know if I should alphabetize each year separately, or put all ten years together. I didn't know what to do about the names. I didn't know if it should even be a book, you know?

BLVR: Was there a turning point in the project?

SH: There were a few. Originally every sentence was on its own line, but Lisa Naftolin, who is also a book designer, was playing around with it and she changed it, making the sentences follow each other, so that every chapter was a paragraph. That was a huge turning point. I realized, Oh my god, it's a novel. And the subject of the book is time. That was huge. I showed it to my editor, Mitzi Angel, at a certain point—it was eighty thousand words—and after she read it, we had a phone call, and I could feel the way she experienced it in the way she was responding to it—that she had found it rich and full. She said it made her feel joy, like the joy of being alive. When I heard that, I understood how to edit it further, and it confirmed for me that it was a book, and that its subject matter was also the joy of being alive, just the amazingness of having so many feelings and so many thoughts and things always changing and always staying the same and how miraculous it is. I wouldn't have thought that would be the way a person could feel after reading the diaries until she said it, and then I could finally see the book from a reader's point of view.

BLVR: That feels true to me. There are some passages I keep returning to because they make me alive to that joy.

SH: And the up and down. You realize, Oh, right, that's what life is. It's these ups and downs and the never-standing-still-ness of life, and at the same time, this kind of core that you can never get far away from. There's some self. One is indeed a self. Even if it's not a glorious self, it's still yours.

BLVR: How did writing *Alphabetical Diaries* make you think about selfhood and change?

SH: I think we have this idea that the point of life is to keep changing and growing and getting better and more moral and more efficient, and to do things more right and to dress more right and to have better relationships—and after finishing the book, I began to feel that all that was illusion, fantasy. You don't need to do anything. There's nowhere to go.

BLVR: You're going to be inside there the whole time.

SH: Yeah, you're stuck in yourself. It's OK! There's no getting better, there's no getting worse. There's just this self that you're in, and then you're not in it anymore. I just felt less angst about being me and about there being some fundamental problem.

BLVR: What a relief!

SH: Yeah, it was a kind of relief. You're not so bad, you know?

BLVR: It's such a strange fact of life that your life is the only one you'll get to see from the inside.

SH: Yeah. You can't see your life from the outside; you can't see anyone else's life from the inside. It's such a confusing imbalance.

BLVR: But that's what books can give you: this sense of someone else's life from the inside.

SH: Completely. The book's thoughts become your thoughts. It's so relaxing to be able to read. It's just the nicest feeling.

BLVR: Yeah, you lose yourself, in a way, while also being intensely yourself.

SH: There's just this home feeling when you're reading. It's like Oh, I'm at home. I'm reading. ★

THE UNOFFICIAL COVEN of BLACK VAMPIRES

AKASHA

in *Queen of the Damned*,
directed by Michael Rymer, 2002

AGE: *Ancient and fabulous (4011 BCE)*
BIRTHPLACE: *Uruk (modern-day Iraq)*
TERRITORY PROWLED: *All around the world*
KEY QUOTE: *"My children. Warms my blood to see you all gathered plotting against me."*

In the 2002 adaptation of Ann Rice's novel *The Vampire Chronicles*, Akasha (played by R&B star Aaliyah) is the first vampire in history, and, like all great firsts, she demands acclaim. A swift predator who vows to take over the world, Akasha works her powers of seduction against vampires themselves, turning immortals into either dust or dutiful servants. If you watch her closely, Akasha's movements on-screen feature traces of Aaliyah's rhythmic control; the songstress's sultry cool imbues Akasha's ancient power with a modern edge. Premiering a year after Aaliyah's sudden and tragic death in 2001, the film is dedicated to its star.

LOUIS AND CLAUDIA

in *Interview with the Vampire*, created by Rolin Jones, 2022–present

AGES: *Nearly 150 years old (Louis); 14 going on 40 (Claudia)*
BIRTHPLACE: *New Orleans*
TERRITORY PROWLED: *1910s New Orleans + post–World War II Paris + 2022 Dubai*

KEY QUOTE: *"I am done enduring." (Claudia)*

AMC's adaptation of the Ann Rice novel *Interview with the Vampire* depicts Louis de Pointe du Lac (played by Jacob Anderson) as a magnetic, petty, and closeted Black businessman in 1910s Louisiana, rather than a sullen French émigré from a slaveholding family based in eighteenth-century New Orleans. Claudia (played by Bailey Bass and Delainey Hayles) is no longer Rice's blue-eyed five-year-old white girl but a teenage Black orphan living with her aunt in a brothel, where Louis rescues her from a fire set by white mobs terrorizing their town. Made by the French vampire Lestat, Louis and Claudia form an extrafamilial alliance within their immortal family that is shaped by their shared condition as Black Southerners who remain eternally haunted by the significance of their race. In a scene that has since become a viral meme, Louis places a COLORED ONLY—NO WHITES ALLOWED sign on his business in protest of Jim Crow laws. This short-lived revolt depicts the Black vampire reduced to human-resistance tactics. Even when he kills a racist alderman, Louis learns he is no match for the wrath of the white mob or the guilt he harbors for jeopardizing the mortal Black community of which he once was a conscripted member and to which he is now eternally tethered.

THE PRINCE

in *The Black Vampyre: A Legend of St. Domingo*,
written by Uriah Derick D'Arcy, 1819

AGE: *Unknown (born sometime before the Haitian Revolution)*
BIRTHPLACE: *Guinea*
TERRITORY PROWLED: *St. Domingo (now Haiti)*
KEY QUOTE: *"Vampyres and gentlemen! Shall not the immortal precede the mortal?"*

One of the first published accounts of the Black vampire in the Americas is set during the lead-up to the Haitian Revolution and centers on an enslaved man who is killed by his master—only to return from the dead as a vampire emancipated by immortality and in pursuit of vengeance.

MAXIMILLIAN AND RITA

in *Vampire in Brooklyn*, directed by Wes Craven, 1995

AGES: *30+ mortal years and thriving*
BIRTHPLACE: *Unnamed vampire nation in the Caribbean Islands*
TERRITORY PROWLED: *New York City*

KEY QUOTE: *"A part of me loves you so much, but that part of me must die." (Rita)*

Maximillian (played by Eddie Murphy), the Caribbean protagonist of this dark romantic comedy, is a singular, suave, and calculating immortal on the hunt for a half vampire, half human to wed. Enter Rita (Angela Bassett), an NYPD homicide detective working to uncover a mysterious death, and who, unbeknownst to her, was born of a human mother and a vampire father, making her a dhampir with the unique capacity to grant Maximillian the opportunity to prolong his lineage, which is on the verge of extinction. Torn between the two sides of herself, Rita ultimately denounces her vampire heritage, and in a dramatic turn of events, kills the last vampire of her paternal clan in an act that is both homicidal and suicidal. For Rita, vampirism is a generational curse to cast out without equivocation.

TARA THORNTON

in *True Blood*, created by Alan Ball, 2008–14

AGE: *27 years old and tired*
BIRTHPLACE: *Bon Temps, Louisiana*
TERRITORY PROWLED: *Louisiana*
KEY QUOTE: *"Did you own slaves?"*

Long before Tara (played by Rutina Wesley) was turned into a vampire during the fifth season of HBO's hit show *True Blood*, her mortal existence as a Black woman navigating the racial landscape of her hometown of Bon Temps, Louisiana, was far from easy. As the best friend of the show's white half-fae protagonist, Sookie Stackhouse, and something of a third wheel in Sookie's romance with the vampire Bill Compton, Tara constantly challenges the mythic and material order of *True Blood*, even going so far as to ask Bill, a 173-year-old former Confederate soldier, if he owned slaves (spoiler: he did!).

MAMUWALDE

in *Blacula*, directed by William Crain, 1972

AGE: *More than 192 years old*
BIRTHPLACE: *"Abani tribe... northeast of the Niger Delta"*
TERRITORY PROWLED: *Transylvania + Los Angeles*
KEY QUOTE: *"Well, we can't ignore what the world characterizes as the Black arts, now, can we?"*

In the blaxploitation film *Blacula*, an eighteenth-century African royal from the Niger Delta (played by William Marshall) travels to Transylvania and implores Dracula to help end the transatlantic slave trade ravaging his homeland. After refusing, Dracula transforms the prince into a vampire and exclaims, "I curse you with my name. You shall be... Blacula!" After lifetimes spent sealed away in a coffin, Mamuwalde eventually emerges into a new world, 1970s Los Angeles. The first Black vampire in film (according to the American Film Institute's catalog) bears a complex legacy due to tensions embedded in the film's plot, which is, unquestionably, a kind of slave narrative. The spirit of abolition is what drives Mamuwalde to find Dracula, and yet it is only through bondage that he acquires the power of vampirism. Undead but unfree, Blacula bears his "slave name" and fights to remake himself in unfamiliar lands. Marshall's portrayal of Mamuwalde is not only a testament to the dynamic campiness and political ironies of the blaxploitation era, but also a spirited embodiment of fugitive life after death.

GILDA

in *The Gilda Stories*, written by Jewelle Gomez, 1991

AGE: *At least 200 years old*
BIRTHPLACE: *Born on a plantation in Louisiana*
TERRITORY PROWLED: *Louisiana + California + Missouri + Massachusetts + New York + New Hampshire*
KEY QUOTE: *"Life was indeed interminable. The malignation of her contemporaries to some mortal questions, like race, didn't suit her. She didn't believe a past could, or should, be so easily discarded."*

In this novel, an anonymous enslaved woman flees her 1850 Louisiana plantation and ends up in a brothel run by a vampire madam named Gilda, from whom she acquires vampirism and a new name.

COUNTESS VAMPIRA

in *Old Dracula*, directed by Clive Donner, 1974

AGE: *Ancient but hip!*
BIRTHPLACE: *Unknown origins*
(The trail runs cold after the Playboy Mansion.)
TERRITORY PROWLED: *Transylvania + United States + Brazil*
KEY QUOTE: *"I'm Black."*

In the British horror comedy *Old Dracula*, Count Dracula longs to bring his deceased Countess Vampira back to life, but he faces an unexpected obstacle: the only match for his beloved's rare blood type is a Black *Playboy* model (played by Teresa Graves). In keeping with the fictitious horrors of old-school race science, the blood of this Black woman contaminates its host, transforming the phenotype of Countess Vampira, who, upon resurrection, discovers she is now in the body of a Black woman. While Dracula sets out to make his lover white again, the countess tries on new affectations, slang, and aesthetics. Not only does she embrace her cosmetic Blackness, but with her fanged bite, the countess makes other vampires Black as well, including the anxious count himself.

DR. HESS GREEN AND GANJA MEDA

in *Ganja & Hess*, directed by Bill Gunn, 1973

AGES: *Eternally '70s-era middle-aged*
BIRTHPLACE: *Somewhere in the US*
TERRITORY PROWLED: *New York City (the ancient dagger which grants them vampirism originated in Myrthia, a mythic African vampire nation)*
KEY QUOTE: *"The only thing she could ever bring herself to say is that I was beautiful. And I loathed my beauty for that!" (Ganja)*

Two unlikely lovers are transformed into vampires as a result of an ancient African dagger and the antics of a reckless anthropologist's assistant. In 2014, the film was remade by director Spike Lee as *Da Sweet Blood of Jesus*. A decade later, the film was archived in the Library of Congress's National Film Registry for its cultural significance.

HARRIET BRANDT

in *The Blood of the Vampire*, written by Florence Marryat, 1897

AGE: *Forever 21*
BIRTHPLACE: *Colonial Jamaica*
TERRITORY PROWLED: *Jamaica + England*
KEY QUOTE: *"Was it my love that killed them? Shall I always kill everybody I love? I must know—I will!"*

Published the same year as Bram Stoker's *Dracula*, Marryat's gothic novel follows Harriet Brandt, a mixed-race Jamaican woman born of an English mad scientist and an enslaved Obeah priestess, on a plantation that also serves as an experimental laboratory. Harriet acquires her vampirism through her maternal line: her enslaved, pregnant grandmother was bitten by a vampire bat, which are "said to fan their victims to sleep with their enormous wings, whilst they suck their blood."

LAURENT

in *Twilight*, directed by Catherine Hardwicke, 2008

AGE: *Nearly 300 years old*
BIRTHPLACE: *Paris*
TERRITORY PROWLED: *The world*
KEY QUOTE: *"Let's not play with our food."*

When the Kenyan American actor Edi Gathegi was cast as the vampire Laurent for the film adaptation of Stephenie Meyer's book series Twilight, the news went viral even to the author. As fans of the franchise soon learned, Meyer's conception of vampirism within the novel features a distinctive arc in which all humans, including those with dark skin, would become vampires with "pale glistening skin." This science fiction in which vampirism attacks only those melanocytes that contribute to human skin color resulted in a compromise that allowed a Black vampire with locs to appear in the two films in the Twilight franchise as a central antihero. Laurent belongs to a vampire coven that has pledged to kill the human protagonist Bella. And though he is committed to this pledge, Laurent demonstrates a dual commitment to murder and mercy, warning his enemies of his coven's intentions and promising to kill Bella quickly rather than subject her to torture.

BLADE

in *Blade*, directed by Stephen Norrington, 1998

AGE: *Unknown*
BIRTHPLACE: *A brothel in the Soho neighborhood of London*
TERRITORY PROWLED: *Los Angeles*
KEY QUOTE: *"There are worse things out tonight than vampires."*

The 1998 film adaptation of *Blade* from the Marvel Comics universe centers Blade (Wesley Snipes) as a dhampir vampire slayer. Knowing his unique biology to be the key to a vampire war on human extinction, Blade sets out to wage a secret plot for human extinction. Bringing his dhampir abilities against the supernatural entities that make his power possible. Bringing a brashness and vulgarity to the typical seductive sophistication associated with the vampire, Blade showcases the brutality of vampire life, introducing audiences to a world in which vampires seek much more than human blood and affection. Though the promised 2025 remake, starring Mahershala Ali, appears to have gone up in smoke, the original adaptation is historic for being one of the first commercially successful Marvel films. And thanks to Blade's cameo in 2024's *Deadpool & Wolverine*, Blade and Snipes now hold the records for "the longest gap between character appearances in Marvel films," and the "longest career as a live-action Marvel character" in history. The day-walker takes all.

THE "NEGRO RULE" VAMPIRE

in a comic by Norman Jennett, from Raleigh, North Carolina's *News and Observer*, 1898

AGE: *Thirty-three years a freeman*
BIRTHPLACE: *Postbellum United States*
TERRITORY PROWLED: *Primarily the American South*

For a North Carolina newspaper, political cartoonist Norman Jennett depicted a dark-skinned vampire with textured hair and the words "Negro Rule" on his bat wings. Jennett sought to activate an existing consensus of white racial anxieties by drawing the vampire emerging from a ballot box with large talons outstretched toward an assortment of disproportionately tiny white women. Subtle, he was not!

Black vampires are coming out of the shadows. From the critically acclaimed race-bent AMC adaptation of *Interview with the Vampire*, which reenvisions its infamous protagonists, Louis and Claudia, as Black New Orleanians, to the 2025 release of Ryan Coogler's Great Depression–era vampire thriller, *Sinners*, vampirism has been declared "the new black" in more ways than one. But, as is so often the case with matters of the undead, the trope of Black vampires is much older than current trends would suggest. Despite the Western archetype of the vampire as the pale, perfect, post-human beauty that seduces mankind and Father Time for fuel, our representations of vampires go far beyond a single narrative of the eternally ravenous, inexplicably charming, and unequivocally white bloodsucker.

Rather, Blackness, and all its historic associations with captivity, desire, and deviance, has long inspired depictions of this supernatural entity, enhancing its symbolism in ways that defy and redefine the fear-arousing boundaries between life and death, freedom and slavery, human and nonhuman. These characters, who are often forced to contend with racial politics even after they acquire freedom from mortality, turn the lore of the vampire's limitless power on its head. They push us to ask vital questions about what it means to inherit, experience, and bear witness to history; in doing so, these beings give the face of immortality sharper teeth, and expose how extraction shapes the worlds of both the living and the dead.

—Jordan Taliha McDonald

WATER

THE DIFFICULTIES OF PROCURING WATER AND POWER IN KARACHI, PAKISTAN, WHERE SURGING TEMPERATURES HAVE STRAINED THE CITY'S RESOURCES, AND MUCH MORE

by **RAFIA ZAKARIA**

PRESSURE

DISCUSSED: *Underground Water Tanks, Envy, Climate-Influenced Mood Disorders, A Widow's Home, Dawn, Urban Heat Islands, Nagging Uncertainty, The Pump Games, Karachi's Water Mafia, Candlelight Feasts, The Incredible Magic of Air-Conditioning, Load Shedding, A Family Showdown, Monsoon Season, Microwaves, Rheumatoid Arthritis, Bacteria That Thrive in High Temperatures, Overconsumption, A Bucket and a Cup*

ILLUSTRATIONS BY: Owen Pomery

In the middle of the summer of 2024, when the temperature in Karachi was skirting 104 degrees Fahrenheit, a man was walking past my paternal aunt's house. The sun was high in the sky at midafternoon, and he had just returned from offering his afternoon prayers at the nearby mosque. He did this every Friday, the holiest day of the week for Muslims, and the day on which the week's main sermon is held. When he passed by my aunt's home, he saw that water was overflowing out of her underground tank and onto the street. This annoyed him a great deal. Water envy is common in Karachi, a city that doesn't have enough water for its twenty million or more inhabitants. Water comes through the municipal pipes for only an hour or two each day and sometimes not at all. Many homes that are not apartments have underground tanks in which water from the pipes can be stored. In most single-family homes, including my aunt's, water must then be pumped to an overhead tank on the roof so it can flow out of the faucets.

When the man saw water coming out of the underground tank and onto the street, he knew it meant that the underground tank must be full. Such water abundance in such heat was a bit too much for him to bear on his own, so he stood there calling out for someone to complain to about the terrible waste of water. No one emerged from the house. My paternal aunt is a widow, and even if she did hear him on that scorching afternoon, she chose not to come out and listen to what he had to say. In general, women in Pakistan do not answer the door for men they aren't related to. However, in his frenzy, the man seemed to have forgotten this. Even though his home was just a few houses farther down the street, he had great trouble obtaining water. It irked him that this was, by chance, less of a problem for my aunt. There was nothing he could do about the water that was flowing out onto the street, but he complained about the situation to anyone who would listen, which meant mainly to his wife.

A few weeks went by and the temperature in the city would not relent. Pakistan, which contributes less than 1 percent to global carbon emissions, is now listed by the Climate Risk Index as the country most vulnerable to climate change. The average temperatures have risen by several degrees to create almost uninhabitable conditions—except that millions of people *do* inhabit Karachi. The dense population, the proliferation of concrete surfaces, and the fumes from millions of gas- and diesel-burning vehicles make the temperatures in some areas, including the one my aunt lives in, several degrees higher than those near the shore. There are few trees and almost no shade, and these facts—combined with the lack of water with which to cool oneself and the frequent power outages that have long plagued the city—mean that midafternoons in summer are hotter than hell itself.

One day not long after that sweltering Friday afternoon, so hot that even birds would not fly, this man—who is the sort of vigilante that retired men of a certain age can be—passed by my aunt's house again. He was stunned to see that, yet again, water was flowing out of the underground tank and onto the street's parched asphalt. If last time he had been annoyed at seeing this largesse of water, this time he was angered. In the past week, no water had flowed into his own tank at all. By Thursday the lack of water in his home had become so acute that he had had to purchase a private water tanker in order to shower and do household tasks like laundry and dishwashing. The tanker had not arrived until 9 p.m. the previous evening, an hour by which he would have liked to have been settled in front of the television. As a result, he was cross not only about having to spend money—something he truly disliked—but also about having his routine thrown into disarray.

All this exacerbated his indignation, added to which was the fact that he felt he "deserved" the water more. Why, after all, should a reclusive widow's home be blessed with such a bounty of water when he was being denied his fair share? This time he decided he would not leave until he could deliver his own sermon on waste to the homeowner, loud enough

I heard about this incident on a day in November 2024. It was still very hot in Karachi then, around 95 degrees Fahrenheit during the day. Karachi has never had real "winters," though when I was growing up, temperatures in November used to be at least nine degrees cooler. The evening hour had arrived, but the breeze that blew over the porch of my maternal grandmother's house, which was only a couple of miles from our own, was still warm. My maternal aunt told me the story. She had heard it through the snakes and ladders by which gossip travels in Karachi. The man who was jealous of her water supply had told his wife, who had told another of my maternal aunts, who had then told the aunt who was relaying it to me.

It was my paternal aunt who had thrown rocks at the man. She had never been one to suffer moralizing interlopers gladly, and this man, considered annoying by most of the neighborhood, had received exactly what he deserved, she decided. Her water was not his business, and his persistent harassment of a widow in her late seventies made him the guilty party. Throughout her life, she had often become the unwitting and unhappy subject of neighborhood gossip. If people talked about her now because she had thrown rocks at a man who annoyed her, they could go right ahead.

It is perhaps also true that heat and envy, and the unrelenting nature of both during a Karachi summer, can make you act in wild, reckless, and unpredictable ways. My aunt has never been a violent woman. As a matter of fact, she is usually subdued, and she eventually became reclusive.

Most of the research on climate-influenced mood disorders has been done in the West, and largely on white subjects. Everyone knows about the winter blues caused by freezing temperatures, which are a regular part of life in the rich and temperate areas of the world. Less, of course, is said about the summer furies that plague people in places like Karachi.

The little research that has been done has shown that older adults in fast-heating environments like Karachi are especially vulnerable to mood disorders. One 2021 report found that there was a 2.2 percent increase in mental-health-related mortality and a 0.9 percent increase in mental-health morbidity for every 1.8-degree-Fahrenheit increase in temperature. This study found that these effects are even more acute for people over the age of sixty-five who live in tropical and subtropical climates.

Temperatures in Karachi have shown sharp increases since 2018. A report published in the Pakistani newspaper *Dawn* in September 2024 quoted a Karachi woman, who pointed out exactly why: "After working all day, our walks back home used to be pleasant as a gentle breeze would blow from the sea. Now, high-rise buildings around our neighbourhood have hemmed us in a hot bubble where it is difficult to even breathe." This is exactly what has happened in my aunt's neighborhood. The street she lives on is surrounded by what is now a busy commercial area. The main road adjacent to her formerly sleepy side

---

for all the other neighbors to hear. For this to be possible, he needed someone to answer the door. Standing on the street, as the rivulets eddied around his sandals, he began calling out and ringing the doorbell. He would not, he resolved, leave until and unless someone responded to him.

Ten and then twenty minutes passed as he pressed hard on the bell, hearing its muffled ring tearing through the inside of the house. No one responded and no one came to the door. He was not deterred, the wet waterway from house to street feeding his sense of noble perseverance. Still, there was silence. Other men from the neighborhood who were also returning from the mosque passed by and offered silent greetings. He tried to enlist at least one of them to stand with him in his valiant cause, pointing to the water, the waste, but the men just nodded and kept walking. This was a widow's home, and if she was being blessed with an abundance of water, they likely concluded, then who were they to tell her what to do with it?

Over half an hour passed and no one responded. Then he heard footsteps and shuffling behind the front door of the house. Ha! He congratulated himself prematurely, preparing the first few sentences of his homily. The door opened, but prior to any words leaving his mouth, he felt a small rock graze his elbow. Before he was able to overcome his surprise, he felt another. He soon realized the rocks were coming from inside the house. He cowered, and then moved away. And without having said anything at all, he had to turn around and leave.

street has a huge banquet hall, high-rises, restaurants, and other local businesses, all of which release exhaust fumes and carbon dioxide.

A study on the growth of Karachi, Pakistan's largest city, revealed that its surface area increased from 257 square miles to 276 square miles between 2015 and 2023, an average growth rate of 13.35 percent over those eight years. All uninhabited land, whether agricultural or vacant, has been swallowed up by the concrete jungle. This in turn creates a bubble effect, officially named an "urban heat island" (UHI). UHIs are essentially microclimates created within densely populated cities where heat becomes trapped and has nowhere to go. Roadways, concrete surfaces, and industrial and transportation activities all have thermal properties that amplify the warming. Add to this the fact that high-rises and commercial establishments like those that have popped up around my aunt's street use air-conditioning units. As if the heat were not enough, these buildings release hot air directly into the outside air, making it still hotter.

This contrasts with areas of the city that still have parks and vegetation, and that are spared from urban sprawl because they are either home to the very wealthy or maintained by the country's all-powerful armed forces (which have their own supply of water). Last summer, when the incident with the rocks occurred, the concrete- and asphalt-ridden areas where houses are close together were shown to be much hotter than those areas near the ocean that boast palatial mansions encircled by green spaces and military bases with sprawling colonial-style lawns. Overall, the temperatures recorded in June 2024 in Karachi were the hottest the city had experienced since 2015, when a historic and punishing heat wave killed thousands of people.

Then there are the politics of water, whose accessibility is intertwined with the experience of living in a hot and furious city. Insight into the mechanics of water supply in Karachi can underscore how the climate crisis has begun to weave through the city's web of human relationships. In some areas, for example, the main city water-supply lines don't automatically supply water to homes on side streets. At my father's house, where I was born and raised, water must be suctioned from the main lines into the underground tank.

The problem is that no one knows when there is water in the city lines, so the suction pump must be turned on at various hours to test if there is anything to pull up. Figuring out when water can be sucked in and stored has thus been one of my father's central preoccupations during his retirement years. When my mother was alive, one of the most frequent questions I heard them ask each other was "Did the water come?" Whoever was indoors did the asking, and whoever was outdoors did the answering. If the answer was yes, there were exclamations of satisfaction,

and if not, expressions of consternation. Full tanks meant water security, and empty ones meant nagging uncertainty.

In summer this game of pulling in water became even more stressful. On many occasions, my father, who is a light sleeper and often wakes in the middle of the night, would use that groggy moment of broken sleep at 3 or 4 a.m. to go outside, walk all the way over to the underground water tank, open its heavy cast iron lid, and turn on the pump to see if water was being sucked in. If it was, he could not go back to sleep right away, or else the pump would keep running even after the water ceased to flow. The motor could then overheat, and the pump would burn out. A burned-out pump meant there would be no way to get any water at all. If the pump did not yield anything, however, worries set in about when the water would come.

These pump games, as I call them, are strategies of the middle-class. There are millions of people who live in tiny apartments and do not have private underground tanks. Sometimes these densely packed neighborhoods are not supplied with water for days, completely disrupting any semblance of normal life. Unlike the wealthy, the poor cannot purchase private water tankers to solve the problem and so are often forced to share single kitchens and bathrooms with multiple generations of family members, and are unable able to regularly wash dishes, flush toilets, or wash themselves.

For this, the residents of these areas blame what they refer to as Karachi's "water mafia." According to them, the Karachi Water and Sewage Corporation (the municipal board whose job it is to supply water to the city) is selling the water it should be providing to residents through city water lines to the operators of private tankers instead. These private tankers then capitalize on the plight of citizens who have been deprived of water for days by making them purchase the water they should have received from the government for free. The tanker mafia not only sells to citizens what it has stolen from them, it also is responsible for water price hikes during periods of intense heat, which in Karachi last for many months.

Those who cannot afford the pricey clean water are sold polluted water. No one knows the source of this polluted water, though it is sometimes rumored to be wastewater. Depending on one's level of desperation, ignorance is sometimes better than knowledge. Consumption of this water has led to disease outbreaks, but because the heat also leads to disease outbreaks, it is difficult to assess which can be attributed to which cause. Many Karachi residents, however, do not have the luxury of asking questions about safety and potability. Even dirty water may be more welcome than the stench of waste stopping up toilets and of bodies ripe with sweat and odor.

In 2024, a new form of protest against the tanker mafia took hold. Residents of an area of the city that had not received water for over a week came out onto a major thoroughfare, where they waited for and then began to hijack tankers. The drivers, scared of the mob, soon absconded. Young men in the crowd opened the taps on the tankers, flooding the highways and disrupting traffic. When news crews arrived at the scene, the rioters explained that for days they had been contacting city councilors, representatives to provincial parliament, and anyone else that could have come to their aid. Nobody had responded, and in the meantime, their children were getting sick from the lack of hygiene, bacteria and viruses adhering to their soft, sticky bodies.

This form of tanker hijacking has become more and more prevalent in recent months. In late December 2024, the Karachi police began to register cases against the hijackers. The police in Karachi are also notoriously corrupt, and not at all invulnerable to being paid off by the very mafia that the hijackers are protesting. For its part, the Karachi Water and Sewage Corporation seems adamant about simply denying the widespread nature of the problem. In a statement made to a news organization after the registration of rioting cases began, one spokesperson from the municipality insisted that an "uninterrupted water supply" had been restored to all the localities whose parched residents were revolting on city streets.

It is not only water that Karachi thirsts for. Electricity has become just as elusive in the past two decades, even while many of the country's other urban areas enjoy an uninterrupted supply. When I was growing up in Karachi, and electricity had yet to become such a precious resource, a power outage was a rare and exciting event. The sudden disappearance of all light in the middle of an otherwise ordinary activity, such as a weeknight dinner, gave everything an air of specialness. One moment our family was sitting down to eat rice and fish curry, and within minutes the regular meal was transformed into a mysterious and thus fun candlelight feast. The shadows, the darkened house, the candlelit table, the unusualness of it all—it was a treat. In those days, the power would be out for barely half an hour before coming back on. The last fun bit was blowing out the candles—something we otherwise got to do only on birthdays—and watching the plumes of smoke dissipate as the ordinary world was restored.

This changed a few years later, as the '80s slipped into the '90s. Power outages became more frequent, and a headache. In a telling counterpoint, this was also the time when my family was able to afford our very first air conditioner. It was installed in my parents' bedroom on a momentous day that came only after workmen had smashed a hole in the concrete of which our two-story house was made. Once the air conditioner was set up and the edges around it filled in with plaster, we finally experienced the incredible magic of air-conditioning. It did truly feel like magic. A few hours after turning on this new appliance, my parents' usually hot and uncomfortable bedroom (it bore the brunt of the afternoon sun) was transformed into a cold and relaxing haven. Like most middle-class families, we could at that time afford only one air conditioner, which meant that we kids, who had only just started to sleep in our own room, now spent nights in the deliciously cool air of our parents' bedroom.

But with great ease came great discomfort. The power outages that

became more frequent around that time, in part because of air conditioners, felt particularly onerous when they happened at night. Nothing was worse than walking from the bedroom onto the first-floor balcony—it was like stepping into an oven. But staying in the room with the air conditioner, where all the windows were shuttered to keep the air in, also felt suffocating.

My brother and I often chose the balcony over the bedroom with its closed windows. From the first floor, we could watch how our neighbors were dealing with the outage. If we saw the kids from across the street pile into their car and leave, we felt jealous and terribly sorry for ourselves, because our father would never think of doing that. Often, he tried hard to sleep during the outage, but even if he was awake, he never (unlike our mother) joined us on the balcony. Bitten again and again by mosquitoes who must have loved that our flesh was now so easily available to them late at night, we waited for the moment when the power would return and our neighbors' houses would suddenly light up.

As the mid-'90s approached, that wait got longer. We started to call the outages "load shedding," which meant that the city's electric grid could not meet consumer demand. Nearly every summer night, the outages did not just interrupt sleep but often occurred earlier in the evening. If you happened to be studying for an exam, you had better have a flashlight and batteries on hand, because working by candlelight was difficult if not impossible. Exam season now brought the trepidation of not only the tests themselves but outages that might last hours and leave one in poor shape to do a good job.

My father probably suffered the most from all this uncertainty. While the inconvenience of studying for tests without electricity was considerable, my father had to be at his job at eight in the morning, taking meetings and making presentations all day long. The late evening and night were precious, since they were the only times he was at home. Of course, we never thought then about how the outages that so often took up these hours likely incurred a much bigger cost for him than for any of the rest of us; we just grumbled when he asked us to open the shutters that had been closed while the air conditioner was running. As it was for millions of other men and women in the city, the demands of the encroaching workday would not go away just because there had been no electricity the night before.

One outage changed our neighborhood dynamics forever. It happened in the summer and lasted for days. The food in the deep freezer threatened to go bad, its ice melting into puddles of water on the kitchen floor. All our food had to be taken to my maternal grandmother's house, where there was still power. The lack of electricity meant that the water in our underground tank could not be pumped into the tank on the roof. So to flush the toilets upstairs, water had to be taken from the underground tank and brought through the yard and up the house's two flights of stairs. On one such trip, I slipped on water that had sloshed out of the plastic bucket I was carrying. For days, my shins and knees were covered in spectacular bruises. It was around then that we learned to continually call the electric company to complain about the outage. The local office, which was just a block from our house, seemed to deal with this by taking its phones off the hook so we would encounter a perpetual busy signal.

Many of our neighbors took things into their own hands. The large business family that lived behind our house and whose children were permitted to stay up a lot later than we ever were (we knew this because we sometimes heard them playing in their yard when we were brushing our teeth) obtained a large diesel generator. Now the pain of not having power was heightened by the fact that, if the bedroom windows were open, we could hear the loud, incessant drone of this machine, which felt very much like a dentist's drill boring into our temples.

Within a few years, the generator trend had become so popular that our neighbors on each side of the house had procured one. When we walked onto the balcony to brave another evening of high temperatures with humidity levels above 90 percent, we now also had to endure a domino effect of generators, which were constantly being upgraded to ever-larger capacities. As if this wasn't awful enough, seeing the lights and fans coming back on in their houses was worse. They were comfortable indoors and had little concern that the noise of their diesel-guzzling contraptions was making life unbearable for our family.

My father still refuses to get a generator. By 2000, my brother and I had both moved to the United States. Two and a half decades later, this refusal has, in some ways, torn our family apart. In the States, we set about establishing careers and families abroad even as our hearts remained in overheating Karachi. We got used to water in our faucets and a largely uninterrupted power supply. We also got used to a more temperate rather than a subtropical climate. We left behind the disorder and frustration of a city where no one seemed to have enough, where the heat ensured that people were always in a bad mood, where obtaining water and power required a constant struggle.

We also became wealthier. When we were little, in order to save money, the air conditioner could be turned on only after 9 p.m. and was never allowed to stay on after 6 a.m. Now, our incomes earned in dollars meant that we no longer felt like we had to heed these strict rules when we visited Karachi. Around the time of my brother's wedding in 2009, this led to a big family showdown.

The wedding and weeks-long festivities that preceded and succeeded it were to be held in Karachi. What would be the first of many climate-related fights between my father and brother took place over the couple's decision to have their wedding in July, in the middle of summer and the unpredictable monsoon season. My brother had forgotten what summer in Karachi was like, my father bellowed. He had forgotten the water problems, the electricity problems, and all the other problems that were caused by the combination of those problems.

For his part, my brother insisted with equal obstinacy that the "problems" were all in my father's head and could be solved by throwing money at them. He wanted to install a high-capacity generator. He wanted to install several additional split-unit air conditioners. He would make sure that water could be delivered by private tankers, and he wanted to make plumbing updates and repairs so that he and his wife could take showers in the upstairs bathrooms.

This response only made my father dig in his heels. Shouting matches erupted over the telephone as my brother threatened not to spend any of his time at the house at all, which sent my mother—who saw my brother's wedding as a dream come true—into a near nervous breakdown. My father had little compassion. The house belonged to him. No one would install new air conditioners or showers or diesel generators without his permission.

I felt stuck in the middle. My brother in his ebullient mood wanted to pull out all the stops. In marrying someone who had initially been introduced to him by our parents, he felt he had already fulfilled all the obligations of an obedient son. He saw himself as the new "man of the house" and felt he could ignore the constraints my father put on him. One of his tactics was to make a change—such as purchasing a microwave for the kitchen—and then

to leave to go hang out with his fiancée at her parents' house. My mother, paternal grandmother, and I would be left at home to bear the brunt of my father's rage. If we did not bear it quietly, as I refused to at least once, it only fed his eruptions. "I am going to throw this microwave in the trash right now," he threatened over and over again in the hours after it had been installed. He had it uninstalled and put on a table outside the kitchen. Eventually, my brother would return in a great mood, but we, after tolerating a conflagration all day long, would be sullen and morose. This annoyed him. "Why can't you happy for me?" he would demand.

During the wedding in July, the mood between my parents and my brother was still tense. The sole concession my father had made was to permit the installation of a large-capacity air conditioner in the room where my brother would stay. The bathroom was fixed up and the existing shower repaired to the extent possible. These were not at all the modernizing renovations my brother had hoped for, which would have equipped the house with the workarounds that most affluent Karachiites were accustomed to. Yet for my father, it was not a matter of cost; it was a matter of respect—for his rules and for the value of money.

The monsoon hit the day before the wedding, when the henna ceremony is hosted by the bride's family. As if on cue, the power at our house went out and the streets of the city flooded, as they do every time there is a downpour. My father felt smug. My brother decamped to his wife's family's home. My mother wept the entire time he was

away. For her, this was not a weather event but a metaphor for having lost the son she loved, whose affections were now forever usurped by his new wife.

If my brother was home and there was no power, he glowered; this being his told-you-so moment. To him, the fact that my father would not permit the installation of a generator that would so obviously make life more bearable for his parents, even after the wedding was over, was absurd. He had a retort for each of my father's qualms, such as my father's quibble that he did not want to be responsible for turning the generator on and off. My brother would install a self-starting one, he said, and ensure that a technician came to service the unit so my father did not have to deal with repairs. My father would not relent. "This is my house, and if he wants to disobey me then he should kick me out first," he yelled as my brother slammed the door and left.

In the end no one won. The issue of the generator created a rift between my father and brother that still has not quite healed. My brother saw his expenditures toward making our childhood home comfortable for everyone as his duty. My father, like my paternal grandparents, was set in his ways. Even when we first got the air conditioner and were so dazzled by its capacities, my grandparents had refused to spend any time in the cooled room. The windows in their room provided cross-ventilation, which was enough for them. The power outages were a nuisance, but they preferred the natural temperature to one created by a machine.

Heat and air-conditioning became the center of our family tensions. My brother and I had changed after living in the West. My father had trouble getting to know us as adults. He wanted time to stop when we entered his house. He wanted us to be the teenagers we had been before we left for the United States. In those days, we had complained less about the heat in Karachi, about what didn't work in the house, about his rules, the obedience to which he saw as the ultimate act of love. A happy trip home required us to regress into that earlier time, even as we and the city around us grew older and ever more complicated.

Fifteen years have passed since the wedding, and during that time my father has used every excuse in the book to explain why he still will not allow us to install a generator at the house in Karachi. Most of his excuses are familar: he will have to turn it on and off; he doesn't like the diesel fumes; it could cause a fire, it will eventually stop working, and so on.

When my mother was alive, the generator was a flashpoint issue. My father would insist that the heat did not bother him, as if he were the only one living in the house. But my mother, who had a slew of health problems, also lived there. Her rheumatoid arthritis had destroyed her joints and then attacked her lungs, giving her asthma, which the heat intensified. There was an inherent unfairness to all this: My mother, who had never smoked a cigarette in her entire life, developed chronic obstructive pulmonary disease. She became especially vulnerable to the many respiratory infections borne by bacteria that thrive in high temperatures. My parents'

experiences of the city, the heat, the problems it bred were entirely separate even though they shared the same little piece of home. Their situation is an apt metaphor for the isolation of climate change. Even in crowded environments, the experience of the jagged edges of suffocating smog, particulate matter, and exhaust smoke is singular, and its costs unfairly distributed.

High temperatures also make chronic pain more difficult to endure. Studies have found that blackouts in periods of intense heat, when there is no access to fans or air-conditioning, cause sharp increases in the mortality rates of vulnerable populations, like my mother's. Naturally, the poor bear the brunt of these disruptions, with little access to cooling resources. In the summer heat waves, hospitals fill up with patients with heat stroke, but once they are there, they become prey to hospital-borne illnesses and bacterial infections. Newspapers can hardly keep up with reports of the number of bodies in Karachi's morgues.

It was one such summer when my mother contracted a severe case of pneumonia. One day she was complaining over FaceTime of a slight cough and exhaustion and the next my father was calling from the respiratory intensive care unit at one of the private hospitals in Karachi. After a mad scramble of tickets and layovers in various parts of the world, I arrived at her bedside thirty-six hours later. It was the kind of trip all migrants dread, because it is impossible to tell during so many hours in transit whether there will be an improving or dying parent waiting at the end of the journey. Even at 11 p.m. the temperature was over 89 degrees Fahrenheit with nearly 100 percent humidity. The sweat poured down my face and back as my cousin picked me up in the car to take me directly to the hospital.

I was lucky. My mother was improving and conscious, if still seriously ill and in the intensive care unit. I could see her, touch her, and talk to her, even though the tubes made it impossible for her to talk to me. I spent the night at my maternal grandmother's house, grateful for the air-conditioning that brought the temperature of the room down a few degrees. It was still too hot for me at 2 a.m., so I took a shower and put on my clothes without drying myself. This is an old trick, and it works only if you fall asleep while your clothes are still damp. That evening I was exhausted enough for the trick to work, but even as I fell asleep, I worried about how I would endure the heat of the city.

With terrible heat come terrible tempers. As the crisis of my mother's sudden hospitalization dissipated, our family was once again riven with the same arguments that had begun over a decade ago. In the respiratory ICU, she fought for her life with lungs weakened by pneumonia. Outside the hospital, my father and brother resurrected their old feud, positions unaltered.

The day she came home from the hospital, the temperature was 102 degrees Fahrenheit and the power was out. The only air-conditioned bedrooms were on the first floor of the house, which still could be reached only by climbing two flights of stairs. It took almost half an hour of supporting her as she climbed them, with her ailing lungs. Once we were in the bedroom, we were all dripping with sweat. The room felt claustrophobic, and the relentless sun beating through the windows seemed like a callous torturer, scorching and insistent.

It is true that as immigrants who had become used to the luxuries of the first world, my brother and I felt life in Karachi was broken. At the same time there are reams of data to show that Karachi's heat patterns have changed since we were little. Power outages were never the norm in the way they became in the 2000s and 2010s. The intense growth of the inland city has created UHIs that mean that Karachi cannot benefit from the sea breezes that had cooled us in the past. Nevertheless, to me and my brother, the fact that we could afford to buy privatized power and water in Karachi presented a clear and easy solution to all this. When we got to Karachi as adults, we felt entitled to use the air conditioners and water as much as we wanted. Jet-lagged for at least a week of the two-week vacations we spent at home, we slept until noon or later and (if we had power) with air conditioners running full blast.

My father seemed to identify more with the millions of Karachiites who endure the heat without electricity and water than with us, his children, who

had by now internalized the Western ethos of unexamined consumption. He and my mother saw sleeping beyond 8 a.m. as rude and regarded flouting his still-standing rules of running the air conditioner only between 9 p.m. and 6 a.m. as gluttonous. Karachi's current climate conditions are due in huge part to global warming, a direct consequence of the West's over-consumption of resources. Like other people in the West, we had become comfortable with the premise that we were somehow entitled to these resources, and that people in places like Karachi were accustomed to privation and thus used to discomforts that we could not—and really should not—endure.

My mother passed away in 2015 during another unbearable summer of high temperatures, power outages, and water shortages. The heat and the Islamic prescription for immediate burial meant that neither I nor my brother could get home in time. Without the glue that she represented, our family scattered emotionally and geographically. If my brother and I had become used to justifying our over-consumption, the families we had raised were even less accustomed to the vagaries of scarcity that Karachi presented.

Naturally, our relationship to our hot and poor city suffered. Due to the heat, we no longer visited in the summers. In the monthlong winter when I do visit—Karachi's winter now lasts only from mid-December to mid-January—it's possible to avoid a confrontation about comfort, consumption, entitlement, and climate change. There is still no generator, but

COMPUTER ASSEMBLY PLANT

by Prince Bush

After Betsy

Every night a drove of us leaves
Our work building

And clot the lot's exit up
Till emptied and distant,

No different when I'm stuck
With my key in the ignition,

Not yielding in spite
Of my turning, and as now
The only person

Except for me here, a man
Has knocked on my windshield,

Assuming I'm stuck and asks
To enter my car. He starts it
As if he freed the key

And looks at me
And says *I'm a car thief.*

To get home safely,
You'll need me.
I agree.

I may stop somewhere
Away from work

Or stall, on that clotted street
Where everyone's gone.

---

my father has installed a rechargeable battery that allows a single fan and a couple of electric lights to be operated.

My daughter does not know Karachi in the way I wish she did. Unlike the parents of so many of my friends who moved to the West, our home never became a place where we could safely and happily spend time. At the end of the day, this is not one individual's fault or responsibility. My father is not liable for what has happened in Karachi, or for the vast forces of climate transformation and involuntary migration that have altered the dense urban hinterlands where most of humanity now lives. Our attenuated family ties and our meager, specific gripes are one tiny illustration of what is happening on a much grander scale, a forbidding and frightening change that has already remade the world. This hotter world, thirsting for water, for electricity that can make a too-hot city bearable, is already a reality for people at the periphery of the world's political and literary imaginations. And yet there is no global war on this terror, which has almost completely engulfed the parts of the world less thought about.

The last time I bathed in Karachi, hours before my flight out, I used a bucket and a cup like millions of other people in the city. You use one bucket of water if you are not washing your hair and two if you are. You get your body wet, you soap up, and when that is done, you wash the soap away with water. There is no standing under the shower to cool yourself or to warm yourself as water runs all over you—water that is terribly scarce. It is the most efficient way of washing oneself. ✶

A NIGHT AT THE PICTURES
by Maxime Gérin

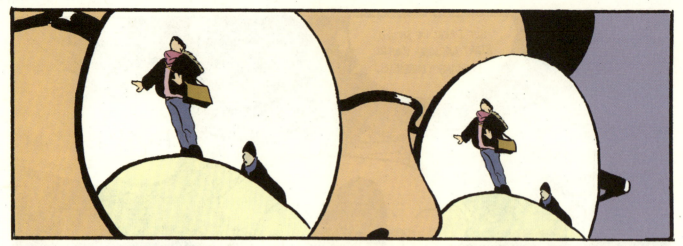

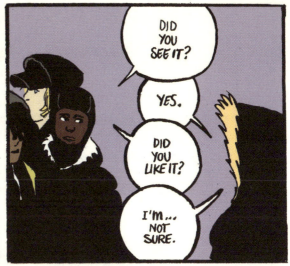

ADVENTURES IN JESUSLAND

CONFESSIONS FROM A FORMER MEMBER OF CAMPUS CRUSADE FOR CHRIST, THE MOST POWERFUL EVANGELICAL GROUP YOU'VE NEVER HEARD OF

by David J. Morris

It was Oscar Wilde who said that "the first duty in life is to assume a pose. What the second is, no one has yet discovered." My pose at Campus Crusade's 2024 Winter Conference in Anaheim, California, was the following: After two decades ensconced in godless academia, I was back to reconnect with my roots, to revisit the scene that had made me, to see what light the current evangelical movement could shed on Trump's America. Studying the schedule at a convention center down the road from Disneyland, and surrounded by kids half my age, I felt like a double agent, which is exactly what I was, in a sense. I'd spent a decade of my life as an evangelical going door-to-door for Jesus and appearing on Christian radio, and years as a Bible study leader in the most powerful evangelical group you've never heard of, the group whose leadership played a central role in ending *Roe v. Wade* and influenced the decision to invade Iraq. Now a credentialed member of the secular humanist establishment, I was everything I had been raised to believe was wrong with America.

I am what has become known as an "exvangelical," a loosely defined identity group that first emerged after Trump's 2016 election that is composed of young people who are unhappy with the church's embrace of militarism, along with its war on science, women, and queer people. While our exact numbers are unknown and our electoral impact is as yet unmeasured, exvangelicals are the vanguard of what pastors Jim Davis and Michael Graham, in their 2023 book, *The Great Dechurching: Who's Leaving, Why Are They Going, and What Will It Take to Bring Them Back?*, called "the largest and fastest religious shift in US history, greater than the First and Second

Illustrations throughout by Andrea Settimo

Great Awakenings and every revival in our country combined… but in the opposite direction."

Inside the convention hall, there were a thousand-odd seats, two camera pedestals, and a stage flanked by two large video screens. A clock on the screens counted down the minutes until the start of the first event, blandly titled "Session 1." Christian anthem rock by an artist I didn't recognize played over the sound system.

With less than a minute to go, the song abruptly switched to Tones and I's "Dance Monkey." The air shifted and I watched in awe as the doors to the ballroom were pried open, unleashing a flood of college students like a Civil War reenactment sponsored by Vans. The first skirmishers through held the doors open for a column of flag bearers. The University of Arizona was first, followed by Utah, Boise State, then Oregon State, then several flags I couldn't make out. The floor was soon awash in a sea of wholesome twentysomethings. I immediately recognized the evangelical look from my high school days: hoodies, black jeans, skate shoes, and messenger bags. I spotted several T-shirts of the officially approved Christian bands from my youth: Switchfoot, Jars of Clay, and P.O.D. The racial makeup looked to be 90 percent white, with occasional Asian American and Black students breaking up long lines of blond hair. The Oregon State flag bearer posted himself two rows away and climbed atop a chair, whipping his black-and-orange flag back and forth, as if he'd just stormed the ridge at Gettysburg.

The bedlam continued for several minutes before everyone rallied around their respective flags. Then a five-piece worship band mounted the stage and began what would turn into a rousing thirty-minute praise-and-worship set. They opened with "Praise," a drum-heavy anthem by a Charlotte, North Carolina, collective known as Elevation Worship. Soon enough, a substantial portion of the crowd was singing with their hands held aloft, as if to signal some sort of spiritual touchdown.

The words rang out, the drums thudding in my chest.

*Let everything that has breath
Praise the Lord
Praise the Lord*

Defenseless against the energy of the room, I was soon singing along, my hands in the air. I'd left this scene behind long ago, and yet through nostalgia's odd alchemy, I saw that nothing had changed. It was 1989 again. I'd had my fair share of life chapters: I'd joined the Marines, gone to grad school, moved to Mexico, worked as a war correspondent, been blown up by a roadside bomb, been diagnosed with PTSD, published two books. Yet a part of me remained that same scared kid who'd given his life to Christ at a beach bonfire years before. Lonely and wide-eyed, the future little more than a slogan printed on a public library poster: THROW OFF THE BOWLINES. SAIL AWAY FROM THE SAFE HARBOR. EXPLORE. DREAM. DISCOVER.

For the longest time I'd looked at my evangelical years as something like a phase. I'd come of age in the Reagan era, just as evangelicalism was becoming a major force in American politics. While I'd personally found Christianity noxious for many years, for my friends who'd remained, I had come to view the religion as similar to Douglas Adams's description of Earth in *The Hitchhiker's Guide to the Galaxy*—"mostly harmless." Now, in the Trump era, with the rise of a militant Christian nationalism whose leaders frequently describe Trump as a leader anointed by God and "an imperfect vessel for God's perfect will," it was starting to sink in that the religion of my youth was, among other things, a handmaiden to fascism.

These days, I teach at a supersize American university where many of the professors come from elite colleges in the Northeast, and whenever my past comes up in conversation and my colleagues discover that I used to be evangelical, things can get a bit weird. I did a stint in the Marine Corps before going to grad school, but somehow the idea that I had been a Bible thumper strikes them as infinitely stranger and more incongruous. I have learned to mostly ignore their incredulity over the years, sometimes dismissing my past as something like a drug phase, which it was, in a manner of speaking. (During my Crusade years I was repeatedly told that it was highly desirable to be "drunk on the Holy Spirit.")

I left the church in the late 1990s, along with my best friend from college, but it wasn't until he died of a sudden heart attack in 2022 that I finally felt free to reexamine my religious past. For reasons I've never understood, Ryan had quietly drifted back to Jesus after college, and, out of a sort of misguided politeness, we'd stopped talking about that part of our past, focusing instead on our replacement religion of surfing, a pursuit that seemed capable of delivering the same type of mystical highs as organized religion but with the added benefit of actually being fun. But with Ryan gone, I felt an urge to figure out what my lost faith had been about and what it had done to me—and by extension what it had done to America. In grad school, I'd come across a line from Jane Austen's *Persuasion*: "She had been forced into prudence in her youth, she learned romance as she grew older—the natural sequence of an unnatural beginning." In my fifties now, my prudence discarded long ago like an old letterman's jacket, I decided to look at my unnatural beginnings for the first time.

This is how you convert people to Christ: You take them to the beach, you build a fire, you invite a bunch of pretty girls, and you make sure that at least one guy with a guitar and a solid handle on some uplifting Jesus-based songs is there. Then, as the sun starts to set, and you're swimming in beauty and wonder, and you've sung some songs glorifying Him—maybe something by Keith Green or Michael W. Smith—you tell everyone to break off into pairs and go pray.

I don't remember the name of the girl who chose me as her prayer partner, but I do remember that she was nicer to me than any girl had ever been before. In a week, I'd be starting my freshman year of high school in suburban San Diego. She was a junior there, and I needed all the friends I could get.

"Heavenly Father…," she began, eyes closed. She was speaking in the soft flower-petal tone that Christians use when they pray out loud. "We just

want to thank you for the gift of this beautiful day…"

After we finished praying, the group reconvened, drawing closer to the fire as darkness fell around us. The guy with the guitar started up again, explaining the process by which one could accept Jesus into one's heart and make Him one's personal savior. For a teenager growing up in Southern California, there were so many dreams on offer (Top Gun, the Navy Fighter Weapons School, was down the road from my house), but none were so powerful as the dream of belonging.

And so I did what kids usually do: I followed the group. I accepted Jesus into my heart.

There were no thunderbolts, no visions, no saints with flaming swords in the sky, no brass trumpets echoing across the heavens, only a vague churchy feeling that started in my chest, catching in my throat. I closed my eyes, and after thirty seconds or so, the spell was cast. I was the property of Jesus.

It was 1985, the height of the Reagan era, and a rough time for my family. My parents had divorced three years before, and the harsh economic realities of being a single mother with three young kids were starting to settle over my mom. At times it felt like life itself was collapsing on us, the hand of fate squeezing us, as we'd been forced to move from a beautiful four-bedroom house at the edge of a canyon with a stream running down it, to a cramped condo on a busy street.

Shortly after moving, my brother Dan and I had launched a multipronged grow-up-quick scheme that involved us covertly subscribing to

Playboy magazine (beating Mom to the mailbox was crucial) and shoplifting cigarettes and porn from a local liquor store whose owners seemed indifferent to the miracles of the modern security camera. Dan and I talked frequently about how to score weed. LSD remained a far-off dream, like the Himalayas. A budding delinquent with an adrenaline streak, I gave a sermon in the form of a dare to my circle of BMX-riding friends: I would steal anything from the local organic market and sell it to them at half price.

Anything, I emphasized. *Anything.*

I was tough, mind you. An inside linebacker in the local Pop Warner league who'd grown up backpacking in Oregon, I'd been nourished on military legends spoon-fed to me by my Vietnam vet dad and a neighbor who was an instructor at Top Gun. Really, I was a white kid ignorant of consequences. I'd been swaddled in the blankets of suburbia and yet a fire burned inside me, lit by the spark of my parents' divorce. Nobody could hurt me. Nothing was my fault. I was ready to take life head-on. Punch its headlights out.

A few years before my freshman year, my older sister had been invited to a beach bonfire hosted by Campus Crusade, followed by my brother. A gifted wrestler and varsity football player with near-perfect grades, my brother was quickly identified as a leader by Crusade staff. He was the perfect fit for Crusade's "key man" strategy, by which they cultivated role models on campus and watched as the student body proceeded to follow their shining example to the Christian faith. My sister left the group after a few months, but by the time I began high school, my brother had risen in the ranks of Crusade and become a student Bible study leader, presiding over long sessions every Wednesday night in our tiny living room.

Not long after the beach bonfire I attended, an adult Bible study leader from Crusade named Mike picked me up at my house and drove me to a nearby strip mall with a Carl's Jr., a fast-food restaurant favored by Crusaders because the founder of the chain was an ardent supporter of various pro-life charities and made sure that a large American flag was flying at every location. Seated in a booth, I looked around, staring idly at the families surrounding us: older sons in their oddly authoritative Members Only jackets (this was the '80s, mind you); younger sons looking tortured and trussed-up like draft horses in their orthodontic headgear; middling, perpetually grossed-out and bored daughters sporting exquisitely large updos—hair lifted and arcing heavenward in a victorious topiary hedge sculpture as if to celebrate the sheer, unfettered Technicolor abundance of America.

Against all this cultural white noise sat Mike, a veritable bulwark of Midwestern restraint, armed only with his weathered polo shirt, metal ballpoint pen, and a fresh copy of a Campus Crusade pamphlet known as the "Four Spiritual Laws." To look at Mike was to take in a straightened version of America where the '60s had never happened, something I would later learn was no accident but was, in fact, an expression of Crusade's personnel policy and

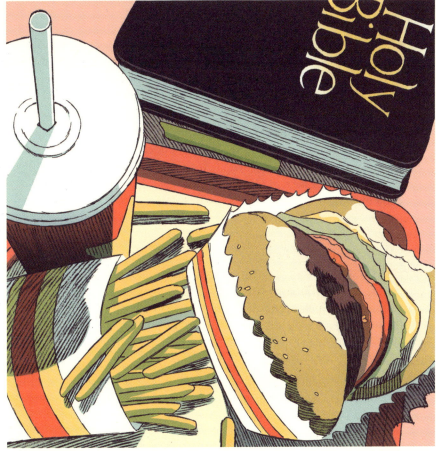

its grand vision for the world—a pre-feminist, pre-*Roe*, pre-Vietnam, Disneyfied America dominated by nuclear *Leave It to Beaver* families. Crusade was many things—a youth group, a social experiment, a Christian madrassa system—but at its core, it reflected the larger project of evangelicalism, which is to say it was a time machine fueled by a kind of nostalgia for a lost America that had never really existed. Back then, my impression of Mike was that he was something of a spiritual trainer, a coach putting a team together.

Because my eternal fate was at stake, Mike needed to make sure I had all my various celestial boxes checked, and as we sat there, wreathed in the smell of burger smoke, he walked me through Bill Bright's pamphlet version of the Gospel. (Law 1: "God loves you and offers a wonderful plan for your life.") This was, I would later learn, completely in keeping with Crusade's vision of itself as a Jesus-based guerrilla unit operating behind enemy lines, one that was "in the world, not of the world."

We said a brief prayer together, the awkward seconds ticking by, transformed by a sort of Bible-based magic into nervous holy expectation. All that was, all that is, all that would ever be ripped through my heart like a righteous tornado, sweeping me and all my dreams up into the sky. Technically, I'd been saved at the beach a few days before, but because this meeting was presided over by an adult, this time felt extra official.

My immortal fate secured, Mike explained to me that a freshman Bible study was starting up and asked if I'd like to join.

Looking back, I can see that Mike was asking me something else. This was a threshold moment, like someone handing you a pen to sign military enlistment papers. To balk now would be to court rejection by my brother and, by extension, my family. High school was a place crowded with invisible rules, the violation of any one of which threatened ostracism. The only rule I knew for sure was the obvious one: in the wilderness of high school, you needed a pack to run with.

As I would later learn, Campus Crusade for Christ was a student movement modeled in part on the very communist groups it opposed, groups that began with small, ideologically committed cells that would serve as cadres for the inevitable revolution to come. In order to withstand the threat of godless communism, America needed Christian kids with a case-hardened dedication to struggling against a belief system that threatened the very fabric of the nation.

Mike wasn't just asking me if I wanted to attend a once-a-week Bible study. He was asking me if I wanted to join an army, to become an insurgent, a revolutionary for Christ. Because he knew Dan, and knew that I was just a younger version of him, he surely knew the likelihood was high that I'd want

to join. Looking back, I sometimes wonder if Mike might have seen me for who I actually was: a bad kid who wanted desperately to be good, a kid whose broken home had left him open to whatever huckster happened along.

He was asking me if I wanted to have a crew, if I wanted to belong.

I nodded and told him I did. More than anything.

Bible study, led by Mike, was held at another student's house, a junior-varsity water polo player named Steffan. There were ten of us, all freshmen from good homes, impressionable as balls of Play-Doh. Most of us were athletes, though I was the only football player. Steffan's mother, who was from Sweden, baked a plate of cookies each time. I went every week for the entire semester, hungry for Steffan's mom's cookies and hungrier still for the Word of God. I could feel my life coming into focus.

That fall, Steffan and I started attending a local nondenominational church that met in an elementary school auditorium, and we talked frequently in his bedroom about the Bible and how to improve our walk with Jesus. I'd been a Christian for only a couple of months, but my previous life as a shoplifting punk seemed like it had been lived by a completely different person, a person I recognized as misguided, lost, and spiritually dead toward God. In Jesus I'd found something real and enduring. Just sitting down and reading the Scripture made me feel like I had been given access to the secrets of human existence, and that the author of the

universe was smiling down upon me, despite my zits and my mustard-gas breath.

In December, my Bible study went to the annual Winter Conference at Campus Crusade's world headquarters at Arrowhead Springs, a luxury resort in the mountains above Los Angeles that in its heyday had been a playground for Hollywood deities like Elizabeth Taylor and Humphrey Bogart. A weeklong program of carefully staged sermons, training seminars, and sing-alongs, it was like the annual sales convention for Jesus Incorporated. My conference admission was paid for by my parents and a Christian English teacher who'd taken an interest in me, and it was my first encounter with the stagecraft and high production values of a faith that took its cues from the movies as much as from the Bible.

Campus Crusade for Christ (now known as "Cru") is one of the largest parachurch organizations in the world, comprising an evangelical empire that stretches across the globe with more than nineteen thousand staff members working in 190 countries, and an annual revenue of over $700 million. While its core mission remains to convert students to Jesus, Cru maintains a vast network of ministries and political influence groups, including FamilyLife and Athletes in Action, along with the Christian Embassy in Washington, DC. In 1994, Cru's leaders cofounded the Alliance Defending Freedom, the legal advocacy group that successfully litigated the end of *Roe v. Wade* in 2022.

Founded in 1951 by Bill Bright, the clean-cut son of a cattle rancher from

Coweta, Oklahoma, who moved to Los Angeles in 1944 to pursue an acting career, Cru has carried the stamp of Hollywood into the present day. When he was disqualified from the military draft because of a burst eardrum, Bright began working with a friend who owned a candy company. After several weeks, Bright bought out his friend's stake, founding what would eventually be called Bright's California Confections. The business was an immediate success because of Bright's organizational acumen and indomitable drive for growth at all costs. It wasn't long before he found himself living the high life: driving a convertible, dressing in expensive suits, and riding horses in the Hollywood Hills. When he wasn't managing his growing business, Bright took acting classes at Hollywood Talent Showcase.

Though Bright had always been somewhat spiritually indifferent, the trajectory of his life was altered forever when he began attending the First Presbyterian Church of Hollywood at the urging of his landlord. It was the largest Presbyterian church in the US at the time, and according to the daughter of one of its former pastors, had "millionaires falling out of every pew." Bright had stumbled into a hotbed of revivalist energy and was suddenly surrounded by wealthy businessmen who seemed to be enjoying all God's blessings. Yet they all insisted that their relationship with Jesus was far more important than any of their worldly achievements. After a particularly powerful Bible study session where the topic of discussion was Paul's conversion on the road to Damascus, Bright returned home, got onto his knees, and accepted Jesus into his heart.

Following his conversion, Bright began practicing street evangelism with the College Department of Hollywood Presbyterian, traveling to towns across Southern California with paper tracts wrapped in cellophane. As Bright would later write in his 1987 book *Witnessing Without Fear: How to Share Your Faith with Confidence*, he was at first "scared to death" of talking to others about Jesus, but after a few early successes (including a convert who eventually went to seminary), Bright discovered that he had a knack for communicating the basics of the Gospel to strangers. By August 1945, Bright had come to believe that God was calling him to the ministry.

In the summer of 1946, at the urging of Henrietta Mears, an influential Hollywood Presbyterian leader who had also mentored the mega-evangelist Billy Graham, Bright enrolled in Princeton Theological Seminary. Uninspired by the curriculum at Princeton, Bright eventually transferred to Fuller, a new seminary in Pasadena, which allowed him to keep tabs on his candy business, which had struggled in his absence. In time, however, Bright became disillusioned with theological studies, declaring to a friend: "I'm not going

---

A PARTIAL LIST OF VERY SMALL TOWNS WITH THEIR OWN BOOKSTORES AND LIBRARIES

★ Monowi, Nebraska (~1 person)—Rudy's Library
★ Matinicus Isle, Maine (~85 people)—Matinicus Island Library
★ Bovill, Idaho (~136 people)—Bovill Community Library
★ Urueña, Spain (~204 people)—Librería Páramo
★ Leonard, North Dakota (~244 people)—Watts Free Library
★ Ingstrup, Denmark (~360 people)—Ingstrup Bogby
★ Hobart, New York (~410 people)—the eight bookstores of Hobart Book Village
★ Chelopek, Bulgaria (~425 people)—Izvor Bookshop
★ Redu, Belgium (~425 people)—the twenty-four bookshops and libraries of Redu Village
★ Tyringham, Massachusetts (~459 people)—Tyringham Library
★ Llanwrda, Wales (~464 people)—Pendleburys
★ Craigmont, Idaho (~509 people)—Craigmont Community Library
★ Montolieu, France (~829 people)—the fifteen bookshops of Montolieu Village
★ Weybridge, Vermont (~836 people)—Cotton Free Library
★ Borrby, Sweden (~840 people)—Antikvariat Bokhuset

—*list compiled by Lula Konner*

to be sitting here studying Greek when Christ comes!"

Like Mears and Billy Graham, Bright had become convinced that America was a nation chosen by the Lord to lead the globe in the struggle against godless international communism. After conferring with Mears, Bright sold his candy business and dropped out of seminary in order to start a nationwide ministry to college students. Bright envisioned this group as part of a crusade against communism and the growing secularization of college campuses, as "shock troops" in a Christian army. Echoing this militaristic theme, a colleague of Mears's suggested the name Campus Crusade for Christ.

Similar to Billy Graham, another Christian hawk kept out of the military by a minor medical condition, Bright viewed his work as opening up a domestic front in the Cold War. Unlike Graham, who preached to the masses, Bright zeroed in on the American college campus as the key battleground that would determine the fate of the globe. In a bulletin promoting his new organization, he warned, "Communism has already made deep inroads into the American campus, and unless we fill the spiritual vacuum of the collegiate world, the campus may well become America's 'Trojan Horse.'" As American troops were fighting communism abroad in Korea with bullets and bombs, Bright saw his mission as fighting communism at home—with preaching and pamphlets. "Christ or communism—which shall it be?" Bright was fond of saying. For his first military objective, he chose UCLA, the "little Red

schoolhouse" down the road from Hollywood Presbyterian.

Through the '50s and '60s, Bright's campus attack strategy evolved into a curious mixture of public spectacle and what one Christian writer called "religion gone free enterprise." Bright had an intuitive grasp of how to market to large groups of people and developed a dumbed-down version of the Gospel, which became the pamphlet I was introduced to decades later, "Four Spiritual Laws." He also didn't shy away from stealing the techniques of the enemy in his war against the moral permissiveness of the '60s counterculture. One "Berkeley Blitz" in 1967, where six hundred Crusaders "invaded" the college campus on a conversion drive, featured a Christian stage magician named André Kole. After learning of the 1969 gathering at Woodstock, Bright came up with the idea for "Explo '72" in Dallas, featuring a slate of popular musicians like Johnny Cash and Kris Kristofferson, intermixed with sermons by himself and Billy Graham. At this patriotic response to Woodstock, the South Vietnamese flag flew onstage, a conspicuous symbol of support for Nixon's war in Southeast Asia. The event, which some dubbed "Godstock," attracted eighty-five thousand high school and college students from across the nation.

As a youth organization unshackled by sludgy church doctrine, Crusade was uniquely positioned to shift its programming to combat the secularizing forces of any given era, a sort of religious avant-garde that was able to probe the front lines of the culture. With the end of the Vietnam War in 1975, it wasn't long before "secular humanism" replaced communism as the main enemy in the broader culture war. Despite Bright's claim that he'd "never been involved in politics," the 1980s saw Crusade parroting Republican talking points centered on "family values" issues such as abortion, homosexuality, teenage pregnancy, and the poisonous influence of feminism. On the tactical level, this translated to abstinence rallies led by Crusade staffers like Josh McDowell, seminars discussing biblical gender roles, and the Christian view of the AIDS crisis, which many evangelicals interpreted as God's punishment for the perversion of homosexuality.

It was at this stage, in an era dominated by Ronald Reagan's Cold War and sexual paranoia, that I entered the ranks of the Crusade army. In time, I would come to see that I'd been a pawn, a demographic entry in the larger body count, a casualty of Bill Bright's war for America's soul.

To call Campus Crusade a cult feels like a cheap shot, a lazy oversimplification. We wore no robes; we wrote no blank checks to the group; we were never made to sever ties with our families and move to a compound in Texas to collect firearms and await the apocalypse. And yet as I learned over the course of my first Crusade Winter Conference, just months after joining, this was no run-of-the-mill church youth group—this was a *movement*, a Christ-centered combat unit committed to spiritual warfare, and as such I was expected to conduct myself as a chaste soldier, a radical evangelizer who would help light my campus on fire for Jesus.

Shortly after I arrived at Arrowhead Springs, things got serious. After softening us up with motivational speakers, some surprisingly funny skits, and hours of praise and worship sing-along sessions, the boys and girls were separated into groups and ushered into different buildings for a full day of talks about the biblical views of gender and sexuality, led by Crusade staffers.

Premarital sex, they explained to a room full of adolescent boys, wasn't your average sin. It was a contagion that was polluting the nation, rotting it from within, aided by Madonna, George Michael, and a godless secular media. Further, as Christians personally selected by God to save America and, by extension, the world, we were now squarely in Satan's crosshairs and should expect—expect? no! feel joyously validated by!—the parade of carnal temptations that would henceforth follow us to the ends of the earth. If we strayed, there would be consequences: AIDS, gonorrhea (if we were lucky and God was feeling especially merciful that day), teenage pregnancy, porn addiction—plus a variety of nightmarish scenarios limited only by the human imagination. What's more, indulging in impure thoughts was, in God's eyes, functionally the same as having actual premarital sex, so I was in far deeper trouble than I'd imagined. Resisting the devil, they continued, required a 24-7 system of restraint and responsibility between brothers, and if we wanted to be Christian leaders, we should seek out "accountability partners" to help keep each other from straying.

I left the seminar room in a daze of conviction. All those sexual visions, the lurid parade of adolescent fantasies that had captivated me since I was twelve, were permanently out the window now, banished until that shimmering honeymoon night when I could join my bride in holy matrimony. All those sexual thoughts I'd harbored over the years had wounded God deeply. So deeply. How could I have been so callous? So unmindful of my Creator, when all those tears were running down Jesus's face?

As I would learn many years later, there is a substantial body of psychological research that indicates that if you're trying to ruin sex for people and damage them for the rest of their lives, forcing them at a young age into a strict regimen of thought control and social surveillance, of the sort that Crusade was promoting, is a really good way to do it—and I now think, with the benefit of hindsight, that injecting this much sexual fear into teenagers' hearts was not only unethical but genuinely evil. In his pioneering study of mind control in communist China, *Thought Reform and the Psychology of Totalism: A Study of "Brainwashing" in China*, the psychiatrist Robert Jay Lifton argues that "by defining and manipulating the criteria of purity, and then by conducting an all-out war on impurity, the ideological totalists create a narrow world of guilt and shame. This is perpetuated by an ethos of continuous reform, a demand that one strive permanently and painfully for something which not only does not exist but is in fact alien to the human condition."

The problem with totalist movements like Crusade is that while they market themselves as wholesome youth groups, they often traffic in a warlike rhetoric that echoes the paranoia of the McCarthy era—a world divided into realms of black and white, good and evil, pure and impure. And as I learned at my first Winter Conference, you were either all in or you were all out. The last thing I wanted to do was disappoint my brother, Mike, Steffan, and the rest of my Bible study, so whatever doubts I may have harbored, inside I knew I had no choice—I was in. All in. I had to be.

My junior year Steffan and I were tapped to lead a Bible study of our own. My brother had graduated the previous spring and gone off to glory at UCLA, the birthplace of Crusade. God's plan was working; new leaders were needed. To be chosen like this was to show everyone in my life that I was following in my brother's footsteps.

This promotion came down from Mike as he was driving me to one of our customary Carl's Jr. meetings one afternoon. "God has big plans for you and your brother. But Dan is gone now and it's time for you to step up." Weeks later, as I looked out over the bright young faces of my freshman Bible study, my fears for the future and my feelings of apartness dissolved. I was raising up the next generation of Christian men.

For the first time in my life, I felt useful and important. I'd found my place.

The only problem with this was that it wasn't true. I hadn't really found my place, and with my brother gone, the pressure to perform and to live up to a certain Christian ideal was gone too. After the sugar high of my conversion, my faith hadn't deepened, and I could feel myself starting to lose interest in Crusade's version of Christianity, which at times seemed like a glorified pyramid scheme—the focus was always on numbers and bringing in new members to the group using the "Four Spiritual Laws."

Steffan, by contrast, had embraced this ethos wholeheartedly, and began insisting that we forgo eating and spend our entire lunch period sharing our faith with our classmates instead. Crusade had stopped my shoplifting and cigarette smoking, but beyond that, it didn't seem all that useful as a lifestyle. Mostly, it was a giant buzzkill, a police roadblock on the fun interstate. Added to this, I was struggling in math, a subject that had always been my brother's forte. I'd long been seen as my brother's protégé—an idea reinforced by Mike—but as the Ds and Fs piled up, I learned to recognize the look of disappointment on my teachers' faces when they realized that, unlike my brother, I was no whiz kid.

By the end of my junior year, I'd been demoted to sophomore algebra, which I proceeded to flunk, mostly out of stark-raving boredom. (Let x find itself, I reasoned.) After word of this got around, Mike took me back to Carl's Jr., which had long since lost any meaning as a restaurant and become an off-campus vice principal's office.

"Struggling in your classes isn't a sin, but Christian leaders shouldn't have report cards full of Ds and Fs," he explained. Mike was reinforcing Crusade's "key man" method: my life was supposed to be a beacon to others, a veritable lighthouse perched atop a rocky shore whose lamp cut through the fog of iniquity.

When I talked to my brother about this one day during a weekend visit to UCLA, he told me that learning wasn't really the point. The point was the discipline itself—it was a way of honoring the Lord. To my searching mind, this seemed like a hollow, robotic faith. Life, intended to be a wide-ranging experiential symphony, reduced to a single note played over and over again: *duty, duty, duty.* My freshman year, at one of the very safe parties Crusade threw, a mutual friend had put on Huey Lewis's "Hip to Be Square" and publicly dedicated it to my brother ("Now I'm playing it real straight. / And yes I cut my hair. / You might think I'm crazy. / But I don't even care. / 'Cause I can tell what's going on. / It's hip to be square"). I just laughed at the song, but later it struck me as apt. My brother had always had this "model citizen" way about him that I resented, but I didn't yet have the eyes to see that our differences were at core more temperamental than theological. Rules and order and the strictures of faith suited him, gave him an ease with religion that I lacked.

The larger problem I had was less religious than hormonal. I'd fallen hard for a cheerleader at our rival high school who was involved in the Crusade chapter there. Liz, known as "Lizard" or "Reptile" to her friends, was blond, zany, and optimistic, a vision of clean Christian California. Her parents were divorced, like mine—a rare thing in '80s San Diego—which served to cement our bond. Our romance unfurled in my mind like a Hollywood film.

Because Liz was a cheerleader, she was considered a "key woman" in Jesusland and was expected to be "above reproach," in accordance with 1 Timothy 3:2 After a group retreat where Liz and I had been spotted briefly holding two fingers together (even in our fervid state we wouldn't have dared to hold whole hands), she broke the news to me. Her Bible study leader had taken her aside and explained that Jesus had big plans for her and that she wasn't yet ready for a relationship.

"The Lord comes first," she explained.

Then, senior year, I got a three-hundred-dollar speeding ticket that required me to quit the football team and get a job at the mall to pay for it. Losing my wonder-boy status had a curiously dispiriting effect on me, and before I knew what was happening, I had failed almost all my classes. I was allowed to attend the graduation ceremony that spring even though I was two classes shy of my degree.

When I walked off the stage and uncorked my diploma tube, I saw that it was empty. Some metaphors write themselves.

In time, I was able to claw my way out of the hole I'd dug for myself. I got a job at a nearby television factory and took remedial math at a junior college. With the credits I earned there, I was provisionally admitted to Texas A&M the next fall and got involved with the Crusade chapter there.

As part of my admissions agreement, I was expected to join the A&M Corps of Cadets, a full-time ROTC program that functioned like a military academy within the larger university. The structure was good for me. My grades rose. For a couple of years, I colored within the lines, dutifully attending a cadet Bible study led by a Crusade staffer who was also a reserve army officer. Then a rather predictable thing happened: My junior year, I took a philosophy class and I began to reconsider my faith. I read some existentialism and started keeping a journal. The seeds of doubt, planted in high school, bloomed.

The disillusionments of high school had tested my spirit but spared my faith, but what finally separated me from Christianity was a growing boredom and a kind of emptiness when I realized that my brother was right—the discipline of faith was the point, not any of the supposed truths of Christianity. Religion is where the irrational meets the political.

My senior year, I enrolled in an intellectual history class, along with Ryan, my best friend from Crusade, where we were introduced to the Antichrist himself, in the form of Friedrich Nietzsche. Nietzsche opened the door to a banquet of questions, and within a year the whole core of my thinking had shifted dramatically. I saw that Christianity was little more than a system of control with a toxic history, not a serious theory about how the universe worked.

I'd been lied to. Worse yet, I'd spread this lie to others, participated in its propagation on an industrial scale. Quietly and without fanfare, Ryan and I stopped attending Crusade meetings and spent our free time reading and discussing philosophy. That summer I reported to Marine Officer Candidates School at Quantico, Virginia. Years later, I would see this for what it was: another coded attempt to prove myself to my family and a way to beat my brother at his own game—in the process distinguishing myself by the mark of martial discipline. We may leave religions, but they don't leave us. As the psychologist Erik Erikson observed in his landmark 1950 study *Childhood and Society*, "The individual unconsciously arranges for variations of an original theme which he has not learned either to overcome or to live with" and manages his anxiety by "meeting it repeatedly and of his own accord."

At the end of my junior year, my brother graduated from UCLA, joined Campus Crusade staff, and departed on a yearslong mission to Russia. Somehow, despite my spirited rejection of Christianity, a residue of shame remained. There was a time when I'd believed in clean getaways, the idea that you could just start over, reboot your existential operating system; but when you give yourself completely to a cause, as I'd done with Crusade, it's impossible to just walk away. Part of you stays there forever, trapped in the amber of memory.

Nearly thirty years would pass before I told my brother that I was a traitor to the faith.

Back in Jesusland, inside the cavernous Anaheim convention hall for Cru's 2024 Winter Conference, things had settled a bit. The uplifting music had stopped and a Korean-Mexican-American pastor from Sacramento was up onstage, explaining to us the importance of acknowledging the Lord as Our Father. The pastor was a gifted orator, and I could feel my heart moving in the old holy ways, and I could sense certain questions stirring that I'd long ago dismissed as the province of idiots. Christianity was, as I'd explained to my brother a few months prior, "a moral catastrophe and perhaps the greatest conspiracy ever inflicted on the human race."

But here in a sea of happy believers, who exactly was I to judge? Like any religion, Christianity was just a dream, after all. Everyone deserves a dream, something to console them when life takes a turn for the worse, something to get them through the night, as Frank Sinatra put it. The questions kept swirling, going nowhere in particular, and when I finally snuck a look at my phone, it was nearly midnight. And yet I wasn't tired. No one was.

A lot had happened since I'd left Crusade: the internet, social media, Bush, 9/11, Iraq, Trump, the end of *Roe v. Wade*. The evangelical movement, which had begun as a wholesome American project to spread a stripped-down version of Christianity, had metastasized into a pro-fascist interest group. The resort at Arrowhead Springs had been sold in the early '90s and Cru's headquarters relocated to Orlando. Bill Bright had died in 2003, but not before signing off on a final crusade, affixing his name to what became known as the "Land Letter," a missive sent to President Bush encouraging him to invade Iraq, claiming, with the perverted logic common to all fundamentalists, that God approved of the king's war. With Bright gone, Campus Crusade began a slow process of rebranding, and in 2011, it changed its name to "Cru," a move that drew the ire of some conservative Christians, who viewed the deletion of "Crusade" as a concession to those who felt the name was a bit too reminiscent of the actual Crusades, which had resulted in the deaths of millions of Muslims.

Throughout his life, Bright had always insisted that he'd "never been involved in politics," but looking back on my time in Cru, I could see that this was a lie. At every stage of its history, Cru had championed the conservative cause du jour, creating what amounted to a guerrilla academy for the American culture wars. In the '50s, the cause had been anti-communism. In the '60s, it was fighting the antiwar counterculture and sex, drugs, and rock and roll. In the '80s, Crusade had taken up the cause of "family values," brainwashing me and my friends about the horrors of premarital sex, abortion, and homosexuality. In the Trump era, Bright's project continued to bear fruit in the work of the Alliance Defending Freedom, litigating the end of *Roe v. Wade* in the Supreme Court.

Looking over the 2024 Winter Conference schedule, it appeared that Cru was engaged in the culture wars yet again, albeit in an unexpected way. While the second afternoon of the conference had the traditional "Day of Outreach" to the local community, interspersed between the main sessions were events like a "BIPOC Lunch" and a series of discussion groups aimed at Asian American students. On a nearby table lay books for sale. *Indigenous Theology and the Western Worldview: A Decolonized Approach to Christian Doctrine* sat next to *Redemptive Kingdom Diversity: A Biblical Theology of the People of God*, along with other books about how to run an inclusive ministry.

Could it be? Had Cru gone woke?

Later that week, I spoke to John G. Turner, a historian of religion at George Mason University and author of a history of Cru, who explained to me that in the wake of George Floyd's death there had been some division in Cru over how to respond to the nationwide calls for racial justice. A letter had been sent to Cru's leadership, demanding change. "I think Bill Bright's successors have been less interested in public right-wing politics than he was," he explained. "My sense is that Cru's leadership attempted to do enough to satisfy those who cared about racial justice without alienating those who reject those moves. And given the current political and theological landscape, that balancing act has become much harder." It's difficult to know what Bright would've made of Donald Trump, though Bright had no problem with Richard Nixon or the American war in Vietnam, and it's likely he would've found a way to support Trump, as most evangelicals have.

They say the personal is political. Ask any Marine who lost his legs in Iraq, or a pregnant fifteen-year-old girl in Texas. For me, there was never an opportunity to unlearn Cru's political system and its claims on my body. I never discovered how to rewrite my emotional software. To this day, romance carries with it the stain of sin, an echo of Liz, a lingering expression of what Robert Jay Lifton called the "shaming milieu." When you're programmed as a kid to believe that physical intimacy is literally the devil's handiwork, you don't just wake up one day and have a healthy sex life. I scarcely dated in college, fearing the reproach of an invisible Bible study leader. I never married.

My plan in coming to the conference had been to do a sort of reconnaissance, to get a sense of how Cru had changed by standing back and watching. And yet here I was, singing and clapping along like the collegiate believer who had long since passed away. As I would learn later, talking with some staffers, Cru had undoubtedly changed, its politics tacking with the winds of the zeitgeist for once, but its ability to draw people to Jesus and make them feel accepted and loved hadn't changed at all. Driving the music was the same beat I'd heard on that San Diego beach decades before, that singular commandment stamped on the drumhead: *Belong. Belong. Belong.*

I turned to the woman sitting next to me, whom I'd met earlier in the evening: an Oregon State senior named Ava, majoring in psychology. Ava, it turned out, was going to grad school the next fall to become a Christian counselor. Driving to Anaheim, I'd assumed that I'd be greeted with suspicion and maybe even asked to leave. But Ava and all the students I talked to all had such warmth. It just flowed out of them like a holy pheromone.

"What are you hoping to get out of the conference?" Ava asked.

The two of us chatted for a few minutes, eventually exchanging prayer requests, a transaction that was for me both an obvious lie and a charming gesture at the same time.

An unmarried academic in a big American city, I'd forgotten that community could be so easy. In a time of social rupture, an era dominated by distrust and skepticism and paranoia, I could feel my heart melting. It struck me then that the name change to Cru, i.e., "Crew," was apt. On some deeper level, I knew this was a nostalgia ambush I was undergoing, not a rebirth of faith, but why not enjoy the reverie, I reasoned, and see where it led? Sure, Cru had hijacked my youth and stolen my sexuality, but now wasn't the time to dwell on such matters. I have always been a soldier of memory, and I knew I would go back and count the costs, replay the scene.

A few minutes later, the music stopped. The house lights came up. It was time to go, the reverie over. I walked back to my hotel room alone, my steps still marking the beat. A seductive lie in the form of a code, still broadcasting after all these years and likely to call out forever and ever, amen: *Belong. Belong. Belong.* ✱

CHARLES JOHNSON

[WRITER, CARTOONIST, PHILOSOPHER]

"THERE ARE ALWAYS COUNTEREXAMPLES OF HEROISM, SURVIVAL, AND RESILIENCE. THAT IS WHAT I MEAN BY RESPONSIBLE FICTION."

Places Charles Johnson's drawings appeared when he was a young cartoonist:
A catalog for a magic company
Mimeographed church bulletins
The Daily Egyptian
The Southern Illinoisan

For more than forty years, Charles Johnson has been a fixture on the literary scene in Seattle, along with two other African American writers, both transplants: the late Octavia Butler and the late August Wilson. Like they did, Johnson has produced work his own way, avoiding the expectations that many would impose on a Black writer. This journey of distinction for Johnson began in 1982, with his second published novel, Oxherding Tale, a quasi–slave narrative and rogue's narrative steeped in both Eastern and Western philosophy. Johnson has since published twenty books, and has received numerous accolades for his work, including the National Book Award for Fiction for his novel Middle Passage, a MacArthur Fellowship, and a Guggenheim Fellowship.

Born in 1948, Johnson grew up in the Chicago suburb of Evanston, home of Northwestern University. He first came to prominence as a political cartoonist and illustrator when he was still a teenager: At the age of fifteen, he was a student of cartoonist

Illustration by Kristian Hammerstad

and mystery writer Lawrence Lariar's. In 1969, he attended a lecture by Amiri Baraka, which inspired him to draw a collection of racial satire titled *Black Humor,* which was published by Johnson Publishing Company, the publisher of the widely read magazines *Ebony* and *Jet. A second collection of political satire,* Half-Past Nation-Time, *was published by Aware Press in 1972. During this period, Johnson earned a BS degree in journalism at Southern Illinois University. He then went on to earn his MA in philosophy at the same university, while taking fiction-writing classes with the legendary John Gardner. In 1976, Johnson joined the faculty in the Department of English at the University of Washington, where he taught until his retirement in 2009.*

I sat down with Johnson on a mild afternoon at Third Place Books in Seattle's Ravenna neighborhood, not far from Johnson's home. To take advantage of the weather, we opted for an outside table, where we enjoyed good coffee, good food, and good conversation. Preferring the nickname Chuck, Johnson is confident but humble and soft-spoken; his eyes sparkled with intelligence. He keeps his hair in a short Afro, completely gray, with a well-groomed halter-like connected beard, also gray. As we spoke, I observed something of the scholar about him, in the way that his spectacles dangled against his chest from an elastic cord encircling his neck.

—Jeffery Renard Allen

I. TWIN TIGERS

THE BELIEVER: How do you define yourself as a writer?

CHARLES JOHNSON: I don't call myself a writer. One of my books is titled *I Call Myself an Artist.*

BLVR: So you're an artist?

CJ: Yes.

BLVR: I'm going to phrase the question differently. Would you call yourself an experimental writer in the usual sense of whatever that term means: someone seeking to innovate, break rules?

CJ: I'm a philosophical writer because my background is in philosophy. I work with different forms and genres to realize, I hope, fiction that is philosophically engaging and capable of transforming our perception in some way. As for experimentation, Clarence Major—he's an experimental writer. And Ishmael Reed is as well. I'm not an experimental writer. The thing about it, too, is I started out as a cartoonist, as a visual artist and journalist. When I was in my teens, drawing was my first passion. Still is to a large extent. So I'll say I'm an artist. Today I might be doing visual art. Tomorrow I might be doing literary art. Last night I got together with some old buddies for Wednesday-night martial arts class. We've been doing this since 1981, training together, every Wednesday night. As an artist, there are different ways to express myself.

BLVR: You see martial arts as a form of self-expression?

CJ: It is. Well, when I was young, back in my teens, it seemed to me reasonable that I needed to develop myself in three areas, to the best of my ability. One was mind, one was body, one was spirit. For mind, I chose philosophy, which seduced me when I was an eighteen-year-old undergraduate at Southern Illinois University. Even though I was a journalism major, I stayed on and got my master's in philosophy. And then I kept going until I got my PhD in philosophy at Stony Brook University. So that was for mind. For body, I chose martial arts when I was nineteen. My first dojo was in Chicago, and was a little like a monastery. I began working out there, without knowing anything about the world of martial arts. It was a cult in the sense that the members of the school blindly followed the leader, but I didn't know it. This was during the time of the Chicago Dojo Wars, as they were called. My school was in competition with another school, run by a flamboyant guy who called himself Count Dante. Count Dante. You'd see him sometimes in the martial arts magazines. [*Laughing*] I don't know anything about his system or his style, but I do know that somebody from his school came by our school one night to invite us to participate in a tournament. He was really arrogant. He said, *If you think you're up to it, you can come try out in our tournament.* Our master wasn't there that night, but when he found out, he told all of us, *Somebody comes in like that again, tell them to leave. They don't leave, you go over here to the wall and take down a weapon. Give one to him and you take one.* Now, these were traditional weapons, Chinese weapons, you know—spears and staffs and swords. *And if he won't leave, kill him.* I'm thinking, What? He's telling us to kill. He said killing was within our rights when somebody invaded our space and we gave them fair warning. It was a rough school. I thought some nights I'd die in there, but I stuck with it until I got my first promotion. Southern Illinois University was about six hours away. I couldn't keep up at that dojo, but I continued with karate on campus. I went through three karate systems, you know, and then settled on Choy Lee Fut kung fu in 1981 when I went down to San Francisco to work on a Black PBS TV show called *Up and Coming.* Wherever I lived, I always looked for a school to train at.

When I came out this way, I discovered there were branches of the Choy Lee Fut school, one here in Seattle and one over in Bremerton. I was able to continue training here in Seattle until the one school here closed. After it closed, our teacher, Grandmaster Doc-Fai Wong, gave me and a buddy permission to start classes in Seattle. He gave us the name Twin Tigers. We taught for ten years. My buddy passed away a couple of years ago, but I still get together with a couple of old friends on Wednesday nights. We go through our empty-hand sets. Then we go through our weapons sets so we don't forget them. Choy Lee Fut has over 130 sets because it combines three martial arts lineages, one from Mr. Choy, one from Mr. Lee, and another one from Chan Yuen-Woo, who taught Fut Gar. Choy Lee Fut is one of the old Shaolin monastery fighting systems.

So mind, body, and spirit. For spirit I chose Buddhadharma. Buddhadharma, for training and cultivating the spirit. I was born a cradle Christian, and I still am to a degree. But the Buddhadharma offered something that was good for me when I was young.

BLVR: How old were you when you were introduced to Buddhism?

CJ: Fourteen.

BLVR: And how did it happen?

CJ: Back then, my mother was an avid reader and a member of three book clubs. One of the books that came into the house was on yoga. I read a chapter on meditation and afterward I told myself, Let me see what this is like. For half an hour, I practiced the method of meditation described in this chapter. It was amazing. My consciousness changed during that half hour of focusing. I'd never done that before, and the experience affected me for life. It made me more conscious of the operations of my own mind and it also made me have more compassion for people around me, more empathy. I began to approach the study of Buddhism and other Eastern philosophies in a scholarly way and read everything I possibly could. As both an undergraduate and a graduate student, I took courses in Hinduism and Taoism.

BLVR: That was back in the '60s?

CJ: Yes, back then, when there was all kinds of stuff floating around.

BLVR: You mean people like Alan Watts?

CJ: Yes, Alan Watts. And D. T. Suzuki was very important at the time because he interpreted Japanese Zen for a Western audience. He did it in a particular way to make it intellectually interesting to academics. Something I didn't care for was what I call "fuzzy-bunny Buddhism," the feel-good stuff. With Buddhism, you must get it right. It's not any old thing you make it out to be.

Buddhism grows and evolves in every country it goes to. It has a particular flavor here in America, because Americans are very interested in politics and social justice. I think this is because we draw on Christianity's emphasis on the social gospel about changing the world that had such an impact on Martin Luther King Jr. So there is that quality to the American Buddhist convert community.

BLVR: What impact has Buddhism had on literature in our country?

CJ: There's very little written about the spiritual register in our literature, especially in fiction. Truth to tell, I don't know American poetry as well as I know the fiction.

BLVR: In terms of my question, I'm thinking about two

aspects of American fiction: the tradition that deals with spiritual questions, and the tradition that deals with philosophical questions. Would you say there's also a lack in terms of philosophical fiction?

CJ: Going all the way back to the nineteenth century, Americans have been anti-intellectual, very suspicious of intellectuals, particularly of European intellectuals. The emphasis is on the common man, so to speak, right? You see that bias starting with Jefferson in the eighteenth century. The century that followed gave us philosophically interesting writers like Hawthorne, Melville, and Emerson the transcendentalist. But then something happens around the turn of the twentieth century with the rise of naturalism. Our writers become less philosophical and less focused on the spiritual register. Part of that has to do with the fact that naturalism in fiction is a subset of naturalism in science and sociology. Naturalism does not involve spiritual experiences. Of course, naturalism offers a deterministic view of the world. Biology, the environment, cause and effect—that's all that really matters in the naturalistic orientation.

I think there's more to human experience—and that experience is much, much larger than that.

In the twentieth century we don't have much in the way of a spiritual/philosophical register in American fiction. William Gass, a trained and important philosopher, was one such writer. My former teacher John Gardner wasn't a trained philosopher, but he explored ideas like Sartrean existentialism in his novel *Grendel*.

And then among Black writers I would say that Jean Toomer is philosophically interesting. Toomer was a follower of Gurdjieff. I wrote a preface for Toomer's collection of aphorisms, *Essentials*, which was edited by the late Rudolph Byrd. Richard Wright is also interesting, even if he was largely a Marxist thinker.

BLVR: I would argue that Wright became an existentialist.

CJ: He was by the time he moved to France. Of course, over there he hung out with Sartre and Simone de Beauvoir. And he started getting into phenomenology. He owned a copy of a philosophical work by the founder of phenomenology, Edmund Husserl. I read, in fact, that he worked with it so much he had to get another cover for it because it was falling apart.

Ralph Ellison is also worthy of attention as a philosophical writer. In *Invisible Man* he addresses Marxism and existentialism, then plays on Freud, and so forth.

BLVR: Ellison seems to define the idea of race and racism as ultimately absurdist in an existentialist sense.

CJ: His novel is absurdist. Those writers to me are the ones I found to have a philosophical kind of register. Still not, though, a spiritual register. Not in Wright, not in Ellison. Only in Toomer.

II. A BIRD IN THE BUSH

BLVR: Please talk some about how you became interested in writing fiction.

FASHION ANACHRONISMS IN FAMOUS MOVIES

★ *Braveheart* (set in the thirteenth century)—kilts
★ *Unforgiven* (set in the nineteenth century)—belt loops
★ *Quadrophenia* (set in 1965)—Motörhead shirt
★ *X-Men: First Class* (set in 1962)—miniskirts
★ *Pride and Prejudice* (set around 1790)—Wellington boots
★ *Dirty Dancing* (set in the 1960s)—denim short shorts
★ *Amadeus* (set in the eighteenth century)—zippers
★ *Django Unchained* (set in 1858)—sunglasses; cigarette holders
★ *The Godfather* (set in the 1950s)—hippie fashion
★ *Marie Antoinette* (set in the eighteenth century)—solid-colored fabric; nineteenth-century jewelry
★ *Glory* (set in 1863)—a digital wristwatch
★ *The Great Gatsby* (set in the 1920s)—pink fur
★ *Pompeii* (set in the first century)—stirrups
★ *Indiana Jones and the Last Crusade* (set in 1938)—M43 field caps; World War II combat medals
★ *Gladiator* (set in the second century)—a corset

—*list compiled by Su Ertekin-Taner*

CJ: Well, I didn't enjoy journalism, since I wanted to be in philosophy instead. However, it was good training. Before World War II, how did writers learn their craft? They learned it from newspapers, for the most part. I was also an avid reader because stories fed my imagination as a cartoonist and illustrator. When I was in high school, I made a point of reading a book a week, outside of class, and then sometimes it would be two books a week. Another week it might be three books. By the end of my freshman year of college, I still thought I wasn't reading enough.

BLVR: What years were you in college?

CJ: I started in '66, and I graduated in '71. I took an extra, fifth year because I was doing all these philosophy courses while doing my bachelor's degree in journalism. And then two years for a master's degree in philosophy, and then three years at Stony Brook for the PhD.

The interesting thing about that period, of course, is that it was during the time of the Black Power movement and the Black Arts movement.

BLVR: Did you have any involvement with any of those Black Power or Black Arts movement groups, like OBAC [the Organization of Black American Culture], in Chicago?

CJ: I was not involved with any group, although I had a couple of friends who were Black Panthers, including a poet friend of mine named Alicia. For a time, I became Marxist, from '71 to maybe '73. My master's degree was a study of Wilhelm Reich as influenced by Marx and Freud. But I was not involved in the Black Arts. Again, I was a journalist and a cartoonist. I didn't know many writers or poets. Those were not the people I was hanging out with. However, in 1970, when I was twenty-two, I decided to write a novel about the martial arts kwoon I had gone to in Chicago, Chi Tao Chuan of the Monastery. That first novel was called "The Last Liberation." I wrote the book over the summer.

BLVR: You never published that one.

CJ: It was a learning novel, because then I wrote five more novels in two years, teaching myself what I hadn't known in the previous book for the next book. One of those books was an early version of *The Middle Passage*. I started the research when I was still an undergraduate, because there were essentially no Black teachers at Southern Illinois University. However, a Black visiting professor came from St. Louis and taught a course, and I took it. I asked him if I could do my research on the Atlantic slave trade, and he told me I could. But I wasn't ready to write the novel yet, because I hadn't immersed myself in fiction enough.

Around that time, Black graduate students formed the first survey course on Black history at Southern Illinois University. And one of my friends, Thomas Slaughter, a graduate student in philosophy, and some other Black students brought Amiri Baraka to campus. I was one of ten undergraduates who Tom selected to be discussion-group leaders. For the past year or so, I had been avidly reading everything I could about Black history and culture. Then one time in my discussion group, one of the grad students in history was lecturing on the Middle Passage. I remember sitting in this big auditorium when he put up that cross-section of the slave ship with dozens of the slaves arranged in spoon fashion. That burned itself into my mind. I hadn't seen an image this startling before. So when the visiting Black professor came from St. Louis, I did some research under his direction.

BLVR: How did you develop as a writer?

CJ: By the time I started my seventh book, *Faith and the Good Thing*, I had taught myself everything I could about writing fiction. One novel I finished was called "Youngblood" and it was about a Black musician. I had a friend who was a musician, and he taught me how to play the piano for this novel. That book was accepted for publication with a start-up publisher in New York. By that time, however, I had started working on *Faith*, with John Gardner looking over my shoulder. I remember I said to him, "Look, I have three chapters of this book, and I don't know if I can finish it, but it's radically different from the other six books I've written." The other six were all naturalistic, because I was reading Baldwin, John A. Williams, Richard Wright, and other writers like that. But with *Faith and the Good Thing*, I got to a place where I could write a philosophical book. It's a tale, a total break from the other books.

I asked Gardner, "What should I do? Should I let them publish 'Youngblood'?" The publisher liked the book because it reminded them of Baldwin. Well, I'm not Baldwin. I was developing my own vision. Gardner said something very wise. He said, *If you feel you're gonna have to climb over it later, don't publish it.* So I wrote them. I said, "I'm sorry, but I don't want to publish the novel." That was like a bird in the hand as opposed to, you know, one in the bush here. I didn't know if I could finish *Faith*, but I did. Gardner got me his agent and it came out a year later. I wrote it in nine months.

The other six books I wrote in ten weeks, one every ten weeks for two years. *Faith* I spent nine months on. I thought it was a long period of time to spend on anything, but I learned better after that, because with the next novel, *Oxherding Tale*, I began to see what was at stake.

When you set out to do something, and you're a literary writer, you have to recognize that this book could be your last will and testament in language. Every book of fiction I've done has transformed me in some way, from the research to the writing. You write trying to get it right, not for fame and fortune. The novel is a form of communication through the best technique and the best thought and feeling that I can bring to bear. *Oxherding Tale* took five years to write. *Middle Passage* took six years. *Dreamer* took seven. Each book is the best I can give in terms of whatever I've learned in the way of craft, human experience. That's why art matters.

III. "JACK KIRBY WAS MY HERO"

BLVR: Tell me about how you started publishing your comics.

CJ: My freshman year at Southern Illinois University, I sold six scripts to Charlton Comics. I took the stories I had done in high school and turned those into one-page comics. And they bought them, although they didn't have me illustrate them, because they had an in-house illustrator. I was seventeen years old. I had finished a correspondence course with Lawrence Lariar when I fifteen years old and still in high school. He was a well-known cartoon editor at the time.

Around that time, one of my buddies was doing catalog illustrations for a magic company in Chicago. So I said, "Well, I'm going to work for this guy." I went and showed him my drawings from high school, and I got a job. They paid me to draw six magic tricks for their catalog. I still have that first dollar. I framed it. It's in my study right now. Because that's the day I got paid to do art. See, my passion as a cartoonist was to publish as much as I could, wherever I could.

You know how churches put out a mimeographed bulletin for members? I went and talked to whoever did that at my church. I said, "Let me do one of those." They did. I looked for every opportunity, because I wanted to see my work in print. That was the main thing.

When I started college, I went right to the campus newspaper, *The Daily Egyptian*, showed them my swatch. I went on to draw hundreds of cartoons for them. I did everything. I even drew illustrations for ads. Then I went up to the town paper, *The Southern Illinoisan*, showed them my swatch, and I started doing editorial cartoons for them. My mindset as a cartoonist was to sell my work anyplace I could. Cartoons are not a way to make a living, not unless you get a syndicated strip, which is rare. But money didn't become a serious issue for me until I had a kid and had to support a family.

BLVR: Because Afrofuturism is a trend, there's been a lot of interest in going back and looking at Black cartoons. I remember reading things like Luke Cage, Green Lantern, and Black Panther as a kid in the '60s and '70s.

CJ: That was '66. That was the first issue. Stan Lee and Jack Kirby created the Black Panther for an issue of *The Fantastic Four*. I remember the year, because that was the same year I went off to college. I was reading all the Marvel comics and collecting them. I know they'd be worth a fortune now, those original issues, and I have few that are in mint condition. But I had started collecting comics in the '50s.

BLVR: Did those cartoons make any impression on you?

CJ: Oh, Jack Kirby was my hero. I started reading his comics in '55 when I was seven years old. What he did was like nobody else, and he was prolific. Everything that guy did—from the late '30s all the way up to maybe the '90s, when he died—is amazing. As I see it, his best period was from about '55 to '65. He worked everywhere and for everybody. He had to go to war. He came back. He did many years of romance comics. He had his own comics company at one point. But then around '65, he started to repeat imagery, started drawing the same thing over and over.

BLVR: You grew up in the '50s, while I grew up in the '60s, and many people in the Black community today think we lived in the Dark Ages. I'm getting into one of my pet peeves. There is a kind of simplistic assumption that there were few Black comics when we grew up, and no Black science fiction, because there weren't Black people in comics or science fiction. Because of this lack of representation, we couldn't imagine ourselves in those spaces. Correct me if I'm wrong, but my impression is that you don't feel you suffered a limitation.

CJ: No, I didn't. When I would read literature or comics, I would be with the characters. They didn't have to be Black for me to relate to them. Now, if I came across something racist that pulled me out of the story, I'd have to stand back and look at it. But you're going to find that, unfortunately, with just about every American writer.

BLVR: Or British, for that matter.

CJ: Yes, the British. You see racist imagery sometimes, even in comics. It's there in the '40s. It's there in animated films in the '40s, Disney and Warner Bros. It's just part of American culture, white American culture. Now, we don't want to show these things today, because we're embarrassed by them. But they exist. I saw them. I grew up with them, but this didn't stop my passion for creating.

IV. "THE GOOD, THE TRUE, AND THE BEAUTIFUL"

BLVR: You studied with John Gardner when you were a graduate student at Southern Illinois University. What strikes you now about him as a teacher?

CJ: On the one hand, he was remarkable. On the other, he had his limitations.

BLVR: Please explain.

CJ: He was the best creative-writing teacher we had in the country. He produced three important books on the subject: *The Art of Fiction*, *On Becoming a Novelist*, and *On Moral Fiction*.

I used *The Art of Fiction* for thirty-three years at UW. Every quarter, I had my students do the exercises in the back of that book. Gardner sent me those questions before the book was published, as soon as he learned I was going to teach. The book was still unfinished when Gardner died. It was brought together by our friend Nicholas Delbanco, who directed the writing program at the University of Michigan.

BLVR: He was also one of Gardner's students.

CJ: Gardner introduced me to Nick, saying, "You two are the best young writers in America. You should know each other."

BLVR: You said earlier that Gardner had some limitations.

CJ: Yes. Gardner was very Western, very white. I mean, we eventually parted ways as student and teacher. He was good with his comments for me on *Faith and the Good Thing*, but he did not support *Oxherding Tale* at first, because he did not understand it. There was a resistance to Buddhism. He sent me a letter where he wrote, *If Buddhism is right, then I've lived my life wrong, and I refuse to believe that.* Yet just before the book's publication he volunteered himself to write a blurb that says, "A true storyteller… *Oxherding Tale* is a 'classic' in the noblest sense."

BLVR: There it is.

CJ: He was initially responding to the novel, not in terms of craft, but rather in terms of a personal issue that he had with Buddhadharma and probably a fear of it as well. He

---

FICTIONAL CHARACTERS WHO PEAKED IN HIGH SCHOOL

✶ Biff Loman—*Death of a Salesman*
✶ Heather Chandler—*Heathers*
✶ Harry Angstrom—*Rabbit Run*
✶ Uncle Rico—*Napoleon Dynamite*
✶ Brooke Cardinas—*Mistress America*
✶ Blanche DuBois—*A Streetcar Named Desire*
✶ Mavis Gary—*Young Adult*
✶ David Wooderson—*Dazed and Confused*

—list compiled by Lula Konner

could not understand that his way of looking at and experiencing the world was not the only way. And the publishing industry at that time largely shared his perspective. I didn't know that the book would be rejected two dozen times, like Pirsig's *Zen and the Art of Motorcycle Maintenance*. For many Westerners, this is a book they cannot easily wrap their minds around. But my feeling about art is that it changes your perceptions. It will help you to see something that you've never seen before within the limited world you have been in.

BLVR: Did you work with any other creative-writing teachers when you were in college?

CJ: No. I'm a philosopher, so there was no way I was going to take a philosophical manuscript into the kind of creative-writing classes you had in the '70s. Interestingly enough, Gardner was described as a philosophical writer when he published *The Sunlight Dialogues*. I was at his farmhouse one Christmas when he showed me the book. He had just gotten copies of it. *Grendel* had been critically acclaimed, but *The Sunlight Dialogues* would be his first bestseller. For ten years he was like a comet across the literary landscape. The hardest-working writer I think I've ever seen, and generous toward his students.

BLVR: How do you feel about the position that Gardner takes in *On Moral Fiction* when he argues that experimental fiction is immoral? He argues that fiction should be about what he calls "the Good, the True, and the Beautiful."

CJ: I believe fiercely in "the Good, the True, and the Beautiful." I wrote a response to Gardner's book called "A Phenomenology of *On Moral Fiction*." As I argue in that piece, "*responsible* fiction" would have been a better title for John's concerns. Permit me this analogy. No matter how bad the world is, as a parent you're not going to tell your kids that the odds are stacked against them. Instead, you have to give them, despite all the negativity, a sense of hope and personal agency. There are always counterexamples of heroism, survival, and resilience. That is what I mean by responsible fiction. I will never write a book that offers no hope. By every metric, America right now is trending down in too many ways, on the decline. Whether it's the quality of life, the state of education, the teacher shortage, homelessness, or, in a place like Chicago, where you and I come from, the gangs, the relentless killings. However, it would be immoral for you as a writer to dump all that negativity on the reader. You can write about bad shit happening all day long and it's just bad shit happening all day long. I don't need to contribute to that.

BLVR: Are there subjects you won't write about?

CJ: I don't like writing about slavery. If you're going to be honest to your characters, you have to be those people, imaginatively. You have to project yourself thoroughly and fully into them, like I tried to do in my stories for the history book *Africans in America*, a companion volume to the PBS series produced by WGBH in Boston. I wrote twelve stories for that book, every one about a slave. They wanted me to do twelve stories that would dramatize the historical record and let viewers know what it felt like to be a slave or a master. To do that, you have to be these characters, and that means you have to experience their pain and you have to experience their hatred, sometimes even murderous hatred. You have to inhabit the heart and soul of your character. If that character is good, then you've got to be good. If that character is evil, then you've got to be evil. Every fiction writer knows this. You are every performer on the stage of the page. At least that's what I've experienced. I put off writing the stories until the last minute. I wrote them all in a month, three a week, just to get it all done and out of my system. However, I still carry scar tissue from that experience.

America right now is suffering from a massive mental health crisis. You read about it every time you open a newspaper. It's good that people are talking about the issue, that they're not ashamed. However, as a Buddhist, I feel we have to have a spiritual practice that allows us to get rid of the sewage in our spirits that we may have picked up in our childhood or early in life or through our bad experiences and conditioning. For this reason, I don't like to take on those assignments that will require me to dwell on ill will, hatred, or evil, because if we dwell on those things, they get into our minds and hearts and can do serious damage. I like to "accentuate the positive," as the song used to say. And my Buddhist practice allows me to cleanse away the grit and grime.

V. "SMELL THE TRUTH"

BLVR: As a writer, do you consciously see yourself as working in a tradition? Do you see yourself as an African American working in an African American tradition? Or as a Chicago writer? A Seattle writer?

CJ: I don't like labels. I don't like boxes. When I was starting out as a writer, I wanted to contribute to the very small tradition of American philosophical fiction. That's why I got a doctorate in philosophy, to know Western intellectual history front to back. Then I needed to know more—namely, the tradition of Eastern philosophy. We all have to develop our own individual vision. And it seems to me that critics often don't know what to make of us, we writers and other artists. Sometimes I think that artists are too complex for some critics. I have had six books published about my work, but only three out of the six are good.

Critics talk about a writer only in terms of what they know and understand. If you don't know anything about Eastern philosophy, then you can't address that aspect of a writer's work. Or if you don't know anything about cartoons, how can you examine me as a cartoonist?

BLVR: Do you think that someone who doesn't know your comics but discovers them will then have a different perspective when they go back to your fiction?

CJ: Jonathan Little published the first critical book about my work, a book called *Charles Johnson's Spiritual Imagination*. He looks at how my comic art influences my fiction, including in *Oxherding Tale*. I really love the book *The Writer's Brush: Paintings, Drawings, and Sculpture by Writers*. Many writers are more than just writers. I've fought my entire life against ideas, labels, and situations that try to limit me, because I think our talent is God-given.

The Writer's Brush is good because what it tells us is that an individual may wake up one day and decide, Let me work on a short story. And the next day you may wake up and think, I'm really interested in the mind-body problem. Let me write a philosophical response to or essay about that. Or you might wake up and think, I want to do a sketch or a drawing. It's all part of the same global talent within an individual. It's a way of being in the world.

BLVR: I have not heard you say anything about music.

CJ: That's not my orientation. My orientation is sight, although of course I love music. When I write fiction, it's my visual imagination that goes into the description. I like detail. Strong, bold outlines. Even in writing I like composition and I think about foreground and background. That's my visual imagination. I have to work hard at getting in the other senses—smell, sound, taste, and touch. Though we have five senses, we tend to be sight-dominated in the West. We always say, *Oh, I see the truth*. We don't say, *I smell the truth*. I'm really amazed by writers who can capture the other senses, like Upton Sinclair in *The Jungle*, writing about the Chicago stockyards. He gets the smell. He describes it in a way that in your imagination you smell it too.

BLVR: One final question. As a Buddhist, how do you deal with the reality of evil in the world? I mean, for example, I know you practice nonviolence, but obviously when you face a Putin or a Hitler or a Stalin or a Mao, nonviolence isn't something they understand.

CJ: That's the dilemma. I'm nonviolent, but then again, I'm a lifelong martial artist. I truly believe in self-defense. I don't believe in letting anybody physically violate me or anybody I care about. Now, that is the dilemma for a pacifist. As you said, the problem with bullies is that violence is the only language they understand. The only thing that will stop them is fear of their own death. If you have to deliver that to them to stop them, to prevent others from being harmed by them, then it's necessary.

When I collaborated with Steven Barnes on his book of Black horror stories, *The Eightfold Path*, he asked me if there are any stories about the Buddha killing somebody. I do remember that in all the stories told about the Buddha's previous lives before he became the Buddha, in one of them he is on a boat with some people, and he realizes one of them is going to kill everybody and rob them. So he kills that person, knowing that he has condemned himself to long rounds of rebirth before he ever achieves liberation. But it was for the sake of the other people that he had to eliminate this robber and murderer. You cannot let evil continue in the world. ★

A REVIEW OF
THE ISLAND
BY ANTIGONE KEFALA

At the beginning of Antigone Kefala's *The Island*, a university student named Melina is offered a theory by her boss, a researcher. He argues that the only people capable of understanding history are those who live across cultures, inhabit multiple worlds: who belong to no single place. "People in between," he says, have a special way of seeing.

Melina is one of those "people in between." Her origins, loosely sketched, are in an old Europe, a place of bathhouses and ornate furniture and brocade curtains, but when she was young her family was displaced by war. They became refugees, living among "the breaths of people stale and tired" in a hotel by the sea, before making their way to the titular "island," a place of rainy green hills, "with sheep permanently grazing in the same spots, as if they had been painted there." Melina's memories of her past are partial and hazy, formed mostly from secondhand stories, but they color her vision and intervene upon the present. She is here on the island, but she is also, always, elsewhere.

First published in Australia in 1984 and newly rereleased by Transit Books, *The Island* is a beguiling portrait of Melina's fragmented consciousness. Equally, it is a portrait of a young woman trying to figure out who and how to be. The places aren't named, but the protagonist's path trails Kefala's. The author was born in Romania in 1931, and after the Soviet occupation she fled to refugee camps in Greece before migrating to New Zealand and finally Australia, where, in her fourth language, she began to write poetry and fiction.

Oblique and impressionistic, the book hinges not on plot but on Kefala's fertile, intensely observant prose. As Melina goes through the motions of a young person's life—roaming the city with friends, studying at university, singing in concerts, learning the thrills and disappointments of love—she feels endlessly alone, estranged from the people around her. She is restless and desirous, "full of longing for unknown things… a longing for something that would raise us, as in

Publisher: *Transit Books* **Page count:** *128* **Price:** *$18.95* **Key quote:** *"The secret heart of the land seemed to be yearning for that uninterrupted silence free of humans that had been there before, the presence of that time still in the land's memory."* **Shelve next to:** *Etel Adnan, Italo Calvino, Clarice Lispector* **Unscientifically calculated reading time:** *One sun-dappled afternoon beside a river*

Byzantine paintings, make us float through the air, disappear in shafts of light, become a line in space." She and her family are haunted by a sense of dislocation, but their nostalgia for a lost home also gives them an identity. The past is "a sort of breath that moulded us and which we could no longer escape," offering "a value and a weight that nothing around was capable of giving us."

Melina perceives the world at a heightened remove, which suffuses her everyday life with mystical strangeness. Cellos at a concert are "golden totem poles bathing in electric suns… and the bells, exotic primitive silver gods waiting to be touched." Her emotions are like a paintbrush over the world, creating a constant interplay between interiority and exteriority; everywhere, she sees her psyche reflected back at her. A bleak morning is "charged with the cry of lawn mowers." Like her, a tree is "vulnerable and young, glass tears hanging from its arms." A glass of water on her bedside evokes her own existential fears: "The light caressing the water with the hands of a lover, the transparent shades that stirred in it… I was afraid for it, a fragile, marvellously balanced beautiful thing that could not possibly last."

This is a slim book, but its dense lyricism makes it feel expansive. As Kefala roves across Melina's memories, dreams, and daily rhythms, often in a single page, the distinctions between those realms start to collapse. Her dreams are often more detailed than her memories, and scenes from her lived reality are imbued with the surreal. Time stretches and contracts, reflecting the nonlinearity of displacement and movement, the migrant's ability to exist in different places simultaneously. Often it is hard to know whether a day has passed in the book, or several months, but it doesn't matter. The pleasure of *The Island* is in its layered sentences, which ask to be unraveled and savored. Like an abstract painting, the book is an atmosphere, a universe with its own rules rather than a linear experience. And it reveals itself slowly, with patient looking.

—*Meara Sharma*

Illustration by Pete Gamlen

A REVIEW OF

FUEL

BY ROSIE STOCKTON

Late in Rosie Stockton's new, apocalyptic book of poems, their narrator remarks: "You must want entirely / or not at all." This could easily be the thesis of *Fuel*, their second book of poems from Nightboat Books. In taut, opaque compositions, Stockton's poems toil over the painful ecstasy of desire and pleasure in a world overburdened by capitalist exploitation. Empty big-box stores serve as symbols of our modern, crumbling Roman Empire. "Geologic sluts" wander the postindustrial landscape, seeking out reservoirs and oil reserves. Making something grow in such a hostile climate is nearly impossible—least of all something as fragile as love.

Stockton was born in New Mexico but now lives in Los Angeles. Their first full-length poetry collection, *Permanent Volta*, was released by Nightboat Books in 2021. Summoning swamps and sweat, Stockton's work often dives into the disconnection between labor and environment, love and drudgery, time and loss. Stockton is also an academic—a PhD candidate in the Gender Studies Department at UCLA—and has written for the contemporary analytic journal *Parapraxis*. Their writing uses psychoanalytic and Marxist frames to parse the troubling effect of capital on our personal lives. In their critical prose, as in their poetry, Stockton is especially interested in psychology's complicated relationship to notions of domesticity, stability, and power.

In this new book, the contemporary and the ancient are often juxtaposed alongside each other. Homer and Ovid make cameos but the speaker is also "turbulent with Lexapro." Stockton plucks out vicious nouns where other poets often fall into inane truisms and cheap simplicities. Their poems feature sharp lyrical quips like "never wanted to invade / anyone's oblivion, but there / was no other place" or "all the ways / I know harm are legal." There is no way to "unsubscribe" from the horrors of modernity. In our time of decay, how can we connect across the chasm of disconnection? Can we? As time stops and starts, Stockton ventures a few guesses, courting the edge of oblivion with a wry smile.

After each long poem, Stockton writes a letter. They start each epilogue with "Dear End...," as if writing to a real or imagined lover. There's a boyish charm to Stockton's references, and a focus on gender. One poem finds the narrator boiling a packer, getting ready to prowl the night for a possible lover. In another moment, Stockton writes, "I could pout tauter than a ratchet strap." The time it takes to prepare for a carnal encounter slows down the electric rod of passion. They reference cars and shaving, "boxy glam" and "sulk[ing] emasculating Mars," even the "RPMs of Jello shots." The maintenance of masculinity needs upkeep, Stockton suggests; the illusion of the petulant, suave Romeo costs an arm and a leg. Do we have the time? Desire often requires that limitations be pushed out of the way. It dies in the daily hum of life, the litany of "idyllic chores." Falling in love is a lot easier when you don't have to go to work the next day.

The "bumping staccato" of Stockton's poems leads eternally to the grim realization that breakups are always metaphysical: "it's not love that we give up. it's being bound to days." Stockton illustrates the pitfalls that await love in our capitalist hellscape. What do we owe one another, we "Utopian simp[s]?" We must outrun premature death and taxes, cops and climate collapse, if we have any chance of maintaining our fragile romantic bonds. We must "want entirely or not at all." Stockton knows the role these issues play in our intimate relationships. These boundaries all too often determine the ways we chase desire. In their poetry, Stockton asks: How do we plant bonds that endure? Perhaps the brutality of the end days can open us up to more intimate encounters. "Our horizon exists only in destruction of time," Stockton writes. As we look underneath our fingernails, we can see the ephemeral erotics left behind. There lie the power of language, the wounds of love.

—*Grace Byron*

Publisher: *Nightboat Books* **Page count:** *88* **Price:** *$17.95* **Key quote:** *"like light, you hit me / when I ask you to"* **Shelve next to:** *Italo Calvino, Lauren Cook, Bernadette Mayer, Irene Silt* **Unscientifically calculated reading time:** *A half hour spent pacing around the garden and one long ride through the Tunnel of Love*

Illustration by Pete Gamlen

A REVIEW OF
FORECLOSURE GOTHIC
BY HARRIS LAHTI

About halfway through Harris Lahti's debut novel, *Foreclosure Gothic*, there is a photograph of two raccoons. One, apparently dead, has been laid on a bed of fruit. The other is attempting to have sex with it. The original image is taken from the multimedia series *Nature Studies* by Brazilian photographer Mari Juliano, which begins with several enchanting photos of levitating bones and flowers and concludes with footage of curious deer and drone shots of Juliano's cabin. These surprisingly ordinary final images are the most effective in the series because, coming after the raccoon necrophilia that appears in the middle of the sequence, they seem to show Juliano's shame, her search for a less-mediated representation of the natural world.

In Lahti's novel, it's Heather Greener, an actress turned farmers' market vendor, who photographs the raccoons in her backyard. She wants to show them to her husband, Vic, a former *Days of Our Lives* star who drinks to cope with his shattered dreams and exhausting job. To Heather, Vic and the libidinous creature have something in common: They embody "the ways in which natural instincts—such as earning money—can sometimes lead to maladaptive behavior in the artificial world we live in." Before Heather has the chance to explain this connection, Vic insists on hanging her work on their office wall, and the couple makes love for the first time in months, right there on the floor in front of it. An unconventional marital aid, no question. As in Juliano's series, in Lahti's fiction, to experience horror is to receive a moral shock treatment.

Foreclosure Gothic is a twisted melodrama animated by close encounters with addiction, incest, and death by misadventure. But it's also an earnest heartland romance. Upon meeting on the Venice boardwalk in 1980s Los Angeles, Vic and Heather learn that they grew up a few New York State Thruway exits apart. As scene partners, they "Yes, and?" each other until they're soon life partners. When Vic's soap money runs out, they swiftly return to the East Coast. Tinseltown exists in this novel only to become a memory of fame. Junior is born. The family eats what Heather can't sell from her garden. (Oops! All cauliflower.) Vic claims he'll audition again once their finances are stable. Meanwhile, he buys foreclosed buildings at auction to remodel and rent them, just as his father did. The Greeners' mantra: "Try to see the house behind the house." It's both sound development advice and a sentimental reminder of the difference between a house and a home.

Over the years, the Greeners amass eight properties. For one last hurrah before he joins the family business, a college-aged Junior takes a trip to Costa Rica. Enamored with the tropics, Junior renounces his place in the line of succession. He decides he'll build a hut, surf every morning, and write the millennial *Robinson Crusoe*. Or so he thinks. As Hollywood was to Vic and Heather, Ostional is to Junior, who calls his parents for return airfare the moment he runs out of Spanish words and colones.

Though we spend more time with his parents, *Foreclosure Gothic* is ultimately Junior's story. When he gets home and ditches the artist's way to flip houses with his father, he learns to love sanding hardwood like the men in Caillebotte's *Raboteurs de parquet*, finding beauty in the long, steady strokes. If this is good news for New York's housing crisis, it also provides a grim outlook for American literature. The omniscient narrator scolds Junior for fiddling with his short stories amid "high unemployment, low wages, and little opportunity—the opposite of what Vic offered."

But Lahti himself has found the middle way: Since finishing his MFA, he's managed to publish his debut while painting houses upstate. Lahti knows that, for most artists, making a living off art will remain a fantasy. *Foreclosure Gothic* is more than a fable about embracing tradition; it's a rejoinder to the horror of modern life. Vic Greener's offer—the novel's, too—is an escape from escapism.
—*Kenneth Dillon*

> **Publisher:** *Astra Publishing House* **Page count:** 240 **Price:** $26.00 **Key quote:** "*In fact, he feels wonderful. Completely lobotomized. Sun-kissed and sleepy. Nostalgic, even.*" **Shelve next to:** Jordan Castro, Bud Smith, Gabriel Smith **Unscientifically calculated reading time:** *An afternoon drive to the dump*

Illustration by Pete Gamlen

A trio of independent bookstores in San Francisco.

Hosting author events, most of them free, at our Books on the Park location 2–3 times a week.

GREEN APPLE BOOKS
506 Clement Street (Since 1967)

BROWSER BOOKS
2195 Fillmore Street (Since 1976)

BOOKS ON THE PARK
1231 Ninth Avenue (Since 2014)

greenapplebooks.com

COVER TO COVER

SURVEYING THE COVERS OF GREAT BOOKS AS THEY CHANGE ACROSS TIME AND COUNTRY.
IN THIS ISSUE: *A TREE GROWS IN BROOKLYN* BY BETTY SMITH

Compiled by Lula Konner

CHINA
Zhejiang
2024

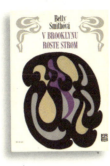
CZECH REPUBLIC
Práce
1970

FINLAND
WSOY
1956

GERMANY
Bastei Lübbe
1978

UKRAINE
BookChef
2019

GREECE
Plume
1988

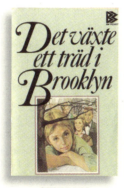
SWEDEN
Metaixmio
2023

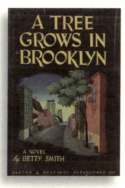
UNITED STATES
HarperCollins
1943

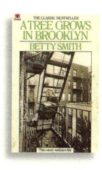
UNITED KINGDOM
Pavanne Publishing
1985

TURKEY
Epsilon Yayinevi
2023

TURKEY
Altin Kitaplar Yayinevi
1979

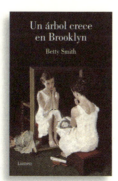
SPAIN
Lumen
2008

RUSSIA
Izdatelstvo Eksmo
2020

JORDAN
Al Dar Al Ahlia
2011

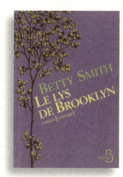
FRANCE
Belfond
2014

An indisputably enjoyable section of **GAMES & PUZZLES**

THE PUZZLE OF INCREDIBLY WIDE AND DEEP KNOWLEDGE

IF YOU COMPLETE THIS PUZZLE, YOU ARE A GENERALIST OF BROAD SKILL AND GREAT RENOWN

by Wyna Liu; edited by Benjamin Tausig

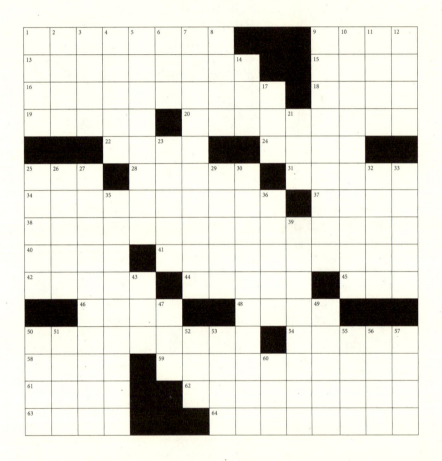

48. Wee
50. Hypes too much
54. Not as nice
58. Singer Aimee
59. Like some members
61. Prefix with septic
62. Pup that's always by your side, informally
63. Crane construction
64. Preps for print

DOWN

1. Accessory for an angel
2. Letters by "0"
3. Portion (out)
4. Got things all wrong
5. Aquatic insect whose presence indicates clean water
6. Birth control method: Abbr.
7. Bladed sporting equipment made from willow wood
8. Numbers game that originally involved betting on homing pigeons
9. 2023 jukebox musical whose name is a state pun
10. Happy accident, cutely
11. "I'm buying"
12. Within reach
14. Briny
17. "u sure?"
21. Air producer
23. Necklace component
25. Rings up
26. Sparkle
27. They generally change throughout the day (and night)
29. Places for 6-Downs
30. Without any consideration
32. "M is for Maud who was swept out to sea / N is for Neville who died of ___" ("The Gashlycrumb Tinies")
33. Big name in reference works
35. "Flipping heck!"
36. "Merry Xmas Everybody" band
39. Need for making lasagna or kugel
43. Palindromic relative
47. "The Simpsons" character who says "Oh, the network slogan is true. Watch Fox and be damned for all eternity!"
49. You can rock the baby with them
50. Home of the Nizwa Fort
51. A rooster might be seen on one
52. Word on a candy heart
53. Early internet alphabet that would render itself as "1337"
55. Pirate ship, for one
56. "People think it's funny when I sneeze, but it's ___" (groaner)
57. Products of layers
60. Drug referenced in Basquiat's "Dustheads"

(answers on page 128)

ACROSS

1. Missing one's own bed, perhaps
9. Legend
13. Irises control them
15. Single
16. Place with a fountain and stools
18. Capital city known as "El Pulpo" ("The Octopus")
19. Make like a peacock
20. Loretta Lynn's father, for one
22. Something cut before a deal
24. Big jerk
25. Dragon's place
28. Violette, par exemple
31. Less forward, in a way
34. Milky summer pick-me-ups
37. Fig. on a license
38. ABCs of salesmanship?
40. Columbo's org.
41. Thoroughfare with a terminus at Union Square
42. Attempts, so to speak
44. Diacritic used to mean "approximately"
45. Stuff to get you started, say
46. Ancient archaeological find

JACKET CAPTCHA
CAN YOU IDENTIFY THESE NINE BOOK COVERS?

COPYEDITING THE CLASSICS

10 ERRORS HAVE BEEN INERTED INTO THIS PASSAGE. CAN YOU FIND THEM?

by Caitlin Van Dusen

PASSING (1929)
by NELLA LARSEN

When she was dressed in the shining black taffeta with its bizarre trimmings of purple and cerise, Fru Dahl approved her and so did herr Dahl. Everything in her responded to his, "She's beautiful; beautiful!" Helga Crane knew she wasn't that, but it pleased her that he could think so, and say so. Her Aunt Katrina smiled in her quiet, assured way, taking to herself her husband's complement to her niece. But a little frown appeared over the fierce mustache, as he barked, in his precise, faintly feminine voice: "She ought to have ear-rings, long ones. Is it too late for Garborg's? We could call up."

And call up they did. And Garborg, the jeweler, in Fredericksgaarde, waited for them. Not only were ear-rings bought, long ones brightly enameled, but glittering shoe-buckles and two great bracelets. Helga's sleeves being long, she escaped the bracelets for the moment. They were wrapped to be worn that night. The ear-rings, however, and the buckles came into immediate use and Helga felt like a veritable savage as they made their leisurely way, ambling across the pavement from the shop to the waiting motor. This feeling was intensified by the many pedestrians who stopped to stare at the queer dark creature, strange to their city. Her cheeks reddened, but both Herr and Fru Dahl seemed oblivious of the stares or the audible whispers in which Hegla made out the one frequently reoccurring word, "sorte," which she recognized as the Danish word for "black."

Follow The Chicago Manual of Style, *17th edition. Please ignore unusual spellings, hyphenations, and capitalizations, and the that/which distinction. All are characteristic of the author's style and time.*

NOTES ON OUR CONTRIBUTORS

Cara Blue Adams is the author of *You Never Get It Back*, a *New York Times* Editors' Choice. Her work appears in *The New Yorker*, *Granta*, and *The Kenyon Review*. She is an associate professor at Temple University and lives in Brooklyn, New York.

Jeffery Renard Allen is the author of six books of fiction and poetry. Allen's accolades include the *Chicago Tribune*'s Heartland Prize for Fiction, a Guggenheim fellowship, the Ernest J. Gaines Award for Literary Excellence, a Whiting Award, and many residencies and other fellowships. He was also a finalist for both the PEN/Faulkner Award and the Carnegie Medal for Excellence in Fiction. Allen is the founder and editor of *Taint Taint Taint* magazine and is the Africa editor of the *Evergreen Review*. His latest books are the short-story collection *Fat Time* and the memoir *An Unspeakable Hope*, which was coauthored with Leon Ford. Allen makes his home in Johannesburg, South Africa, and New York. Find out more at writerjefferyrenardallen.com.

Prince Bush is a poet from Nashville, Tennessee, whose poems appear in *Cherry Tree*, *The Drift*, *The Cortland Review*, *Northwest Review*, and elsewhere. Currently an Albert C. Yates Fellow and PhD student in creative writing at the University of Cincinnati, Prince Bush earned his MFA in creative writing as a Truman Capote Literary Fellow from the Iowa Writers' Workshop.

Grace Byron is a writer from the Midwest based in Queens, New York. Her debut novel, *Herculine*, is out this October.

Paul Collins is the author of ten books of nonfiction. A newly revised edition of his collection *Banvard's Folly: Thirteen Tales of People Who Didn't Change the World* is now available as an audiobook. He is a professor in the creative writing program at Portland State University in Oregon.

Kenneth Dillon is a writer from New York. His work has appeared in *The Baffler*, the *Los Angeles Review of Books*, *Publishers Weekly*, and other publications.

Maxime Gérin is a French Canadian cartoonist and illustrator living in Montréal. He has been self-publishing comics and partaking in anthologies since 2018. His latest release is *Hats Off!* #1.

Gish Jen's short stories have been included five times in *The Best American Short Stories*, including in *The Best American Short Stories of the Century*. A fellow of both the American Academy of Arts and Letters and the American Academy of Arts and Sciences, she has been the recipient of a Lannan Literary Award as well as a Mildred and Harold Strauss Living Award. She has also been awarded National Endowment for the Arts, Fulbright, Guggenheim, and Radcliffe Fellowships. Her work has appeared in *The New Yorker*, *The Atlantic Monthly*, and *The New York Times*. Her most recent book is a collection of stories titled *Thank You, Mr. Nixon*, and she has a new novel coming out in October, titled *Bad Bad Girl* (Knopf).

Nora Lange's debut novel, *Us Fools*, was a finalist for the National Book Critics Circle Award in Fiction, received the Sue Kaufman Prize for First Fiction from the American Academy of Arts and Letters, and was named a "Best Book of 2024" by *The Boston Globe* and NPR. It was also a *Los Angeles Times* bestseller and a *New York Times* Editors' Choice. Her short writing has appeared in *BOMB*, *Hazlitt*, *Joyland*, *American Short Fiction*, *Denver Quarterly*, *HTMLGIANT*, and elsewhere. Lange has received fellowships from Brown University and is currently a fellow at the Los Angeles Institute of the Humanities at the University of Southern California. She recently moved to Salt Lake City with her family.

Melissa Locker is a writer and music podcast impresario in the making. She lives on the internet and runs on coffee. You can follow her at @woolyknickers but not in real life.

Jordan Taliha McDonald is an essayist, critic, editor, cultural worker, and (sometimes) poet from Seat Pleasant, Maryland. She is currently a PhD candidate in English at Harvard University with a secondary field in the history of science. Her public writing, journalism, and cultural criticism have appeared in *New York* magazine, *Artsy*, *Vulture*, *Africa Is a Country*, *The Offing*, *Harvard Review*, *Lux*, *Complex*, and other publications. Her newsletter, *East Coast Lit(erary) Thot*, can be read on Substack.

David J. Morris is the author of two books of nonfiction. *The Evil Hours: A Biography of Post-Traumatic Stress Disorder* was a finalist for the Los Angeles Times Book Prize. He is a former war correspondent, and his work has appeared in *The Surfer's Journal*, *The New York Times*, and *Virginia Quarterly Review*.

Annalee Newitz writes science fiction and nonfiction. They are the author of three novels: *The Terraformers*, *The Future of Another Timeline*, and *Autonomous*, which won the Lambda Literary Award. As a science journalist, they are the author of *Stories Are Weapons: Psychological Warfare and the American Mind*, *Four Lost Cities: A Secret History of the Urban Age*, and *Scatter, Adapt, and Remember: How Humans Will Survive a Mass Extinction*, which was a finalist for the Los Angeles Times Book Prize in Science and Technology.

Cecily Parks is the author of three books of poetry, including *The Seeds* (Alice James Books, 2025), poems from which appear in *A Public Space*, *The Nation*, *The New Yorker*, and elsewhere. She teaches in the MFA Program in creative writing at Texas State University and lives in Austin.

Meara Sharma is a writer and artist. She is the senior editor of *Elastic*, a new magazine of psychedelic art and literature. With roots in Massachusetts and India, she currently lives in Scotland.

Evie Shockley thinks, creates, and writes with her eye on a Black feminist horizon. Her books of poetry include *suddenly we* (NAACP Image Award; National Book Award finalist), *semiautomatic* (Hurston/Wright Legacy Award; Pulitzer Prize finalist), and *the new black* (Hurston/Wright Legacy Award). Among the honors for her body of work are the Academy Fellowship for Distinguished Poetic Achievement, the Shelley Memorial Award, the Lannan Literary Award for Poetry, the Holmes National Poetry Prize, and the Stephen Henderson Award. Her joys include participating in poetry communities and collaborating with artists working in various media. Shockley is the Zora Neale Hurston Distinguished Professor of English at Rutgers University.

Joan Silber is the author of ten books of fiction. Her newest, *Mercy*, will be out in September. *Secrets of Happiness* was a *Washington Post* 2021 Notable Work of Fiction and a *Kirkus Reviews* Best Fiction Book of 2021. Her novel *Improvement* was the winner of the National Book Critics Circle Award and the PEN/Faulkner Award. She also received the PEN/Bernard and Ann Malamud Award for Excellence in the Short Story. Her book *Fools* was longlisted for the National Book Award and was a finalist for the PEN/Faulkner Award. Other works include *The Size of the World*, a finalist for the Los Angeles Times Book Prize for Fiction; and *Ideas of Heaven*, a finalist for the National Book Award and the Story Prize. She lives in New York and has taught at Sarah Lawrence College and in the Warren Wilson College MFA program.

Pitchaya Sudbanthad is the author of the novel *Bangkok Wakes to Rain*, selected as a notable work by *The New York Times* and *The Washington Post*; it was also a finalist for the Center for Fiction's First Novel Prize, the Chautauqua Prize, the Casa delle Letterature "The Bridge" Book Award, and the Edward Stanford Travel Writing Award. He has received fellowships in fiction writing from Civitella Ranieri, MacDowell, and the New York Foundation for the Arts.

Shruti Swamy is the author of the story collection *A House Is a Body* and a novel, *The Archer*. She lives in San Francisco.

Rafia Zakaria is an author, most recently of *Against White Feminism: Notes on Disruption* (2021), which has been translated into eight languages. In 2025, she was awarded the Pushcart Prize for her essay "The Crows of Karachi."

IN THE NEXT ISSUE

Not all contents are guaranteed; replacements will be satisfying

The Last Resort . . . . ASH SANDERS
At Bombay Beach, a half-ruined former resort town on the edge of the Salton Sea, absurdist philosophers, artists, and everyday townsfolk have undertaken a postapocalyptic experiment in radical living.

The Labyrinth . . . . MONA KAREEM
Building a library, by any means necessary, in 1990s Kuwait.

The Haunting of Pennhurst Asylum . . . . OLIVER EGGER
Contradiction and fear at America's only physical museum of disability.

SOLUTIONS TO THIS ISSUE'S GAMES AND PUZZLES

CROSSWORD
(Page 124)

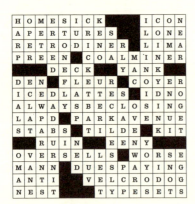

JACKET CAPTCHA
(Page 125)

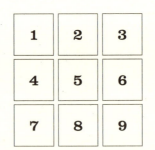

1. *Martyr!* by Kaveh Akbar
2. *Neuromancer* by William Gibson
3. *Invisible Man* by Ralph Ellison
4. *Crush* by Ada Calhoun
5. *The Grapes of Wrath* by John Steinbeck
6. *James* by Percival Everett
7. *Knife* by Salman Rushdie
8. *Good Material* by Dolly Alderton
9. *The Message* by Ta-Nehisi Coates

COPYEDITING THE CLASSICS *(Page 126)*

When she was dressed in the shining black taffeta with its bizarre trimmings of purple and cerise, Fru Dahl approved her and so did herr (1) Dahl. Everything in her responded to his, (2) "She's beautiful; beautiful!" Helga Crane knew she wasn't that, but it pleased her that he could think so, and say so. Her Aunt (3) Katrina smiled in her quiet, assured way, taking to herself her husband's complement (4) to her niece. But a little frown appeared over the fierce mustache, as he barked, (5) in his precise, faintly feminine voice: "She ought to have ear-rings, long ones. Is it too late for Garborg's? We could call up."

And call up they did. And Garborg, the jeweler, in Fredericksgaarde, waited for them. Not only were ear-rings bought, long ones brightly enameled, but glittering shoe-buckles and two great bracelets. Helga's (6) sleeves being long, she escaped the bracelets for the moment. They were wrapped to be worn that night. The ear-rings, however, and the buckles came into immediate use and Helga felt like a veritable savage as they made their leisurely way, ambling (7) across the pavement from the shop to the waiting motor. This feeling was intensified by the many pedestrians who stopped to stare at the queer dark creature, strange to their city. Her cheeks reddened, but both Herr and Fru Dahl seemed oblivious of the stares or the audible whispers in which Hegla (8) made out the one frequently reoccurring (9) word, (10) "sorte," which she recognized as the Danish word for "black."

1. Herr: Titles are capped when they immediately precede a name. In this case, *Herr* is the German equivalent of "Mr."
2. No comma is needed here, as the dialogue is the direct object of *his* (as in: "Everything in her responded to his [remark].")
3. Either delete *Her* before *Aunt* or lowercase *aunt*; kinship titles are lowercased unless they are used in place of a name; when they are modified by a possessive adjective, such as *her*, they are lowercased.
4. compliment: *Complement* (meaning something that completes something else) and *compliment* (meaning an expression of praise) are frequently confused.
5. Change *barked* to *said* or a similar dialogue tag; the harshness implied by *barked* seems contradicted by "in his precise, faintly feminine voice."
6. Flip the opening single quote mark to make it a possessive apostrophe.
7. Suggest cutting *ambling*—it is redundant with "made their leisurely way."
8. Helga: Names are frequently misspelled, as they eye tends to glance over them.
9. recurring: *reoccurring* and *recurring* are often confused—not only because one has two *c*s and the other only one, but also because *recur* means "to repeat frequently, often at fairly regular intervals," whereas *reoccur* means "to happen again but not necessarily repeatedly." Here she seems to mean the former.
10. Delete the comma, as *sorte* isn't the only "frequently recurring word."